Internet of Energy Handbook

Internet of Energy Handbook

Edited by

Pawan Kumar
Srete Nikolovski
Z Y Dong

CRC Press
Taylor & Francis Group
Boca Raton London New York

CRC Press is an imprint of the
Taylor & Francis Group, an **informa** business

First edition published 2021
by CRC Press
6000 Broken Sound Parkway NW, Suite 300, Boca Raton, FL 33487-2742

and by CRC Press
2 Park Square, Milton Park, Abingdon, Oxon, OX14 4RN

© 2021 Taylor & Francis Group, LLC

CRC Press is an imprint of Taylor & Francis Group, LLC

Library of Congress Cataloging-in-Publication Data
Names: Kumar, Pawan, 1977- editor. | Nikolovski, Srete, editor. | Dong, Z.
Y., editor.
Title: Internet of energy handbook / edited by Pawan Kumar, Srete
Nikolovski, and Z.Y. Dong.
Description: First edition. | Boca Raton, FL : CRC Press, 2021. | Includes
bibliographical references and index. | Summary: "The Internet of Energy
(IoE), with the integration of advanced information and communication
technologies (ICT), has led to a transformation of traditional networks
to smart systems. This handbook of research on Internet of Energy
provides updated knowledge in the field of energy management with an
Internet of Things (IoT) perspective. It explains the technological
developments for energy management leading to reduction in energy
consumption through topics like smart energy systems, smart sensors,
communication, techniques and utilization. Dedicated sections cover
varied aspects related to renewable sources of energy, power
distribution and generation and so forth"-- Provided by publisher.
Identifiers: LCCN 2020055216 (print) | LCCN 2020055217 (ebook) | ISBN
9780367499648 (hardback) | ISBN 9781003048343 (ebook)
Subjects: LCSH: Electric power systems--Automatic control. | Electric power
distribution--Data processing. | Energy conservation--Data processing. |
Internet--Industrial applications.
Classification: LCC TK1007 .I75 2021 (print) | LCC TK1007 (ebook) | DDC
621.310285/4678--dc23
LC record available at https://lccn.loc.gov/2020055216
LC ebook record available at https://lccn.loc.gov/2020055217

ISBN: 978-0-367-49964-8 (hbk)
ISBN: 978-0-367-49965-5 (pbk)
ISBN: 978-1-003-04834-3 (ebk)

Typeset in Times
by SPi Global, India

Contents

Foreword vii
Preface ix
Editor Biographies xv
Contributors xix

Chapter 1   A Framework of Internet of Energy for Coordinated
Operation in Power Delivery 1

                     Pawan Kumar and Anjali Uppal

Chapter 2   Evaluation of Soft Computing Techniques and IEC61850
Protocols for the Development of the Internet of
Energy Framework 41

                     Anjali Uppal and Pawan Kumar

Chapter 3   Internet of Energy for Plug-In Hybrid Electric Vehicle 71

                     Arush Singh, Saurabh Ranjan Sharma, Vivek Kumar Tripathi,
                     Deepanshu Singh Solanki, and Raj Kumar Jarial

Chapter 4   Assessment of Plug-in Hybrid Electric Vehicle (HEVs)
Through Big Data Analysis 107

                     Vikas Khare, Cheshta J. Khare, Savita Nema,
                     and Prashant Baredar

Chapter 5   Estimation of Fault Location Using Cyber Physical
System in WAMCP 139

                     Ankur Singh Rana, Shufali Ashraf Wani, Nisha Parveen,
                     and Mini Shaji Thomas

Chapter 6   The Role of Blockchain and IoT in Modern Energy Systems 159

                     Wesley Doorsamy and Babu Sena Paul

Chapter 7   Solar Energy Generation and Internet of Energy (IoE):
Challenges and Purview 175

                     Sanghita Baidya and Champa Nandi

Chapter 8   IoE for Energy Efficient Buildings: Challenges
and Solutions 193

Meet Kumari

Chapter 9   Battery Management of Automated Guided Vehicles
Via System Dynamics 209

Arzu Eren Şenaras and Onur Mesut Şenaras

Index 217

Foreword

I am extremely honored and delighted to write a Foreword to this book, as its scope and content offers the prospective readers with insights on the role, use, and application of Internet of Energy (IoE) in different industrial settings in power and energy systems.

The role and impact of electricity in governing our modern society are significantly amplified through information and communications technology (ICT), and it is the proliferation of ICT within and beyond the electric infrastructure that merits the focus of this book. With the extensive deployment of heterogeneous Internet of Things (IoT), the Industrial Internet of Things (IIoT), and IoE technologies, smart grids have been transformed into a complicated ecosystem of smart sensing, measurement, monitoring, and intelligent infrastructure capable of monitoring, informing, or controlling most of the energy use and distributed generation in industrial, commercial, residential and mission-critical premises. The increased penetration of variable renewable and other distributed energy resources, smart/energy-efficient buildings, electric vehicles, and energy storage requires the power grid to be even more resilient and responsive to fast changing conditions to ensure access to secure, reliable, safe, and affordable energy.

Additionally, major outages in the electric sector are often caused by a lack of adequate situational awareness on the power grid conditions, insufficient control assets to react to disruptions, aging electrical infrastructure and the increasing complexity and variability in electricity generation portfolios and demand profiles, and the escalating frequency and intensity of extreme weather events, cyber-attacks, terrorist attacks, and human and system errors. Coordinating with these populations of smart and connected machines extends the operational performance, including maintaining a resilient and high-quality energy supply to critical facilities.

There has been a national and international push to conceive and develop integration approaches of the vast sensing, intelligence and energy flexibility resources represented by the IoT, IIoT, IoE, and analogous emerging machine platforms growing at the grid edge. Through IoT and IoE technologies, cutting-edge sensors can rapidly gather data from grid-connected assets and about prevailing conditions to provide operators better insight into infrastructure performance or offer improvements in data integrity and data quality. Local communications and data exchange can also lead to more resilient distributed and fault tolerant control systems. Discussing and discovering knowledge, technologies, tools, and solutions that help unlock and achieve coordination across these boundaries with negligible risk are essential and the focus of this book.

This handbook provides answers to different challenging questions dealing with the deployment, implementation, and instrumentation interoperability of IoE in a variety of use cases in the electric sector. The content provides the energy infrastructure community with robust and scalable approaches to interfacing with advanced and rapidly developing IoE technologies that will enhance their operational capability to maintain energy surety to transmission or distribution connected facilities and their surrounding communities. This handbook comprises nine chapters, covering a myriad of interesting topics ranging from IoE for coordinated operation of power delivery infrastructure, to IoE for battery storage, electric vehicle, and energy-efficient building management, and blockchain interactions with IoT and IoE technologies.

I recommend this handbook to researchers and practitioners in the field, and for scientists and engineers interested or involved in IoT and IoE applications in the power and energy sector. I really appreciate the timely efforts of all the editors to compile this book. The managing editor, Dr. Pawan, and his team have meticulously collected the chapters, reviewed, and placed them in an appropriate structure for better in-depth understanding. I believe the readers will enjoy and benefit from the work presented in this book.

Prof. Payman Dehghanian
Assistant Professor and Director, GW SmartGrid Laboratory
Department of Electrical and Computer Engineering
The George Washington University, Washington DC, USA

Preface

Technological innovation is a key driver of economic growth and human well-being. In the modern world, the major challenges in technological innovations are smart energy, smart governance, smart transportation, smart traffic, and smart education.

Prima facie 'smart energy' is an important aspect because per capita energy consumption defines the living standard of the people of any nation. In recent trends, the energy demand has grown exponentially, and it endeavors to reframe energy-saving opportunities by considering every aspect including social, technical, and environmental. As a consequence of this, energy efficiency continues to be the top priority for any organization to become more cost-competitive in the open marketplace and meet the international objective of enhanced energy efficiency. Further, in a smart city environment, energy management needs to be done at the primary and secondary distribution of power.

The energy management at primary and secondary distribution level can performed with and without the external energy resources. Therefore, the energy management schemes that involve the external energy resources are viewed as active energy boosters (AEBs) whereas the other schemes that are being implemented without external energy resources are viewed as passive energy boosters (PEBs). However, in advanced power and energy systems, the AEBs and PEBs are realized through smart systems and, therefore, it needs to develop a new framework of internet of energy (IoE).

Online monitoring and subsequent analysis tend to improve system performance with no extra cost and IoE provides an extraordinary platform for energy efficiency in the process and or operation. However, the operation, control, and monitoring of the power systems need to be aligned with international standards. In this regard, the recent development of IEC61850 protocols has been explored by the researchers for online energy management. The online data management and operating strategies, i.e. involvement of Internet and cloud/grid computing, have revolutionized the research in a new direction. Recently, this has coined a new term, which is 'Internet of Energy' (IoE). The IoE is an interdisciplinary area of research where several processes such as computation, communication, monitoring, and management have to be performed simultaneously.

This handbook aims to be an essential reference source, building on the available literature in the field of IoE. This specific text is expected to provide the primary and major resources necessary for researchers, academicians, students, faculties, and scientists, across the globe, to adopt and implement new inventions in the area of power generation from conventional and non-conventional resources and their utilization and energy management. Therefore, this book aims to provide a platform to share up-to-date scientific achievements in the core as well as related fields. The main objectives of this book can be underlined as:

a. To explore the scope of Internet of Things in smart energy systems
b. To identify a new framework of energy management at building and substation level
c. To explore various methods/approaches/technique for energy efficiency in generation, transmission, distribution, and utilization.

Recent trends show that the researchers are more focused on active or passive energy boosters, electric vehicles, fault analysis, and energy efficiency through artificial intelligence. This tends to develop a smart energy system that will control, monitor, and operate the system for the benefits of the customer and utilities simultaneously. One of the most recent communication technologies is the Internet of Things (IoT), which has provided the development of numerous different communication protocols. The IoT can be exploited to ensure communication between devices employing dissimilar data types. Also, in order to present a communication platform in both machine-to-machine (M2M) and human-to-machine (H2M) environments, IoT technologies utilize several communication mediums, protocols, and layer architectures. Charging demands differed among different types of electric vehicles and influenced by charging location. Random variables, such as technical characteristics and drive patterns, are considered to estimate the electric vehicles charging demand over time. The optimal location of charging stations also plays a critical role. Time-of-use (ToU) price is applied to influence the electric vehicles charging behavior of EV owners so that the charging demand can be reduced during peak hours and shifted to the off-peak hours. Due to ToU, the overall energy demand can be cut down.

Therefore, considering the above aspects this book is comprises nine chapters and these chapters are summarized below.

Chapter 1: This chapter presents a framework of IoE for coordinated operation in power delivery. Energy management has assumed a critical role in our pursuit of sustainable development. During the past ten years increasing productivity trends are visible in the industry sector and at a macro level, the energy intensity of industry is decreasing as well. However, technical and non-technical barriers continue to inhibit the adoption of many long-term energy efficient options that are economically and environmentally sustainable. These options need to be harnessed rapidly in order to enhance competitiveness and profitability, energy security, and environmental quality. This requires the development of a new framework for the energy efficiency in process or operation. With the growing energy demand, the network complexity has also increased. In a sustainable grid scenario, the energy efficiency performance can be analyzed through a passive energy booster (PEB) and active energy booster (AEB). In modern power and energy systems, the AEBs and PEBs are realized through smart systems and, therefore, a new framework of Internet of Energy (IoE) needs to be developed. An IoE is the merging of two techniques, namely internet of things (IoT) and energy efficiency. Under frequent changing in the operating conditions, the IoE allows monitoring, analyzing, and implementing of the new techniques through internet sources. Conversely, in the traditional automation system instantaneous monitoring is not possible; rather, these systems operate more or less when the contingency has occurred. Online monitoring and the subsequent analysis tend to improve the system performance with no extra cost and IoE provides an extraordinary platform for energy efficiency in the process and or operation. This chapter presents the new framework of the Internet of Energy for coordinated operation of power distribution systems.

Chapter 2: This chapter presents the evaluation of various soft computing techniques and IEC61850 protocols for the development of IoE framework. In recent years, the application of soft computing techniques has involved research in the field of power and energy systems optimization and management. As the consequence of this the conventional methods of energy management have become obsolete. Online energy management is an effective means of controlling and reducing energy consumption. This brings benefits to customers and utilities by reducing costs and maximizing their profits. The performance of online configuration of the energy management is usually evaluated by the computational time and the reliability of the communication signals. In the past, several soft computing techniques have been proposed by researchers and the application of these techniques may be suitable under different operating conditions. With different objective functions the operating constraints may also affect the performance of these techniques. Therefore, in recent years the standard communication protocols have been developed and followed worldwide. In this regard, the IEC61850 has been extensively studied by the researcher and it is implemented effectively in the substation automation and building energy management systems. The implementation of IEC 61850 has allowed the development of a new framework of Internet of Energy, which enables online monitoring and control of power and energy systems.

Chapter 3: This chapter presents the Internet of Energy for plug-in hybrid electric vehicles. In the present world, energy consumption is increasing day by day, and the primary source of energy is fossil-based resources, which will fade away shortly. A new concept called 'Energy Internet' has been recently introduced to deal with these challenges. The Energy Internet (EI) vision tends to overcome some critical problems, such as improving sustainable and eco-friendly energy sources, new models for hybrid energy sources, more secure and effective energy management, and control systems. The wired and wireless communication technologies, such as ZigBee, WiMAX, cognitive radio, cellular communications, and the software-defined network (SDN), which are managed via the network system, are applied in the EI system to carry out monitoring, controlling, and management of transactions in real time.

The chapter begins with a brief overview of the process of power delivery from generation site to load center, the role of demand side management and the challenges and opportunities provided by electric vehicles to the grid. Subsequently, the fundamentals of electric vehicles have been discussed along with an extensive coverage of various practices associated with information sharing and energy management in plug-in hybrid electric vehicles using vehicle-to-grid technology. Afterward, the Internet of Energy is discussed along with the process of information flow and various communication technologies are discussed. Lastly, a hypothetical analysis reflects on the impact of the exchange of information and energy between vehicles and the grid for a city with a significant number of electric vehicles.

Chapter 4: This chapter presents an assessment of hybrid plug-in electric vehicle (HEVs) through big data analysis. Big data refers to large databases that are obtained from a number of data foundations for commercial requirements to disclose a new vision for automated decision-making. The integrated plug-in electric vehicle using the advanced technology of a converter, a battery, and an electric drive system is a transformation of automobile systems and a step towards a pollution-free existence and continuous development of an electric drive system. The application of broad data analysis based decision-making and control in the electric vehicle is primarily concerned with three aspects: data stream side management of the electric vehicle, storage side management, and load side management of the electric vehicle. The goal of this chapter is to present a web-based technical platform for the management of large quantities, variety, and speed of plug-in electrical vehicle related information through major data tools such as Hadoop to support the assessment of plug-in electrical vehicles. The framework involves device design, storage, management, monitoring, and forecasting on the basis of a large amount of data needed to test the electrical vehicle plug by means of a large data analysis. This chapter also includes application of the MapReduce algorithm for electric vehicles.

Chapter 5: This chapter presents a robust and straightforward four-step method for locating faults in an electrical power system using PMU data that is collected through advanced information and communication technologies (ICT), from both the terminals of the faulted line. For better utilization of electrical energy, real-time estimation of the power flow is required. To collect this real-time information about the energy requirements, a fast and reliable Cyber Physical System (i.e. communication architecture) is essential. Hence, nowadays CPS proves to be bottleneck for power engineers. When normal conditions exist in a power network, information provided by relays is sufficient for supervising the functioning of network. It is during contingencies that power engineers require advanced relays (Intelligent Electronics Devices) producing relevant information to cope-up with the situation. With the advancement in technology, relays with Global Positioning System (GPS) functionalities such as Phasor Measurement Units (PMUs) were developed that can generate ample information. The adequate data supported by advanced CPS will enable power engineers to provide solutions for real-time applications even under contingencies. Power system contingencies such as transmission network faults require special attention because of associated economic reasons.

The phasor information is sensed and can be transmitted over an Internet of Things (IoT) based medium even from remotely located transmission lines. Hence WAMCP, which is one of the major components of smart grid along with IoT can be combined to provide a vision of the Internet of Energy (IoE). The chapter is devoted to fault estimation application of WAMCP. Various types of faults including symmetrical and asymmetrical are simulated at various positions on the line and distance to fault in each case is determined in this chapter. Two different phasor measurement methods are used for extraction of current and voltage in the form of phasors. The synchro phasor-based measurements are used for calculating sequence components, which are in turn used in locating the fault distance. Solutions for asymmetrical and symmetrical faults are also provided and the method is also tested for different fault resistance values. Results reveal that the proposed method is accurate besides being immune to fault resistance in case of asymmetrical faults.

Chapter 6: This chapter presents the role of blockchain and IoT in modern energy systems. Blockchain and IoT are emerging as key features of the modern energy system. This chapter focuses on these technological advancements in the context of transition of the energy sector into the Internet-of-Energy (IoE) environment. Here, authors explore how Blockchain and IoT fit into this transition and deal with issues relating to their development and deployment in the sector. Although the interest in Blockchain- and IoT-based innovation in energy is growing, its widespread deployment usage is rightly encumbered by the critical nature of the application that necessitates proven reliability and alignment with the future goals of the sectors through rigorous development, implementation, and testing. It also investigates how applications of Blockchain and IoT principles progressively seek to meet the demands of future energy systems and extricate the current and future challenges with respect to inter alia context, architecture, regulations, security, and uptake. The chapter also unpacks the details of the various challenges with the different components and subsystems of Blockchain- and IoT-based technologies developed for the energy sector that affect security, privacy, and reliability and offer technical insight into opportunities and resolutions pertaining to the same. Moreover, this chapter is intended to provide researchers, developers, and policymakers with an understanding of the possibilities of Blockchain and IoT in the energy sector through equipping them with knowledge of the application principles, state-of-the-art, technological limitations/barriers as well as current and future developments encompassing this technological confluence.

Chapter 7: This chapter presents the challenges in solar energy generation and Internet of Energy (IoE). IoE presents an efficient means for the amalgamation of renewable energy-based distributed power generation to the conventional utility grids. But the integration of distributed energy sources to the utility grids introduced several challenges regarding protection of the system, the safety of information transfer, maintenance of privacy in energy trading, and so on. IoE technology provides an effective, highly reliable, and better communication network based on a real-time approach and a secure platform for the energy market. This chapter presents an extensive evaluation of different IoE features with their roles in the power system. The possible challenges while implementing IoE technology in existing power grids are also reviewed here. The areas for improvement through the IoE technology and future research directions that can enhance the development of the energy market are outlined in this chapter.

Chapter 8: This chapter presents the IoE for energy-efficient buildings with challenges and solutions. Nowadays, the concept of energy efficiency has become a globally remarkable and concerning challenge for feasible economic development. The increasing demand for energy efficiency leads to degradation in network power quality and congestion problems. Thus, IoE is defined as an Internet-style energy solution that has been chosen as an addition to smart devices for the energy-efficient network. IoE integrates the features of the Internet of Things (IoT) and the smart grid. This chapter describes the features and concept of IoE and indicates its relations to energy-efficient buildings for sustainable urban development. It also presents the concepts and achievements in this field and describes the driving forces for the evolution of IoE for energy-saving building. It is shown how the IoE plays a vital role in the evolution of energy-efficient buildings as smart renewable sources and heterogeneous renewable energy resources. Also, the potential applications of IoE in the commercial and residential buildings have been discussed. This chapter present an extensive literature review and supplies insights to the users regarding the future of energy-efficient buildings in the context of IoE. Furthermore, major challenges for implementing IoE in buildings along with their solutions are discussed. Finally, the future trends of IoE are discussed.

Chapter 9: This chapter presented the battery management of automated guided vehicles via system dynamics. This study aims to analyze Automated Guided Vehicle (AGV) battery management using system dynamics modeling. The battery management system is crucial in AGV systems. Different methods can be implemented in a real system. If it is tried in a real system, costs will increase. The system dynamics (SD) model will be developed in Vensim PLE software. The model will provide analysis of different scenarios. After developing AGVs' battery management model, different policies will be able to be designed. This model will enable us to choose a more efficient policy for AGVs. With a system dynamics model, energy management projects related to AGV systems can be evaluated by decision makers effectively.

This book contains nine chapters of high-quality contributions from international leading researchers in the field of energy management. In this book it is observed that energy efficiency is the major concern in the present scenario since every single unit saved is viewed as the energy resource when existing resources are depleting day by day and the energy demand has grown exponentially.

Editor Biographies

Dr. Pawan Kumar, PhD, (MIEEE): Dr. Kumar works as a Professor (Assistant) with Thapar Institute of Engineering and Technology, Patiala, Punjab, India, in the department of Electrical and Instrumentation Engineering. He received his B. Tech from Kurukshetra University, M. Tech from Indian Institute of Technology, Delhi, and completed his PhD from Jamia Millia Islamia, New Delhi, in the years 2001, 2010, and 2016, respectively. He is a Certified Energy Manager cum Auditor (Bureau of Energy Efficiency). He has developed an independent research center while working as the Coordinator of Energy Elite Club. He is actively working as Principal Investigator for the university-funded project on 'Power and renewable energy management through strategic auditing and benchmarking.'

Dr. Kumar worked as the Managing Guest Editor for the Special Issue on "Innovative Technologies for Micro-grid and Smart-grid Systems" of *Computers and Electrical Engineering*, an Elsevier Journal. Dr. Kumar has also served as a reviewer for reputed journals and conferences including: IEEE Transactions on Industrial Informatics, IET-Generation, Transmission and Distribution, Elsevier-Electrical Power and Energy Systems, Computers and Electrical Engineering, Springer-Electrical Engineering, IJITWE IGI Global USA, JCIT IGI Global USA, 12th IEEE INDICON-2015 and 2018. He has published several papers/books/book chapters with various journals/conferences of repute including IEEE, IET, Elsevier, and Taylor & Frances etc. He has worked as Session Chair and reviewer for ICICS-2016 for the tracking of power, energy, and control. He has also received Best Paper Award during the ICICS-2016 International Conference.

Dr. Kumar is the editor of the book *Handbook of Research on Power and Energy System Optimization* (IGI Global, USA). He has delivered expert lectures on Energy Efficiency in Electrical Utilities in various institutions. His areas of current interest include: energy efficiency in electrical utilities, optimization in power system's operation and planning, distributed generation, load management and energy auditing, computational intelligence, and innovative technologies for micro-grid and smart-grid systems.

Prof. (Dr.) Srete Nikolovski, PhD, (SMIEEE): is a Full Professor, Head of Chair of Power Networks and Substations, responsible for development of the faculty and for research and teaching at Power Engineering Department. Prof. Nikolovski received his PhD in Power Systems from the Faculty of Electrical Engineering and Computing, Zagreb. His research fields of activities include active involvements in power and energy systems.

Prof. Nikolovski was the coordinator of TEMPUS EU project EMSA 'Electricity Market Simulation and Analysis Curricula for Engineering Education,' EU ITEA 2 project ESNA 'European Sensor Network Architecture.' Prof. Nikolovski worked as the main researcher of the Croatian project MZOS Nr. 0165116 Reliability of Electric Power System in deregulated electricity market and MZOS Nr.165-1651481-1482 Quality and Reliability of Croatian Electric Power System on Regional Electricity Market. He teaches courses at graduate level: Electrical Networks, Power System Protection, Power System Reliability, Transmission and Distribution of Electrical Energy, and Protection Coordination of Active Distribution Networks. He teaches MSc and PhD study courses: Power System Reliability and Monitoring of Electric Power Quality.

Prof. Nikolovski has delivered 67 technical projects, studies for HEP-Croatian National Grid company and other industry companies. He is the leader on more than 200 graduated works and supervisor on five M.Sc. degree these and six Ph.D. theses. In addition, Dr. Srete has published more than a hundred papers, several books, research works in scientific journals and national and international conferences. His research fields of activities include power system analysis including power flow, short circuit, and harmonic analysis. His research field of activities also include power system protection and integration of RES and reliability analysis of transmission and distribution systems. He has made significant contributions in these fields as evidenced by his above 200 research publications in journals of repute at national and international levels. He is a pioneer researcher on reliability analysis in Croatia and for his work he received IEEE PES Chapter Outstanding Award for his contribution in the field of Power System Reliability in 2014.

Dr. Nikolovski has authored seven books including: *Power System Protection* (2005, 2008), *The Basic of Reliability Analysis of Power System* (1995), *Introduction to Electricity Market* (2010), *Electrical Network I – Solved Problems* (1989, 2000), *Program Packages for Power System Analysis and Simulation* (1997, 2003). Prof. Nikolovski received the Hrvoje Požar National Award (2011) for his professional and scientific contribution in power engineering (Croatia) in recognition of his significant contribution in his professional and scientific work in power engineering. He is on the editorial board of *Technical Gazette Journal*, published by The J. J. Strossmayer University of Osijek (UNIOS) and *International Journal of Electrical and Computer Engineering Systems*, published by Faculty of Electrical Engineering, J. J. Strossmayer University of Osijek, Croatia. Recently, Prof. S. Nikolovski was also reviewer of several journals by Elsevier, *Electric Power System Research*, the IEEE Association such as *IEEE Transaction of Fuzzy Systems*, *IEEE Transaction on Power Delivery*, and Springer, *Electrical Engineering*, *Neural Computing and Applications*, and *International Journal of Electrical and Computer Engineering* (IJECE), official publication of the Institute of Advanced Engineering and Science (IAES).

Prof. (Dr.) Z Y Dong, PhD, (FIEEE): Professor Dong is a Professor in the School of Electrical Engineering and Telecommunications, University of New South Wales, Sydney, Australia. He was the Head of School of Electrical and Information Engineering in the University of Sydney, and a contractor with Ausgrid and EPRI, USA. He is now a member of the ARC College of Experts. Prior to joining the University of New South Wales in 2017, he was Ausgrid Chair and Director of Ausgrid Centre of Excellence for Intelligent Electricity Networks (CIEN) at the University of Newcastle, Australia. He has also worked for Hong Kong Polytechnic University and as system planning manager with TAS networks, Australia. Professor Dong's research interest includes power system planning and stability, smart grid/micro-grid, load modeling, renewable energy grid connection, electricity market, data mining, big data analytics, artificial intelligence, and computational methods. He has served as editor for a number of international top journals such as *IEEE Transactions on Smart Grid, IEEE PES Letters, IEEE Transactions on Sustainable Energy, IET Renewable Power Generation*, and *Journal of Modern Power Systems and Clean Energy*. He is an international advisor for the leading Chinese journal *Automation of Electric Power Systems* and a guest editor for *Southern Power System Technology* published by China Southern Power Grid. He also serves as guest editor for *International Journal of Systems Science*.

Professor Dong has been the principal investigator for over 10 EPRI projects, 14 ARC grants, 4 grants under the HK RGC & ITF scheme, and a partner investigator of two theme-based projects in Hong Kong. He has worked on many industrial R&D and consulting projects in power system planning, stability, smart grid, electricity market analysis, load modelling, and data-mining based methods for energy system data analytics. As a consultant, he leads the development of the load models for Western Power Corporation's daily usage in operations and planning of Western Australia's transmission network. He led the gas and electricity network co-planning for the $12.6m CSIRO Future Grid project. He also worked with the government on smart grid cyber security. He is a member of IEEE taskforce on power system cascading failure, a chapter coordinator for the CIGRE work group on load modelling, a core member of the IEEE PES Smart Building, Loads and Customer System Committee coordinating IEEE standards in Load Model and Simulation. He is the Deputy Chair for Smart Grid Australia (SGA) study group and leads its research domain on cyber physical systems, including representing SGA at the International Federation of Smart Grid. He established a team of 28 at Ausgrid Centre for Intelligent Electricity Networks to provide R&D support for the $100m (plus $500m from Ausgrid) Smart Grid, Smart City national demonstration project.

Professor Dong obtained a Ph.D. from the University of Sydney in 1999. He has published over 300 journal papers (mostly IEEE transactions and IET journals), and received over $16 million in research and industrial grants. Professor Dong has supervised or co-supervised over 50 PhD students, many who now work in industry and research/academia in Australia, Europe, Asia, and America

Contributors

Sanghita Baidya
Electrical Engineering
Tripura University
Agartala, Tripura, India

Prashant Baredar
Department of Energy
Maulana Azad National Institute of
  Technology
Bhopal, Madhya Pradesh, India

Wesley Doorsamy
Institute for Intelligent Systems
University of Johannesburg
Johannesburg, South Africa

Raj Kumar Jarial
Department of Electrical
  Engineering
National Institute of Technology
Hamirpur, Himachal Pradesh,
  India

Cheshta J. Khare
Electrical Engineering
Shri G.S. Institute of Technology &
  Science
Indore, Madhya Pradesh, India

Vikas Khare
Electrical Engineering
School of Technology, Management and
  Engineering, NMIMS
Indore, India

Pawan Kumar
Electrical and Instrumentation
  Engineering Department
Thapar Institute of Engineering &
  Technology
Patiala, Punjab, India

Meet Kumari
Electronics and Communication
  Engineering
Chandigarh University
Mohali, Punjab, India

Champa Nandi
Electrical Engineering
Tripura University
Agartala, Tripura, India

Savita Nema
Electrical Engineering
Maulana Azad National Institute of
  Technology
Bhopal, Madhya Pradesh, India

Nisha Parveen
Electrical Engineering
Indian Institute of Technology
Delhi, India

Babu Sena Paul
Institute for Intelligent Systems
University of Johannesburg
South Africa

Ankur Singh Rana
Electrical and Electronics Engineering
National Institute of Technology
Tiruchirappalli, Tamil Nadu, India

Arzu Eren Şenaras
Econometrics
Bursa Uludag University
Bursa, Turkey

Onur Mesut Şenaras
Automotive Engineering
Bursa Uludag University
Bursa, Turkey

Saurabh Ranjan Sharma
Department of Electrical
    Engineering
National Institute of Technology
Hamirpur, Himachal Pradesh, India

Arush Singh
Department of Electrical
    Engineering
National Institute of Technology
Hamirpur, Himachal Pradesh, India

Deepanshu Singh Solanki
Department of Electronics Engineering
National Institute of Technology
Hamirpur, Himachal Pradesh, India

Mini Shaji Thomas
Electrical and Electronics Engineering
National Institute of Technology
Tiruchirappalli, Tamil Nadu, India

Vivek Kumar Tripathi
Department of Electrical
    Engineering
National Institute of Technology
Hamirpur, Himachal Pradesh, India

Anjali Uppal
Electrical and Instrumentation
    Engineering Department
Thapar Institute of Engineering &
    Technology
Patiala, Punjab, India

Shufali Ashraf Wani
Electrical Engineering
National Institute of Technology
Srinagar, Jammu & Kashmir, India

1 A Framework of Internet of Energy for Coordinated Operation in Power Delivery

Pawan Kumar and Anjali Uppal
Thapar Institute of Engineering & Technology, Patiala, Punjab, India

CONTENTS

1.1 Background 2
1.2 Literature Review 3
1.3 Power Distribution Systems 6
1.4 Objectives of Distribution Systems 7
1.5 Classification of Distribution Systems 7
1.6 Connection Scheme of Distribution System 8
    1.6.1 Radial System 8
    1.6.2 Ring Main System 9
    1.6.3 Interconnected System 10
1.7 Requirement of a Distribution System 11
    1.7.1 System Voltage Profile 11
    1.7.2 Availability of Power Demand 11
    1.7.3 Reliability 11
1.8 Mathematical Formulation of Energy Efficiency Parameters 11
    1.8.1 Equivalent Representation of Distribution Line Between
           Two Nodes 12
    1.8.2 Phasor Diagram of Distribution Line Between Two Nodes 13
    1.8.3 Node Voltage Calculation 13
    1.8.4 Power Flow Equation 15
           1.8.4.1 Forward Power Flow Equation 16
           1.8.4.2 Backward Power Flow Equation 16
    1.8.5 Calculation of Power Losses 17
1.9 Calculation of Peak Load Factor 18
1.10 Load Modeling and Their Representations 19
    1.10.1 Load Modeling 19
    1.10.2 Load Growth 20
1.11 Illustrative Example 21

1.12   A Framework of Internet of Energy...23
        1.12.1   IoE Framework at the Primary Distribution
                  System Level..24
                  1.12.1.1   IoE Framework for Network Configuration
                              Management..24
                  1.12.1.2   IoE Framework for Integration of Distributed
                              Energy Resources.......................................26
                  1.12.1.3   IoE Framework for the Integration of Dynamic
                              Voltage Restorer..28
        1.12.2   IoE framework at the Secondary Distribution
                  System Level..30
                  1.12.2.1   IoE Framework for DSM.............................31
                  1.12.2.2   IoE Framework for a Vehicle to Grid and
                              Grid to Vehicle..31
1.13   Results and Discussions...31
1.14   Future Research Directions...35
1.15   Conclusions...35
References..36
Related Reading...39
Keywords and Descriptions...39

1.1   BACKGROUND

In the modern world, the conventional way of controlling the system operation is obsolete now and the most recent research involves various approaches for sustainable energy security. This requires the implementation of software operating systems that can be operated from a remote location through internet services. The involvement of online operations in power delivery has revolutionized the research work for energy efficiency. Therefore, in recent years, energy efficiency has become a burning issue since the energy sources are depleting day by day and the major requirement of today's world is to focus on the best utilization of the available resources. In practice, energy efficiency measures are different for different types of loads and load classes. This is because the loads in the power system are voltage-dependent and the state of the economy of the distribution system's operation can also affect the system's operation. For energy efficiency, in an ever-growing loading scenario, the integration of the distribution system has increased many folds due to the deregulation of power systems.

In addition, with the frequent change in loading patterns, the power utilities are restructuring the network topology. This allows minimization of power loss, relief of overloaded sections, improvement in voltage profile of the system and reliability of supplying power, improved peak loading, and hence increases the overall energy efficiency. Various studies are ongoing to optimize the system operation and the associated network parameters using a variety of techniques. To find the optimal operation of distribution systems, the location and size of distributed energy resources is a big challenge for the researchers under practical loading. In this scenario, it calls for the development of a new framework of the Internet of Energy (IoE) in coordination with the local grid system.

1.2 LITERATURE REVIEW

According to International Energy Agency (IEA) the world's energy need will be more than 50% higher in 2030 compared to today's scenario, assuming that the demand grows at the rate of 1.8% annually. In the ever-growing loading scenario, energy efficiency is the only alternative to sustain the energy required for long period.

Energy efficiency in the distribution systems depends on the type of loading and operating conditions. During operation, a distribution system can achieve this objective by altering network topology, resizing the distributed generation, as per demand, and finding alternative energy devices that consume less input for the same output.

Network reconfiguration is an integral part of the load management at the distribution level. Reconfiguration allows the network topology to be altered for optimal or for energy-efficient operation. However, the optimization function depends upon the operating constraints and it can be formulated for different objectives under different operating conditions. The commonly used objectives in the research work for energy-efficient operation are shown in Table 1.1.

Table 1.1 shows a comprehensive analysis of the energy efficiency performance of the distribution system with PEBs and AEBs. In these studies, authors have considered different loading patterns and/or load models to show the effectiveness of their approach in a practical scenario. From these studies, it has been observed that the voltage-dependent loads can affect the system performance while reconfiguration is performed and the DG or DVR is integrated into the distribution systems.

Further, from the research, it can also be seen that the energy efficiency is not limited to a single parameter – it needs to be evaluated comprehensively. In practice, loads are voltage-dependent, and they can affect the system performance and therefore, for accurate results, the modeling of practical loads is required during online operation and, hence, for energy management. Ideally, practical loads are represented as residential loads, commercial loads, and industrial loads. The industrial loads are the bulk load that is widely studied by the researcher whereas with the involvement of the electronic devices the residential and commercial load characteristics keep on changing every fraction of time. The role of these loads is also studied by the researcher where energy management is performed for the local grid and or microgrid. However, in most of these studies no practical model is developed and the research is conducted based on static data only.

TABLE 1.1

Summary of research work for energy efficiency under different objectives

Ref. No.	Author(s)/et al.	Objectives/Descriptions
[1]	Baran & Wu (1989)	Reconfiguring the distribution system for reduction in losses and balancing in load
[2]	Nara et al. (1992)	Reconfiguring the distribution system for reduction of loss
[3]	Venkatesh et al. (2004)	Rearranging the distribution system for maximization of the loadability
[4]	Sivanagaraju et al. (2005)	Reducing voltage instability by reconfiguring the network of a radial distribution system
[5]	Mendoza et al. (2009)	Reconfiguration of an algorithm by taking power losses and reliability indices into consideration
[6]	Oliveira et al. (2010)	Optimal reconfiguring and placement of capacitor in radial distribution systems for minimization of losses in energy
[7]	Ali et al. (2012)	Impact of patterns of load on system performance of reconfigured medium-sized distribution network
[8]	Gupta et al. (2014)	Reconstruction for improving power quality as well as reliability
[9]	Kumar & Singh (2014)	Redistribution of radial distribution system with static load model to reduce losses
[10]	Kumar & Singh (2014)	Execution of reconfiguring the radial networks with reactive power injection for energy efficiency
[11]	Ali et al. (2015)	Energy-efficient recombination under practical load combinations
[12]	Ali et al. (2016)	Examination of the rearranged distribution system for energy efficiency under practical loads
[13]	Kumar et al. (2017)	Usage of efficient heuristic and meta-heuristic approach to voltage protection and radiality for reconfiguration of a distribution system
[14]	Kumar et al. (2020)	Integrated operation and planning of distribution system
[15]	Haque (1999)	Placement of capacitor in radial distribution systems for loss reduction
[16]	Popovic et al. (2005)	Optimal positioning of distributed generators and reclosers for security of network and reliability for distribution network
[17]	Borges & Falco (2006)	Optimal distributed generation allocation to improve reliability, loss, and voltage
[18]	Gautam et al. (2007)	Optimal placement of DG in the deregulated market of electricity
[19]	Zou et al. (2009)	Voltage supported by distributed generator and shunt capacitor
[20]	Singh & Goswami (2010)	Optimum placement of distributed generations on the basis of nodal pricing to improve voltage, including gain, loss reduction, and including voltage increase issues
[21]	Hemdan & Kurrat (2011)	Efficient combination of distributed generation to meet the increment in load demand
[22]	Banerjee & Islam (2011)	Optimum location of distributed generation on the basis of reliability
[23]	Ali et al. (2011)	Optimal placement of capacitor in smart distribution systems for improving their peak loading and efficiency of energy
[24]	Hung et al. (2013)	Placement of DG in a primary distribution network for the reducing the loss

(Continued)

TABLE 1.1 (Continued)
Summary of research work for energy efficiency under different objectives

Ref. No.	Author(s)/et al.	Objectives/Descriptions
[25]	Kumar et al. (2013)	Distributed resource planning for better voltage stability of radial distribution system
[26]	Kumar & Singh (2014)	Comprehensive analysis of stability for radial distribution system with rising load
[27]	Ahuja & Kumar (2019)	A novel approach for the integrated operating the variable speed wind energy conversion in smart grid applications
[28]	Logenthiran et al. (2010)	Managing the demand side in smart grid using heuristic optimization
[29]	Rad et al. (2010)	Demand-side management on the basis of game-theoretic consuming the energy for scheduling for the future smart grid
[30]	Palensky & Dietrich (2011)	Demand-side management: Demand response, resourceful energy system, and smart loads
[31]	Arora & Kumar (2012)	Structural advancement of energy outlining and energy managing for implementing the smart grid
[32]	Pipattanasomporn et al. (2012)	Algorithm for management of energy for home and analysis of demand response
[33]	Guo et al. (2012)	Optimal management of power for residential customers in the smart grid
[34]	Costanzo et al. (2012)	An architecture for autonomous load management for demand-side in smart buildings
[35]	Agentis et al. (2013)	Scheduling of load for optimization of consumption of household energy
[36]	Zhao et al. (2013)	An optimal scheduling of power for demand response in the home energy management system
[37]	Chiu et al. (2013)	Unbalancing of energy management using a robust pricing plan
[38]	Kumar et al. (2014)	Synchronization of a solar cell, battery, and grid supplies for the developing the smart power systems for the home
[39]	Safdarian et al. (2014)	Improvement in reliability in distribution network in presence of demand response
[40]	Abdelwahed et al. (2015)	To control, power consumption at home: Smart home
[41]	Tsagarakiset et al. (2016)	Cost assessment and impact on environmental residential demand-side management
[42]	Hao et al. (2016)	Transactive control of commercial buildings for demand response
[43]	Rahman et al. (2016)	Development of demand-side management program for commercial customers: A case study
[44]	Facchini et al. (2017)	Evaluation of impact of social interactions on distributed demand-side management systems for home appliances
[45]	Anvari et al. (2017)	Management of energy efficiently for a grid-bound residential microgrids
[46]	Kumar and Thanki (2018)	Synchronization of operation of grid power, solar power, and batteries for smart power management
[47]	Kumar et al. (2018)	Demand-side management: Energy efficiency and demand response
[48]	Kumar et al. (2019)	To outline the perspectives and intensification of energy efficiency in commercial and residential buildings

(Continued)

TABLE 1.1 (Continued)
Summary of research work for energy efficiency under different objectives

Ref. No.	Author(s)/et al.	Objectives/Descriptions
[49]	Kumar et al. (2019)	Assessment of energy efficiency in commercial and residential buildings with DSM: A review
[50]	Kumar et al. (2020)	To frame the network for intensification of energy efficiency in commercial and residential use
[51]	Jowder (2009)	Analysis and design of DVR for deep voltage relaxation and harmonic compensation
[52]	Sasitharan and Mishra (2010)	Constant switching frequency and controlling the load for dynamic voltage restorer
[53]	Jayaprakash et al. (2013)	To control the reduction in rating of dynamic voltage restorer with a battery energy storage system
[54]	Chandrasekaran & Murthy (2016)	Improvement in dynamic voltage restorer for enhancement in power quality
[55]	Galesh & Iman-Eini (2016)	Dynamic voltage restorer for implementing the multilevel cascaded H-bridge inverter

1.3   POWER DISTRIBUTION SYSTEMS

Distribution systems can be defined as distributing or transferring the electric power to the user premises for the local use. The distribution system is normally the electrical system between the transmission system and the substation fed by the consumer's meters. It contains feeders, distributors, and the service mains. Figure 1.1 depicts the single line diagram of a typical low-tension distribution system.

Feeders: A feeder provides the connection between the substation (or local generating station) and the area from which the power is going to be distributed. Generally, to maintain the same current throughout the feeder no tapping is taken from it. The main point to be taken into consideration while designing the feeder is its current carrying capacity.

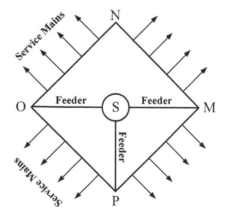

FIGURE 1.1   Single line diagram of a typical low-tension distribution system.

Distributor: A distributor is a conductor from which tapping is carried from supply to the consumers. In Figure 1.1, MN, NO, OP, and PM are the distributors. The current flowing through a distributor does not remain constant because tapping is taken at various places over its length. The voltage drop is the main consideration taken into mind while designing a distributor, as the s voltage variations have the statutory limit of ± 10% of its rated value at the consumer's terminals.

Service mains: A service mains is a short cable connecting the distributor to the consumer terminals.

1.4 OBJECTIVES OF DISTRIBUTION SYSTEMS

The main objectives of the distribution system are as follows,

1. To plan and modernize the power delivery system
2. Providing service connection to all consumers including urban, rural, and industrial
3. Maximal security of power and minimal period of interruption
4. Safety for utility staff and consumers
5. To ensure better quality electricity in terms of the following,
   a. Balanced three-phase supply
   b. Improved power factor
   c. Flickering of voltage within permitted limits
   d. Reduced voltage sags
   e. Minimal interruption in power supply.

1.5 CLASSIFICATION OF DISTRIBUTION SYSTEMS

A distribution system may be classified according to the following,

(i). **Nature of current:** Based on the nature of the current, the distribution system can be classified into

(a) DC distribution system

(b) AC distribution system.

The AC system is simpler than the DC system and it is more economical, which is why it is extensively accepted for the distribution of electric power.

(ii). **Type of construction:** As per the type of construction, the distribution system can be classified as

(a) Overhead system

(b) Underground system.

The overhead system is five to ten times more economical than the underground system, which is why it is mainly employed for distribution. However, the underground system is practiced at places where overhead construction is prohibited by the local laws or impracticable.

(iii). **Scheme of connection:** As per the scheme of connection, the distribution system can be classified as,

   (a) Radial system

   (b) Ring main system

   (c) Inter-connected system.

Generally, in a power distribution system, the above three schemes are followed, and these schemes have their advantages and disadvantages. Therefore, in the subsequent section, the description of these schemes is presented.

1.6 CONNECTION SCHEME OF DISTRIBUTION SYSTEM

The constant voltage system is generally used for the distribution of electrical energy. In practice, the following distribution circuits are generally used:

1.6.1 RADIAL SYSTEM

In this system, different feeders radiate from a single substation and they feed the distributors from one end only. Figure 1.2 (a) depicts the single line diagram of a radial network system for DC supply. The distribution is that where a feeder AB supplies a distributor CD at point 'C'. The distributors are fed at one point only, i.e. point 'C' in this case. Figure 1.2(b) shows a single line diagram of the radial system for AC distribution. Radial systems are employed only when electricity is generated at low voltage and the substation is located at the center of the load. This is the simple distribution circuit with a low initial cost. However, it suffers some drawbacks that are given below:

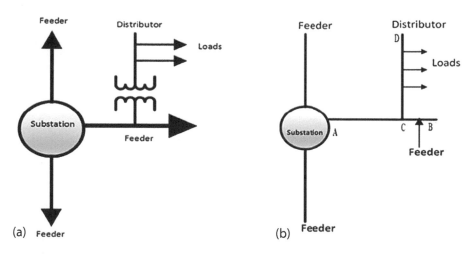

FIGURE 1.2   Single line diagram of radial system.

(a) The distributor end that is near the feeding point will be heavily loaded.

(b) The consumers are relying on one feeder and one distributor. Therefore, if there is any fault on the distributor or feeder it will cut off the supply for the consumers that are staying away from the substation.

(c) The consumers living at the distant end of the distributor will suffer from various fluctuations in voltages when there is a change of load in the distributor. Due to these limitations, this system is restricted for short distances only.

1.6.2 RING MAIN SYSTEM

In this system, a loop is formed by the primary sides of the distribution transformer. The loop circuit starts at the substation bus-bar, which forms a loop through the area served and returns to the substation. The single line diagram of the ring main system for AC is shown in Figure 1.3. Distribution is from where the substation supplies to the feeder through the closed feeder JFIGXZYT via distribution transformers. The main features of the ring main system are as follows:

a. Voltage variations at consumer's terminals are reduced.

b. The system is reliable because each distributor is fed through two feeders.

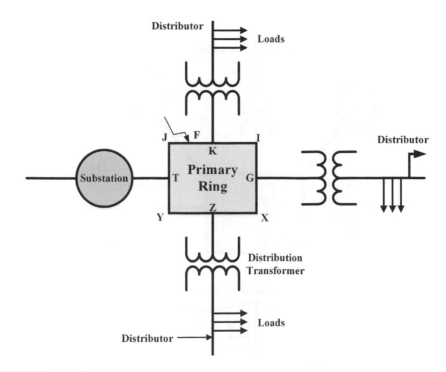

FIGURE 1.3 Ring main systems.

In case of fault on any part of the feeder, the continuity of supply is maintained. For example, assume that a fault occurs at any point F of section TJF of the feeder. The continuity of supply can be maintained to all the consumers through the feeder TYZXGIK if the section TJF of the feeder is isolated for repair.

1.6.3   INTERCONNECTED SYSTEM

When two or more than two generating stations or substations are used to energize the feeder ring, it is known as an interconnected system. The single line diagram of the interconnected system is shown in Figure 1.4 in which the closed feeder ring KLMN is supplied by two substations named S_1 and S_2 at points K and L respectively. D, A, C, and B are the points on the feeder ring where distributors are connected through distribution transformers. The interconnected system has some advantages, which are as follows:

a. It enhances the reliability of the system.

b. During peak load hours, any area received from one generating station can be fed from another generating station. This reduces reserve power capacity and increases system efficiency.

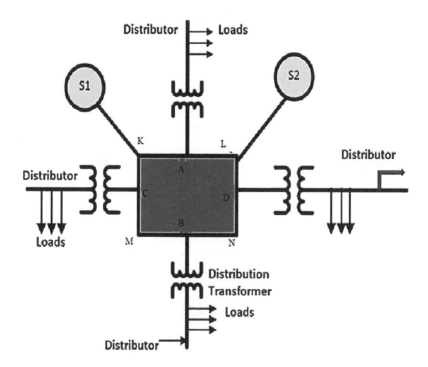

FIGURE 1.4   Interconnected systems.

1.7   REQUIREMENT OF A DISTRIBUTION SYSTEM

A considerable amount of effort is necessary for maintaining an electric power supply within the needs of various types of consumers. Some of the necessities of a good distribution system are reasonable voltage, availability of power on demand, and reliability.

1.7.1   System Voltage Profile

An important necessity of a distribution system is to keep the voltage differences at the terminals of consumers as low as possible. This change in voltage is due to the variation of load on the system. Lower voltage leads to loss of revenue, inefficient lighting, and potential burns from motors. A higher voltage value may cause lamps to fail and other electrical appliances may malfunction. Therefore, the distribution system must ensure that the variations in voltages at consumers' terminals should be in the permissible range. The limitation of voltage difference is ±10% of the rated value at the consumers' terminals. Thus, if the specified voltage is 230 V, then the maximum value of the voltage should not exceed 244 V while the minimum voltage value for consumers should not be less than 216 V.

1.7.2   Availability of Power Demand

Consumers should have electricity available in any amount that they may need from instant to instant. For example, motors can be started or stopped; lights can be switched on or off, without giving warning to the power supply company. It is not possible to store electrical energy, therefore the distribution system needs to be able to supply the load demands of consumers. Operating staff must continuously study load schedules so that they can anticipate in advance major load changes that follow the known schedules.

1.7.3   Reliability

Modern industry relies entirely on electricity for its operation and control. Houses and office buildings are electrically lighted, cooled, heated, and ventilated. They need a reliable service. Unfortunately, electric power, as with everything that is man-made, can never be completely reliable. However, the reliability can be improved to a great extent by (a) a inter-connected system, (b) a reliable automatic control system, and (c) providing additional reserve facilities.

1.8   MATHEMATICAL FORMULATION OF ENERGY EFFICIENCY PARAMETERS

From the literature, it has been observed that the performance of the power distribution system can be evaluated in terms of several parameters. The various energy efficiency defining parameters are described as:

1. Power demands in terms of apparent, active, and reactive components
2. System voltage profile

3. Peak loading limit
4. Power loss during operation
5. Size and location of external energy resources
6. Reliability of supplying power.

The PEBs and AEBs have direct and indirect effects over the above-mentioned parameters. The power demands define the rated capacity of the loads and effect value of the requirement of load demand at a particular time instant. However, power demand varies with the time of operation and the state of the economy. Therefore, a mathematical formulation of this parameter for the analysis and to show their interdependence must be developed.

1.8.1 EQUIVALENT REPRESENTATION OF DISTRIBUTION LINE BETWEEN TWO NODES

The distribution lines are considered as the short lines and these usually vary from 5 to 20 km in length and can be represented in a simple equivalent circuit as shown in Figure 1.5. Here, n_s and n_r are the end nodes whereas r_i and x_i are the line parameters.

V_s = Sending end voltage
V_r = Receiving end voltage
n_s = Sending end node
n_r = Receiving end node
r_i = Resistance of power line
x_i = Reactance of power line

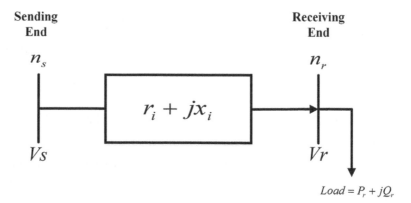

FIGURE 1.5 Single line representation of distribution line.

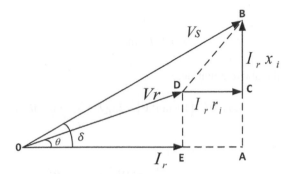

FIGURE 1.6   Phasor diagram of a line segment between two nodes.

1.8.2   PHASOR DIAGRAM OF DISTRIBUTION LINE BETWEEN TWO NODES

For the line segment considered above, as an equivalent circuit, it is considered that the load connected with the receiving end node is inductive and Figure 1.6 shows the phasor diagram for the distribution line between two nodes.

1.8.3   NODE VOLTAGE CALCULATION

For the calculation of node voltages, the following assumptions are made:

a. A balanced three-phase system is represented with a single line diagram.

b. The distribution system is operating at comparatively low voltage and therefore, the effect of shunt capacitance can be considered as negligible. However, if there is any capacitance, it may be represented as a reactive load at the end nodes.

From the phasor diagram,

$$OA = V_s \cos\delta = V_r \cos\theta + I_r r \tag{1.1}$$

$$AB = V_s \sin\delta = V_r \sin\theta + I_r x \tag{1.2}$$

From the above Equations (1.1) and (1.2),

$$V_s^2 = OA^2 + AB^2 = \left(V_r \cos\theta + I_r r\right)^2 + \left(V_r \sin\theta + I_r x\right)^2 \tag{1.3}$$

On solving the Rquation (1.3),

$$V_s^2 = V_r^2 + 2r_i P_r + 2x Q_r + \left(r_i^2 + x_i^2\right)\left(\frac{P_r^2 + Q_r^2}{V_r^2}\right) \tag{1.4}$$

Where

$$P_r = V_r I_r \cos\theta \tag{1.5}$$

And,

$$Q_r = V_r I_r \sin\theta \qquad (1.6)$$

Re-arranging the above equation,

$$V_s^2 = V_r^2 + 2r_i P_r + r_i^2 \cos^2\theta I_r^2 \left(1 + \tan^2\theta\right) + 2x_i Q_r + x_i^2 \cos^2\theta I_r^2 \left(1 + \tan^2\theta\right) \qquad (1.7)$$

From the above,

$$r_i^2 \cos^2\theta I_r^2 = V_r^2 \left(\frac{r_i^2 \cos^2\theta I_r^2}{V_r^2}\right) = r_i^2 * \frac{P_r^2}{V_r^2} \qquad (1.8)$$

And

$$x_i^2 \cos^2\theta I_r^2 = V_r^2 \left(\frac{x_i^2 \cos^2\theta I_r^2}{V_r^2}\right) = x_i^2 * \frac{P_r^2}{V_r^2} \qquad (1.9)$$

Putting the above in Equation (1.12) and then the resultant equation is represented as,

$$V_s^2 = V_r^2 + 2r_i P_r + 2x Q_r + \left(r_i^2 + x_i^2\right)\left(1 + \tan^2\theta\right)\frac{P_r^2}{V_r^2} \qquad (1.10)$$

Using $\theta = \tan^{-1}\dfrac{Q_r}{P_r}$

Therefore, $Q_r = P_r \tan\theta$

Putting Q_r and re-arranging,

$$V_s^2 = V_r^2 + 2P_r\left(r_i + x_i \tan\theta\right) + \left(r_i^2 + x_i^2\right)\left(1 + \tan^2\theta\right)\frac{P_r^2}{V_r^2} \qquad (1.11)$$

Let,

$$V_s^2 - 2P_r\left(r_i + x_i \tan\theta\right) = V_r^2 + \left(r_i^2 + x_i^2\right)\left(1 + \tan^2\theta\right)\frac{P_r^2}{V_r^2} \qquad (1.12)$$

$$V_s^2 - 2P_r\left(r_i + x_i \tan\theta\right) = K \qquad (1.13)$$

Then,

$$K = V_r^2 + \left(r_i^2 + x_i^2\right)\left(1 + \tan^2\theta\right)\frac{P_r^2}{V_r^2} \qquad (1.14)$$

$$V_r^4 + \left(r_i^2 + x_i^2\right)\left(1 + \tan^2\theta\right)P_r^2 - V_r^2 K = 0 \qquad (1.15)$$

Put, $V_r^4 = V_r^2$ and solve the quadratic equation for finding the roots, which yield,

$$V_r^2 = \frac{\left[K \pm \left(K^2 - 4\left(r_i^2 + x_i^2 \right) \sec^2 \theta P_r^2 \right)^{\frac{1}{2}} \right]}{2} \qquad (1.16)$$

Putting the value of K & $\tan \theta$ in the above equation,

$$V_r^2 = \frac{\left[V_s^2 - 2P_r \left(r_i + x_i \tan \theta \right) \pm \left\{ \left(V_s^2 - 2P_r \left(r_i + x_i \tan \theta \right)^2 \right) - 4\left(r_i^2 + x_i^2 \right) \sec^2 \theta P_r^2 \right\}^{\frac{1}{2}} \right]}{2}$$

$$= \frac{V_s^2}{2} - \left(P_r r_i + x_i Q_r \right) \pm \left[\left\{ \frac{V_s^2}{2} - \left(P_r r_i + x_i r \right) \right\}^2 - \left(r_i^2 + x_i^2 \right) \left(P_r^2 + Q_r^2 \right) \right]^{\frac{1}{2}} \qquad (1.17)$$

In generalized form,

$$V_i^2 = \frac{V_{i-1}^2}{2} - \left(P_i r_i - x_i Q_i \right) \pm \left[\left\{ \frac{V_{i-1}^2}{2} - P_i r_i + x_i Q_i \right\}^2 - \left(r_i^2 + x_i^2 \right) \left(P_i^2 + Q_i^2 \right) \right]^{\frac{1}{2}} \qquad (1.18)$$

1.8.4 POWER FLOW EQUATION

For calculating the terms related to the optimization problem described in the action section, a set of power flow equations can be used as these are very conducive to compute efficiently. To explain this, consider the radial network shown in Figure 1.7.

Here, the lines with impedances and loads are represented as constant power sinks,

$$Z_1 = r_1 + jx_1 \qquad (1.19)$$

$$S_L = P_L + jQ_L \qquad (1.20)$$

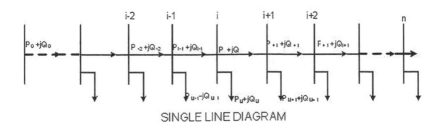

FIGURE 1.7   Single line diagram of a radial network.

1.8.4.1 Forward Power Flow Equation

Forward sweep is a calculation of voltage drop with the desired value of current or power flow updating values. The nodal voltage is upgraded in the forward sweep starting from the branches in the last layer. The main motive of the forward propagation is to find the voltage at each node that starts from the feeder source node. The feeder substation voltage is set at its actual value. The effective power in each branch during forwarding propagation is kept in line with the value obtained in backward propagation.

$$P_{i+1} = P_i - \frac{r_i\left(P_i^2 + Q_i^2\right)}{V_i^2} - P_{Li} \tag{1.21}$$

$$Q_{i+1} = Q_i - \frac{x_i\left(P_i^2 + Q_i^2\right)}{V_i^2} - Q_{Li} \tag{1.22}$$

$$V_{i+1} = V_i - \frac{\left(r_i + x_i\right)\left(P_i^2 + Q_i^2\right)}{V_i^2} \tag{1.23}$$

1.8.4.2 Backward Power Flow Equation

The backward sweep is a power or current flow solution with a permissible range of voltage update. It starts from the branches present in the last layer and moves towards the branches that have connection with the root node. The updated value of effective power flowing in each branch is obtained by considering the node voltages of previous iteration computation. This means that the voltage values received in the forward path are kept constant during backward propagation and updated power flows in each branch are transmitted backward along the feeder using a backward path. This illustrates that the backward propagation initiates from the extreme end node and moves towards the source node.

$$P_{i-1} = P_i + \frac{r_i\left(P_i^{2'} + Q_i^{2'}\right)}{V_i^2} + P_{Li} \tag{1.24}$$

$$Q_{i-1} = Q_i + \frac{r_i\left(P_i^{2'} + Q_i^{2'}\right)}{V_i^2} + Q_{Li} \tag{1.25}$$

$$V_{i-1} = V_i + \frac{\left(r_i + x_i\right)\left(P_i^{2'} + Q_i^{2'}\right)}{V_i^2} \tag{1.26}$$

Here,

P_{i+1} = Real power at the next node to that of ith node

P_{i-1} = Real power at the previous node to that of ith node

P_i' = Sum of the real power flowing next to ith node and load power at that node

P_i = Real power flow from ith node

Q_{i+1} = Reactive power at the next node to that of ith node

Q_{i-1} = Reactive power at the previous node to that of ith node

Q_i' = Sum of reactive power flowing next to ith node & load power at that node

Q_i = Reactive power flow from ith

V_{i+1} = Voltage at node next to ith node

V_{i-1} = Voltage at node previous to ith node

V_i = Voltage at ith node

1.8.5 CALCULATION OF POWER LOSSES

If the line parameters are known, then the real and reactive power loss of branch 'i' is given by

$$P_{LL} = I_i^2 r_i \tag{1.27}$$

$$Q_{LL} = I_i^2 x_i \tag{1.28}$$

By substituting the value of current in Equation (1.27) and (1.28), the active and reactive power losses can be obtained as under,

$$P_{LL} = r_i \frac{\left(P_i^2 + Q_i^2\right)}{V_i^2} \tag{1.29}$$

The total real power losses are given as,

$$TP_{LL} = \sum r_i \frac{\left(P_i^2 + Q_i^2\right)}{V_i^2} \tag{1.30}$$

Here, 'i' varies from 1 to n-1

$$Q_{LL} = x_i \frac{\left(P_i^2 + Q_i^2\right)}{V_i^2} \tag{1.31}$$

And the Total Reactive Power Losses are given as:

$$TQ_{LL} = \sum x_i \frac{\left(P_i^2 + Q_i^2\right)}{V_i^2} \tag{1.32}$$

Here, 'i' varies from 1 to n-1

1.9   CALCULATION OF PEAK LOAD FACTOR

In some industrial zones, it is seen that in case of some critical loading conditions the distribution system undergoes a voltage collapse. Voltage collapse is a localized phenomenon that occurs at a node within a region with a high load and low voltage profile. The occurrence of unexpected voltage collapse due to the rapid increase in power demand of some industrial loads has been experienced. When this kind of collapse occurs, some industrial loads will be automatically cut off due to severe interruption through the cut-off switches.Hence, voltage stability is a major concern that has recently occurred in power distribution systems

This chapter presents a simple criterion of peak load factor (PLF) that measures the proximity of the current position of a line to finite loads in a radial distribution system. The value of PLF provides an estimation of the additional load as a factor of the existing load that can be drawn before reaching the point of peak loading. The value of PLF can be calculated at each node of the radial distribution system. The value of PLF is near to 1.0 indicating that the feeder will not be able to supply any more apparent power by using this method; nodes closer to peak loading can be identified.

$$V_{i+1}{}^2 = \frac{V_i^2}{2} - \left(P_i r_i + x_i Q_i\right) \pm \left[\left\{\frac{V_i^2}{2} - \left(P_i r_i + x_i Q_i\right)\right\}^2 - \left(r_i^2 + x_i^2\right)\left(P_i^2 + Q_i^2\right)\right]^{\frac{1}{2}} = X \pm Y$$

(1.33)

Here,

$$X = \frac{V_i^2}{2} - \left(P_i r_i + x_i Q_i\right)$$

(1.34)

And

$$Y = \left[\left\{\frac{V_i^2}{2} - \left(P_i r_i + x_i Q_i\right)\right\}^2 - \left(r_i^2 + x_i^2\right)\left(P_i^2 + Q_i^2\right)\right]^{\frac{1}{2}}$$

(1.35)

From Equation (1.35), it is clear that a solution does not exist for voltage when the value of Y^2 is becoming negative. Mathematically the solution will exist only when.

$$\left\{\frac{V_i^2}{2} - \left(P_i r_i + x_i Q_i\right)\right\}^2 - \left(r_i^2 + x_i^2\right)\left(P_i^2 + Q_i^2\right) \geq 0$$

(1.36)

Peak loading is reached when $(P_2 + jQ_2)$ is increased to the point where Y^2 becomes zero. To determine the point, the existing load $(P_2 + jQ_2)$ is replaced by the term [PLF *$(P_2 + jQ_2)$] assuming a constant load power factor and equating it to zero to determine the maximum permissible loading as under:

$$\left\{\frac{V_i^2}{2} - \left(PLF * P_i r_i + PLF * x_i Q_i\right)\right\}^2 - PLF * \left(r_i^2 + x_i^2\right)\left(P_i^2 + Q_i^2\right) \geq 0$$

(1.37)

Rewriting the above equation as a quadratic equation in term of PLF and solving it

$$PLF = V_i^2 \left[-\left(P_2 r_i + Q_2 x_i\right) + \frac{\left\{\left(r_i^2 + x_i^2\right)\left(P_i^2 + Q_i^2\right)\right\}^{\frac{1}{2}} * \left(P_i x_i - r_i Q_i\right)^2}{2} \right] \quad (1.38)$$

On loading the feeder, the value of PLF decreases to the value of 1.0. At the point of peak loading, the value of (PLF-1) indicates the maximum additional amount of load in terms of existing $(P_2 + jQ_2)$ load flowing through the branch between nodes n_1 and n_2.

1.10 LOAD MODELING AND THEIR REPRESENTATIONS

1.10.1 LOAD MODELING

In traditional load flow studies, it is assumed that active and reactive power demands are specified as constant values, even if the voltage amplitude is at the same node. Different categories and types of a load may exist in the operation of an actual power system. The active and reactive power of these types of loads depends on the voltage and frequency of the system. Also, load characteristics have a significant effect on the load flow solutions and convergence efficiency. The static load model is expressed in a polynomial as well as in exponential form for active and reactive power calculations. The characteristic equation of the exponential load model can be given as:

$$P_L = P_{LO}\left(\frac{V}{V_0}\right)^\alpha \quad (1.39)$$

$$Q_L = Q_{LO}\left(\frac{V}{V_0}\right)^\beta \quad (1.40)$$

Here, α and β are the voltage exponent corresponding to the active and reactive power components of load demand.

P_{Lo} and Q_{Lo} are the values of the active and reactive power at the nominal voltages, respectively. V and V_0 are load node voltage and load nominal voltage, respectively.

Specific values of the load exponent can be selected to give different load types, like '0' for the constant power, '1' for constant current, and '2' for constant impedance. The polynomial load model is termed as the static load model, which represents the relationship between power and voltage as a polynomial equation of voltage magnitude. The polynomial load model is usually referred to as a ZIP model as it consists of three different exponential load models: constant impedance (Z), constant current (I), and constant power (P) static load models. A common value for the voltage exponent of different types of static load models is given in Table 1.2.

TABLE 1.2

Exponent of different types of static load model [23]

Load types	Voltage exponents	
	α	β
Constant power	0	0
Constant current	1	1
Constant impedance	2	2

TABLE 1.3

Exponent of different load classes [13]

Load class	Voltage exponents	
	α	β
Residential load	1.20	2.90
Commercial load	0.99	3.60
Industrial load	0.18	6.90

For practical application, the evaluation of coefficients np and nq requires the use of parameter estimation techniques. The composite load, for example, consists of 50% constant power +30% constant impedance +20% constant current. Further, the composite load can be classified based on the load area and these loads with their voltage exponents are tabulated in Table 1.3.

1.10.2 LOAD GROWTH

The load growth is modeled as

$$\text{Load} * \left(1 + \frac{g}{100}\right)^n \tag{1.41}$$

In (1.41), load growth = g

Number of years = n

Most of the electrical loads in a power system have connection with the low voltage distribution systems. The electrical loads consist of residential, commercial, industrial, and municipal loads. In a distribution system the active as well as reactive power are dependent on the system voltage and its deviations in frequency. Additionally, characteristics of active and reactive power for various types of load models are different from each other. For static analysis, such as load flow studies, it is assumed that the deviation in frequency is not significant and it has its impact only on the voltage deviation on the active and reactive electrical loads can be considered to obtain better as well as accurate results. These results have the tendency to improve the quality of all subsequent system studies that utilize the load flow results.

1.11 ILLUSTRATIVE EXAMPLE

A sample radial network, as shown in Figure 1.8, is considered and the technical parameters for the same are defined as under,

$Z = r_i + x_i = 2.8 + j\,2.2\ \Omega,$

$S_2 = P_2 + jQ_2 = 2.5\ \text{MVA},$

$V_1 = 1\ \text{p.u.},$

Power factor = 0.8 lagging,

Base MVA = 100 MVA

Base kV = 11 kV

$r_i\ (\text{p.u.}) = r_i * \dfrac{100}{11^2}$

$x_i\ (\text{p.u.}) = x_i * \dfrac{100}{11^2}$

$P_2\ (\text{p.u.}) = \dfrac{2.5}{100} * 0.8,$

$Q_2\ (\text{p.u.}) = \dfrac{2.5}{100} * 0.6$

Using (1.38), the calculation of the PLF is performed and the results are listed below.

In the above calculation, the sending end voltage is assumed to be 1 p.u. The value of PLF is evaluated for various values of power flow through the branch and the results are tabulated in Table 1.4. For each step of loading, the fourth column of Table 1.4 gives the value of the product of load MVA and (PLF-1), which is equal to the

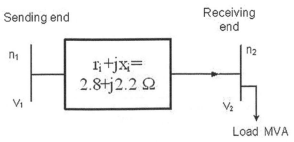

Simple Model of RDS for the calculation of MLI

FIGURE 1.8 Sample radial network for PLF calculation.

TABLE 1.4

Calculation of node voltage and PLF

S. No.	MVA load	The voltage at node 2	PLF	Additional load to reach the peak loading = [MVA load]*[PLF−1.0]
1	2.5	0.9201	3.3984	5.999
2	3.0	0.9022	2.8300	5.499
3	3.5	0.8834	2.4275	4.999
4	4.0	0.8637	2.1240	4.499
5	4.5	0.8429	1.8880	3.999
6	5.0	0.8208	1.6992	3.499
7	5.5	0.7969	1.5447	2.999
8	6.0	0.7710	1.4160	2.499
9	6.5	0.7424	1.3071	1.999
10	7.0	0.7098	1.2137	1.499
11	7.5	0.6712	1.1280	0.999
12	8.0	0.6209	1.0620	0.499
13	8.499	0.5134	1.0000	0.000
14	8.5	No solution	0.9900	−0.099

maximum possible additional power flow in the branch when the value of PLF is greater than 1.0 or the minimum power flow decrement to establish solvability of the power flow equation when the value of PLF is less than 1.0. When the load is 8.5 MVA, the value of PLF is found to be 0.99. This indicates the reduction of the load to the extent of 0.099 MVA will restore the solvability of the power flow equation for that branch and increases PLF to 1.0. In a similar manner at a load of 2.5 MVA, the value of PLF equal to 3.3984 indicates that an increase of power flow by 5.999MVA to reach 8.499 MVA reduces PLF to 1.0 and moves the branch to the point of peak loading condition. Figure 1.9 shows the graphical change in load and its effect on

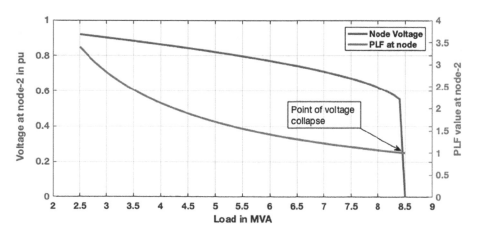

FIGURE 1.9   Graphical representation of PLF, node voltage, MVA load.

PLF and voltage magnitude at node n_2 by considering the sending-end node voltage as constant.

1.12 A FRAMEWORK OF INTERNET OF ENERGY

Recent developments in computational intelligence and later the involvement of internet sources have revolutionized the Internet of Things' (IoT's) new field of research. The major application of IoT has been to improve system performance with every change in operating conditions or not even before. Therefore, the merging of IoT and its application for energy management has coined a new term, the IoE.

$$IoE = IoT + Energy\ Efficiency$$

In a sustainable distribution grid, energy management is usually done at different stages and it needs to develop the IoE framework separately. The classification of the power distribution system can be realized through the level of system voltage and the quantity of load supplied from the substation. On considering the above two aspects, here, the power distribution system is categorized into two parts

1. Primary distribution system, i.e. supply-side management
2. Secondary distribution system, i.e. demand-side management (Figure 1.10).

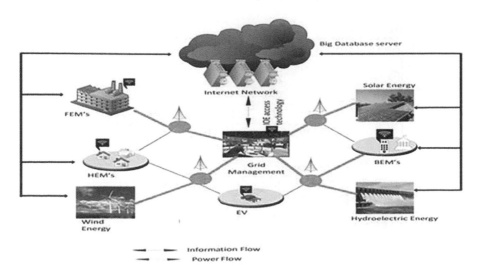

FIGURE 1.10   IoE framework for load and energy management [1].

1.12.1   IoE Framework at the Primary Distribution System Level

In primary distribution, the load demand is managed at a high level of voltage and for large demand. The energy efficiency measures at this level mainly deal with overall system voltage profile, peak loading, and reliability of supplying power. Therefore, the various IoE frameworks at primary distribution can be modeled as,

a. IoE framework of network configuration management (NCM)
b. IoE framework of integration of renewable energy sources (IRES)
c. IoE framework of integration of dynamic voltage restorer (IDVR).

1.12.1.1   IoE Framework for Network Configuration Management

Reconfiguration of distribution systems is an important task during online and offline operations. It is taken into consideration that the most economical way to improve energy efficiency performance (EEP) is by changing the topology of the network. Reconfiguration can be performed within a single radial network fed from a single source and two or more networks fed to a multi-source. The latter case is commonly referred to as node transfer because it leads to an increase or decrease in the number of nodes in the radial structure of EEP by

a. Improving the voltage profile of the node away from the source node
b. Reducing the power loss
c. Improving the peak load capacity of the existing system, without external resources (Figure 1.11).

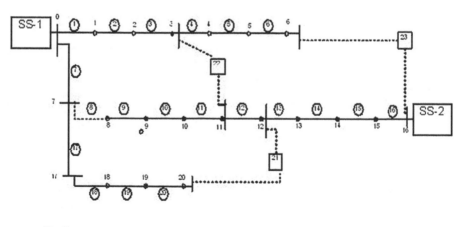

FIGURE 1.11   Network configuration-I.

The limitation of reconfiguration is the switching loss which limits the number of reconfigurations performed in a particular time duration (Figures 1.12 and 1.13)

In the network reconfiguration, the major challenge is the identification of branch number, sending-end and receiving-end nodes, and node beyond branches. Therefore, to illustrate this process, a single line diagram of a 12-node radial distribution system is considered as is shown in Figure 1.14. The information regarding branches, nodes, the total number of nodes, nodes, and branch beyond a particular branch is tabulated in Table 1.5:

For every change in the network topology, the above process is repeated and the new value of system voltage profile, load profile, power loss, and the peak loading factor need to be re-evaluated.

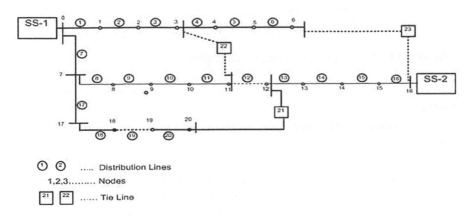

FIGURE 1.12   Network configuration-II.

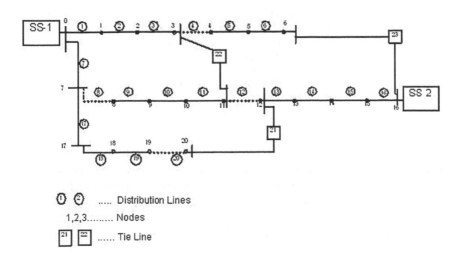

FIGURE 1.13   Network configuration-III.

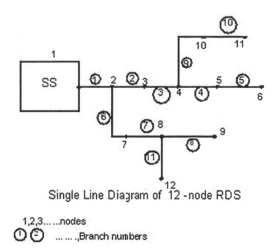

Single Line Diagram of 12-node RDS

1,2,3......nodes

①② ....,Branch numbers

FIGURE 1.14   A sample radial network for illustration.

TABLE 1.5
Branch number, sending end node, receiving end node and node beyond branches

Br. No	Sending-end node	Receiving-end node	Branches beyond of particular branch	Nodes beyond branch	Total number of nodes beyond the branch
1	1	2	2, 6, 3, 7, 4, 9, 8, 11, 5, 10	2, 3, 7, 8, 5, 10, 9, 12, 6, 11	11
2	2	3	3, 4, 9, 5, 10	3, 4, 5, 10, 6, 11	6
3	3	4	4, 9, 5, 10	4, 5, 10, 6,1 1	5
4	4	5	5	5, 6	2
5	5	6	End branch	6	1
6	2	7	7, 8, 10	7, 8, 9, 12	4
7	7	8	8, 11	8, 9, 12	3
8	8	9	End branch	9	1
9	4	10	End branch	10, 11	2
10	10	11	End branch	11	1
11	8	12	End branch	12	1

1.12.1.2   IoE Framework for Integration of Distributed Energy Resources

IoE consists of various renewable energy resources that have connection with the grid for providing clean and green energy. With the advancement of technology, the price of renewable energy resources is reducing, and it helps to enhance the global economy of the country every year. Hydroelectric, wind, solar, etc. are various types of renewable energy resources. Solar energy and wind energy are at the top level in the form of renewable sources of energy. The wind power system uses wind to harness the wind energy through the wind turbine to generate electricity. Figure 1.15

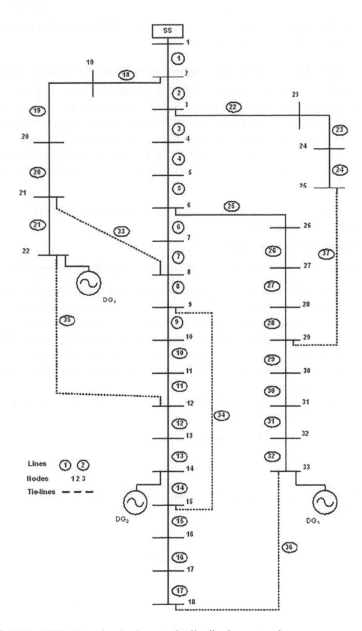

FIGURE 1.15 DER allocation in the sample distribution network.

shows the connection of various distributed energy resources (DER) in the existing system for improving energy efficiency performance while delivering power.

In Figure 1.15, three locations are identified for the integration of DER; however, it is a big challenge to identify the exact size and location of these DERs under frequent changes in the loading patterns. The IoE framework helps to analyze the energy data for a particular area under different operating conditions and a near-optimum value has been selected for economic reasons.

1.12.1.3   IoE Framework for the Integration of Dynamic Voltage Restorer

DVR is the application-specific component for energy efficiency in power delivery. DVR consists of three main components, namely storage device, power converters, and injecting transformer. The frequent variation, due to incremented or decremented rate, in load demand is responsible for voltage sags and swells at the load end. In practice, some loads are highly sensitive to the change in voltage profile, which in turn may damage the load or cause a deterioration in the operating efficiency and thereby,

- a. DVR allows maintaining the voltage by injecting external voltage in phase with the existing system.
- b. It reduces the frequent voltage sags and swells.
- c. It can act as an uninterrupted power supply during interruptions (Figure 1.16).

The limitation of DVR is that it is not economical to install a DVR for every single load in distribution systems. It is difficult to identify the most sensitive load and hence the optimal location of DVR, so it is operated for a group of loads.

The IoE framework helps to identify load sensitivity and dynamics. With load dynamics, the detailed analysis of the load demand and scope of energy management under different operating conditions can be identified for normal and abnormal operations during power delivery.

From Figure 1.17, by applying the KVL, the following can be obtained,

$$\bar{V}_s + \bar{V}_f = \bar{I}_s \left(R_s + jX_s \right) + \bar{V}_L \tag{1.42}$$

$$\bar{V}_L = Z_L \bar{I}_L \tag{1.43}$$

With known line and load parameters, the current flowing in the series circuit can be calculated using,

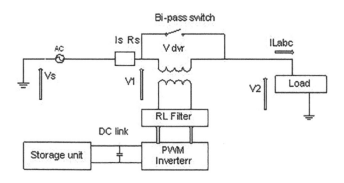

FIGURE 1.16   Dynamic model of DVR.

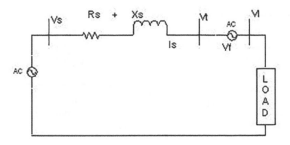

FIGURE 1.17   Equivalent circuit of DVR model.

$$\overline{I}_s = \overline{I}_L = \frac{\overline{V}_s + \overline{V}_f}{Z_s + Z_L} \tag{1.44}$$

$$\overline{V}_L = \frac{\overline{V}_s + \overline{V}_f}{Z_s + Z_L} * Z_L \tag{1.45}$$

With every change in the V_L, it is required to change the magnitude or phase angle of V_f as per the requirement. The IoE framework will manage the same based on the previous trends and the circuit conditions. The different network model of the DVR is shown in Figures 1.18 to 1.20.

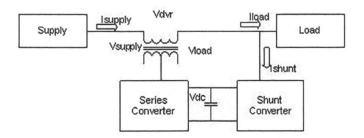

FIGURE 1.18   DVR topology with no energy storage.

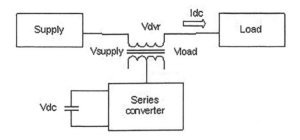

FIGURE 1.19   DVR topology with energy storage (with variable DC-link voltage).

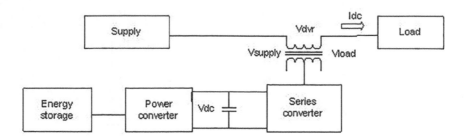

FIGURE 1.20   DVR topology with energy storage (with constant DC-link voltage).

1.12.2   IoE FRAMEWORK AT THE SECONDARY DISTRIBUTION SYSTEM LEVEL

The load demand and the voltage profile at the secondary power distribution level are comparatively low compared to the primary distribution level. Therefore, energy management mainly involves demand response analysis. In this system, the consumer's interest is always at a higher priority.

a. IoE framework of demand-side management (DSM)
b. IoE framework of a vehicle to grid and grid to vehicle technology (V2G/G2V) (Figure 1.21).

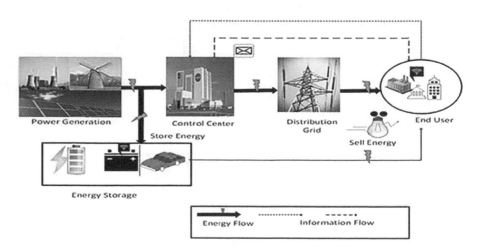

FIGURE 1.21   Generalized IoE framework.

1.12.2.1   IoE Framework for DSM

Buildings are the most energy-consuming areas in the world. Buildings have complex structures and many factors that affect the total consumption of energy in various buildings. Therefore, it is the biggest challenge to manage energy in buildings. Research from various researchers shows that nearly 30% of the total energy in the world is consumed by buildings and 60% of the energy is consumed by buildings for heating and cooling purposes.

Also, traditional buildings are not equipped with a lot of intelligent and intellectual designs. It is worth monitoring the consumption of real energy data and finding key factors as well as patterns through an organized way of modeling and analysis for various types of buildings. Such results can be used to advance and implement an appropriate IoT-based networking system to create appropriate methods and strategies to improve energy efficiency for green and traditional buildings. Building an energy management system using IoE will help to reduce energy consumption by preparing sufficient information related to demand of energy and its supply.

Figure 1.22 shows the functional algorithm for energy management in a commercial building. Here, three parameters are considered, namely several persons involved in the working area, the surrounding temperature, and the light intensity due to natural (sunlight) or artificial (electric lamps) resources.

1.12.2.2   IoE Framework for a Vehicle to Grid and Grid to Vehicle

The interest in the electric vehicles (EVs) sector as a replacement of existing vehicles such as a car, motorbike, etc. is increasing day by day with a rapid increase in the number of EVs on the road every year. EVs can either be a source of power or load on the grid; whether EVs support the grid or not depends on their charging state. In addition, EVs can provide support to the grid by providing power to the load during peak demands, which will improve energy quality, reliability, and efficiency. Therefore, integrating the EV power management system into IoE is one of the major trends today (Figures 1.23 and 1.24).

Table 1.6 shows the key features of the IoE framework and therefore, based upon the significant role that IoE can play in power delivery, the IoE framework can be categorized as follows.

1.13   RESULTS AND DISCUSSIONS

This section presents an illustrative example of the EEP analysis of the distribution system with many objectives solved using soft computing techniques. Here, a 33-node radial distribution network is considered and the effect of PEBs (reconfiguration only) and AEBs (with DER integration only) have been studied.

The 33-node radial network represented in Figure 1.18 is considered to demonstrate the EEP with PEBs and AEBs. Table 1.7 shows the EEP with PEBs under various models of load. Here, it can be observed that the system performance was

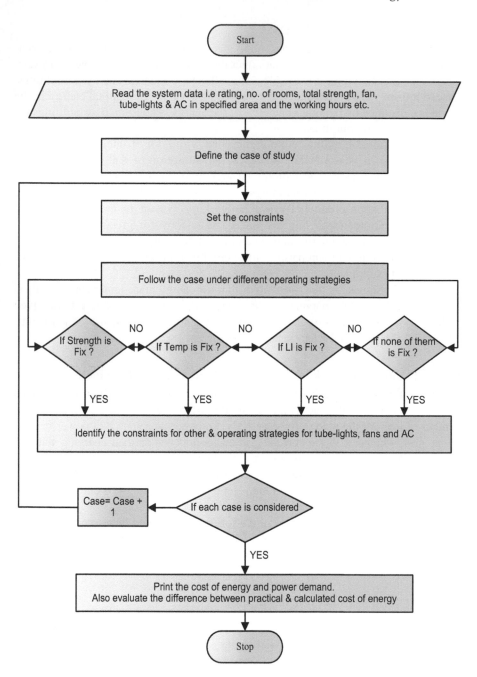

FIGURE 1.22   Flow chart for IoE framework of building energy management.

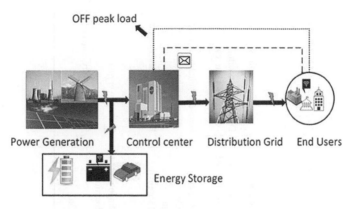

OFF peak load

Power Generation   Control center   Distribution Grid   End Users

Energy Storage

FIGURE 1.23 Charging during off-peak load period.

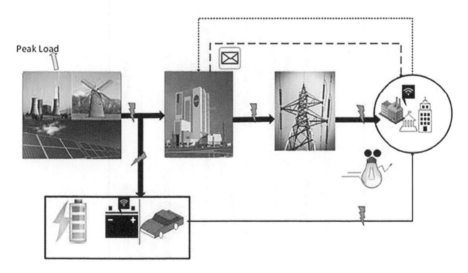

Peak Load

FIGURE 1.24 Discharging during peak load period.

found to be different under different load models. Similarly, in Table 1.8 the EEP is represented with AEBs for load model-1. From the results, it can be noticed that DG locations and sizes are different when single, two, or three DGs are considered. Also, the power demands in terms of active, reactive, or apparent powers are found to be significantly different in each case. This will further affect the system voltage profile, power loss, and the peak loading, and hence the peak load factor.

TABLE 1.6

Key features of IoE framework for load and energy management

IoE framework	Features	Functions	Applications	Advantages	Constraints
DSM	Demand response, energy efficiency	Energy management at demand and supply-side	Commercial and residential building energy management	Reduction of electricity bills, peak demand, and congestion	Data compendium, customer's interest
NCM	Load flow optimization, Altering load profile, energy efficiency	Reconfiguration, Load characterization	The network topology in Primary distribution	Loss minimization, voltage profile improvement	Network radiality, number of switching
IRES	Local power generation, energy efficiency	Integration of solar and wind energy	Generation for a remote location, rural electrification	Reliability of supplying power	Power quality and quantity
IDVR	Stability and energy efficiency	Integration of energy storage system	Voltage stabilization	Improved voltage profile for remote location	Cost, power quality
V2G/G2V	Grid-tie converter and energy efficiency	Vehicle to grid and grid to vehicle charging	Electric vehicles, hybrid electric vehicles	Eco-friendly transportation	Storage capacity, rate of charging

TABLE 1.7
EEP analysis of 33-node network with PEBs under different load models

Parameters	System performance under different load models		
Load models	Load model-1	Load model-2	Load model-3
Configurations	7,14,9,32,28	7,14,9,32,37	7,14,9,32,37
$P_{FD, KW}$	3854.9	3732.0	3733.0
$Q_{FD, KVAR}$	2404.9	2316.4	2073.6
$S_{FC, KVA}$	4543.5	4392.5	4270.3
$V_{i, MIN}$	0.9413	0.9407	0.9440
PLF	85.3419	88.2608	90.6602
$P_{L, KW}$	139.9796	128.7678	118.9440

TABLE 1.8
EEP analysis of 33-node network with AEBs under load model-1

Parameters	System performance under LM-1		
DG generation	DG=1	DG=2	DG=3
Configurations	33–37	33–37	33–37
$P_{FD, KW}$	3179.7	2246.1	1484.4
$Q_{FD, KVAR}$	2393.5	3268.7	2353.6
$S_{FC, KVA}$	3979.9	3268.7	2782.6
$V_{i, MIN}$	0.9272	0.9424	0.9700
F_{sl}	97.9221	121.7364	149.2277
$P_{L, KW}$	141.0509	109.5984	78.2595
DG locations	13	8,27	14,26,32
DG sizes, kw	676.1	966.9,611.5	652.3,999.8,656.7

1.14 FUTURE DIRECTIONS

The conventional method of load and energy management requires large manpower and extensive analysis. This will create the complexity in system operation and information exchange. Therefore, in the present research, the major focus of research is concentrated on online load management. The online management allows huge data gathering and subsequent manipulation with no time. The proposed framework of the IoE is a base model for futuristic research. In this chapter, the results are obtained with static data whereas the dynamic data needs to be considered for future work.

1.15 CONCLUSIONS

This chapter presented the various aspects of the development of the framework of the IoE for a sustainable distribution grid. The features, benefits, application, advantages, functions, and the constraints while developing the IoE framework have been discussed. The IoE framework has its application starting from distribution generation, primary distribution, smart utilization of energy, data history and analysis, system monitoring, and online computation to find the scope of energy saving in process or operation and to contribute to energy efficiency.

REFERENCES

[1] Baran, Mesut E., and Felix F. Wu. "Network reconfiguration in distribution systems for loss reduction and load balancing." *IEEE Power Engineering Review* 9, no. 4 (1989): 101–102.

[2] Nara, Koichi, Atsushi Shiose, Minoru Kitagawa, and Toshihisa Ishihara. "Implementation of genetic algorithm for distribution systems loss minimum re-configuration." *IEEE Transactions on Power systems* 7, no. 3 (1992): 1044–1051.

[3] Venkatesh, B., Rakesh Ranjan, and H. B. Gooi. "Optimal reconfiguration of radial distribution systems to maximize loadability." *IEEE Transactions on Power Systems* 19, no. 1 (2004): 260–266.

[4] Sivanagaraju, S., N. Visali, V. Sankar, and T. Ramana. "Enhancing voltage stability of radial distribution systems by network reconfiguration." *Electric Power Components and Systems* 33, no. 5 (2005): 539–550.

[5] Mendoza, J. E., M. E. Lopez, C. A. Coello Coello, and E. A. Lopez. "Microgenetic multiobjective reconfiguration algorithm considering power losses and reliability indices for medium voltage distribution network." *IET Generation, Transmission & Distribution* 3, no. 9 (2009): 825–840.

[6] Silva Jr, Ivo C., Sandoval Carneiro Jr, Edimar J. de Oliveira, J. L. R. Pereira, Paulo A. N. Garcia, and Andre LM Marcato. "A Lagrangian multiplier based sensitive index to determine the unit commitment of thermal units." *International Journal of Electrical Power & Energy Systems* 30, no. 9 (2008): 504–510.

[7] Ali, Ikbal, Mini S. Thomas, and Pawan Kumar. "Effect of loading pattern on the performance of reconfigured medium size distribution system." In *2012 IEEE Fifth Power India Conference*, pp. 1–6. IEEE, 2012.

[8] Gupta, Nikhil, Anil Swarnkar, and K. R. Niazi. "Distribution network reconfiguration for power quality and reliability improvement using genetic algorithms." *International Journal of Electrical Power & Energy Systems* 54 (2014): 664–671.

[9] Kumar, Pawan, and Surjit Singh. "Reconfiguration of radial distribution system with static load models for loss minimization." In *2014 IEEE International Conference on Power Electronics, Drives and Energy Systems (PEDES)*, pp. 1–5. IEEE, 2014.

[10] Kumar, Pawan, and Surjit Singh. "Energy efficiency performance of reconfigured radial networks with reactive power injection." In *2014 IEEE 6th India International Conference on Power Electronics (IICPE)*, pp. 1–6. IEEE, 2014.

[11] Ali, Ikbal, Mini S. Thomas, and Pawan Kumar. "Energy efficient reconfiguration for practical load combinations in distribution systems." *IET Generation, Transmission & Distribution* 9, no. 11 (2015): 1051–1060.

[12] Kumar, Pawan, Ikbal Ali, and Mini S. Thomas. "Energy efficiency analysis of reconfigured distribution system for practical loads." *Perspectives in Science* 8 (2016): 498–501.

[13] Kumar, Pawan, Ikbal Ali, Mini S. Thomas, and Surjit Singh. "Imposing voltage security and network radiality for reconfiguration of distribution systems using efficient heuristic and meta-heuristic approach." *IET Generation, Transmission & Distribution* 11, no. 10 (2017): 2457–2467.

[14] Kumar, Pawan, Ikbal Ali, Mini Shaji Thomas, and Surjit Singh. "A coordinated framework of DG allocation and operating strategy in distribution system for configuration management under varying loading patterns." *Electric Power Components and Systems* (2020): 1–18.

[15] Haque, M. H. "Capacitor placement in radial distribution systems for loss reduction." *IEE Proceedings-Generation, Transmission and Distribution* 146, no. 5 (1999): 501–505.

[16] Haque, M. H. "Capacitor placement in radial distribution systems for loss reduction." *IEE Proceedings-Generation, Transmission and Distribution* 146, no. 5 (1999): 501–505.

[17] Borges, Carmen LT, and Djalma M. Falcao. "Optimal distributed generation allocation for reliability, losses, and voltage improvement." *International Journal of Electrical Power & Energy Systems* 28, no. 6 (2006): 413–420.

[18] Gautam, Durga, and Nadarajah Mithulananthan. "Optimal DG placement in deregulated electricity market." *Electric Power Systems Research* 77, no. 12 (2007): 1627–1636.

[19] Zou, Kai, A. P. Agalgaonkar, Kashem M. Muttaqi, and Sarath Perera. "Voltage support by distributed generation units and shunt capacitors in distribution systems." In *2009 IEEE Power & Energy Society General Meeting*, pp. 1–8. IEEE, 2009.

[20] Singh, Rajesh Kumar, and S. K. Goswami. "Optimum allocation of distributed generations based on nodal pricing for profit, loss reduction, and voltage improvement including voltage rise issue." *International Journal of Electrical Power & Energy Systems* 32, no. 6 (2010): 637–644.

[21] Hemdan, Nasser G. A., and Michael Kurrat. "Efficient integration of distributed generation for meeting the increased load demand." *International Journal of Electrical Power & Energy Systems* 33, no. 9 (2011): 1572–1583.

[22] Banerjee, Binayak, and Syed M. Islam. "Reliability based optimum location of distributed generation." *International Journal of Electrical Power & Energy Systems* 33, no. 8 (2011): 1470–1478.

[23] Ali, Ikbal, Mini S. Thomas, and Pawan Kumar. "Optimal capacitor placement in smart distribution systems to improve its maximum loadability and energy efficiency." *International Journal of Engineering, Science and Technology* 3, no. 8 (2011): 271–284.

[24] Hung, Duong Quoc, and Nadarajah Mithulananthan. "Multiple distributed generator placement in primary distribution networks for loss reduction." *IEEE Transactions on Industrial Electronics* 60, no. 4 (2011): 1700–1708.

[25] Ali, Ikbal, Mini S. Thomas, and Pawan Kumar. "Distributed resource planning for improved voltage stability of radial distribution system." *International Journal of Advanced Research in Electrical, Electronics and Instrumentation Engineering* 2, no. 1 (2013): 95–101.

[26] Kumar, Pawan, and Surjit Singh. "Comprehensive stability analysis of radial distribution system with load growth." In *2014 IEEE 6th India International Conference on Power Electronics (IICPE)*, pp. 1–6. IEEE, 2014.

[27] Ahuja, Hemant, and Pawan Kumar. "A novel approach for coordinated operation of variable speed wind energy conversion in smart grid applications." *Computers & Electrical Engineering* 77 (2019): 72–87.

[28] Logenthiran, Thillainathan, Dipti Srinivasan, and Tan Zong Shun. "Demand side management in smart grid using heuristic optimization." *IEEE Transactions on Smart Grid* 3, no. 3 (2012): 1244–1252.

[29] Mohsenian-Rad, Amir-Hamed, Vincent W. S. Wong, Juri Jatskevich, Robert Schober, and Alberto Leon-Garcia. "Autonomous demand-side management based on game-theoretic energy consumption scheduling for the future smart grid." *IEEE Transactions on Smart Grid* 1, no. 3 (2010): 320–331.

[30] Palensky, Peter, and Dietmar Dietrich. "Demand side management: Demand response, intelligent energy systems, and smart loads." *IEEE Transactions on Industrial Informatics* 7, no. 3 (2011): 381–388.

[31] Arora, Seema, and Pawan Kumar. "Infrastructural development of energy planning and energy management for smart grid implementation." *Journal of Electrical and Electronics Engineering* 2, no. 1 (2012): 26–31.

[32] Pipattanasomporn, Manisa, Murat Kuzlu, and Saifur Rahman. "An algorithm for intelligent home energy management and demand response analysis." *IEEE Transactions on Smart Grid* 3, no. 4 (2012): 2166–2173.

[33] Guo, Yuanxiong, Miao Pan, and Yuguang Fang. "Optimal power management of residential customers in the smart grid." *IEEE Transactions on Parallel and Distributed Systems* 23, no. 9 (2012): 1593–1606.

[34] Costanzo, Giuseppe Tommaso, Guchuan Zhu, Miguel F. Anjos, and Gilles Savard. "A system architecture for autonomous demand side load management in smart buildings." *IEEE Transactions on Smart Grid* 3, no. 4 (2012): 2157–2165.

[35] Agnetis, Alessandro, Gianluca De Pascale, Paolo Detti, and Antonio Vicino. "Load scheduling for household energy consumption optimization." *IEEE Transactions on Smart Grid* 4, no. 4 (2013): 2364–2373.

[36] Zhao, Zhuang, Won Cheol Lee, Yoan Shin, and Kyung-Bin Song. "An optimal power scheduling method for demand response in home energy management system." *IEEE Transactions on Smart Grid* 4, no. 3 (2013): 1391–1400.

[37] Chiu, Wei-Yu, Hongjian Sun, and H. Vincent Poor. "Energy imbalance management using a robust pricing scheme." *IEEE Transactions on Smart Grid* 4, no. 2 (2012): 896–904.

[38] Kumar, Pawan, Ikbal Ali, and Mini S. Thomas. "Synchronizing solar cell, battery and grid supply for development of smart power system for home." In *2015 Annual IEEE India Conference (INDICON)*, pp. 1–5. IEEE, 2015.

[39] Safdarian, Amir, Merkebu Z. Degefa, Matti Lehtonen, and Mahmud Fotuhi-Firuzabad. "Distribution network reliability improvements in presence of demand response." *IET Generation, Transmission & Distribution* 8, no. 12 (2014): 2027–2035.

[40] Abdelwahed, Ahmed S., Abdel Halim Zekry, Hossam Labib Zayed, and Ahmed M. Sayed. "Controlling electricity consumption at home smart home." In *2015 Tenth International Conference on Computer Engineering & Systems (ICCES)*, pp. 49–54. IEEE, 2015.

[41] Tsagarakis, George, R. Camilla Thomson, Adam J. Collin, Gareth P. Harrison, Aristides E. Kiprakis, and Stephen McLaughlin. "Assessment of the cost and environmental impact of residential demand-side management." *IEEE Transactions on Industry Applications* 52, no. 3 (2016): 2486–2495.

[42] Hao, He, Charles D. Corbin, Karanjit Kalsi, and Robert G. Pratt. "Transactive control of commercial buildings for demand response." *IEEE Transactions on Power Systems* 32, no. 1 (2016): 774–783.

[43] Rahman, Md Aminur, Riazul Islam, Kazi Fatima Sharif, and Tareq Aziz. "Developing demand side management program for commercial customers: A case study." In *2016 3rd International Conference on Electrical Engineering and Information Communication Technology (ICEEICT)*, pp. 1–6. IEEE, 2016.

[44] Facchini, Alessandro, Cristina Rottondi, and Giacomo Verticale. "Evaluating the effects of social interactions on a distributed demand side management system for domestic appliances." *Energy Efficiency* 10, no. 5 (2017): 1175–1188.

[45] Anvari-Moghaddam, Amjad, Josep M. Guerrero, Juan C. Vasquez, Hassan Monsef, and Ashkan Rahimi-Kian. "Efficient energy management for a grid-tied residential microgrid." *IET Generation, Transmission & Distribution* 11, no. 11 (2017): 2752–2761.

[46] Kumar, Pawan, and Dip V. Thanki. "Synchronized Operation of Grid Power, Solar Power, and Battery for Smart Energy Management." In *Handbook of Research on Power and Energy System Optimization*, pp. 255–291. IGI Global, 2018.

[47] Kumar, Pawan, Ikbal Ali, and Dip V. Thanki. "Demand-Side Management: Energy Efficiency and Demand Response." In *Handbook of Research on Power and Energy System Optimization*, pp. 453–479. IGI Global, 2018.

[48] Kumar, Pawan, Gagandeep Singh Brar, Surjit Singh, Srete Nikolovski, Hamid Reza Baghaee, and Zoran Balkić. "Perspectives and intensification of energy efficiency in commercial and residential buildings using strategic auditing and demand-side management." *Energies* 12, no. 23 (2019): 4539.

[49] Kumar, Pawan, Gagandeep Singh Brar, and Lovepreet Singh. "Energy efficiency evaluation in commercial and residential buildings with demand side management: A review." In *2019 8th International Conference on Power Systems (ICPS)*, pp. 1–6. IEEE, 2019.

[50] Kumar, Pawan, Dip Vinod Thanki, Surjit Singh, and Srete Nikolovski. "A new framework for intensification of energy efficiency in commercial and residential use by imposing social, technical and environmental constraints." *Sustainable Cities and Society* 62 (2020): 102400.

[51] Jowder, F. A. L. "Design and analysis of dynamic voltage restorer for deep voltage sag and harmonic compensation." *IET Generation, Transmission & Distribution* 3, no. 6 (2009): 547-560.

[52] Sasitharan, S., and Mahesh K. Mishra. "Constant switching frequency band controller for dynamic voltage restorer." *IET Power Electronics* 3, no. 5 (2010): 657–667.

[53] Jayaprakash, Pychadathil, Bhim Singh, D. P. Kothari, Ambrish Chandra, and Kamal Al-Haddad. "Control of reduced-rating dynamic voltage restorer with a battery energy storage system." *IEEE Transactions on Industry Applications* 50, no. 2 (2013): 1295–1303.

[54] Jayaprakash, Pychadathil, Bhim Singh, D. P. Kothari, Ambrish Chandra, and Kamal Al-Haddad. "Control of reduced-rating dynamic voltage restorer with a battery energy storage system." *IEEE Transactions on Industry Applications* 50, no. 2 (2013): 1295–1303.

[55] Galeshi, Soleiman, and Hossein Iman-Eini. "Dynamic voltage restorer employing multilevel cascaded H-bridge inverter." *IET Power Electronics* 9, no. 11 (2016): 2196–2204.

RELATED READING

[56] Pawan Kumar, Ikbal Ali, Taha Selim Ustun and Surjit Singh, *Handbook of research on power and energy system optimization*. IGI Global, USA, March 2018.

[57] Cao, Bin, Weinan Dong, Zhihan Lv, Yu Gu, Surjit Singh, and Pawan Kumar. "Hybrid microgrid many-objective sizing optimization with fuzzy decision." *IEEE Transactions on Fuzzy Systems* 28, no. 11 (2020): 2702–2710.

KEYWORDS AND DESCRIPTIONS

Active energy booster (AEBs) The means of improving energy efficiency by integrating external energy resources in the existing distribution system while power delivery.

Passive energy booster (AEBs) The mean of improving energy efficiency without integration of external energy resources in the distribution system while power delivery.

Distributed energy resources (DERs) Distributed generation also known as distributed energy resource or on-site generation, which are used for local power generation near to the point of consumer load.

Internet of Energy (IoE)   The Internet of Energy is the amalgamation of two approaches namely Internet of Things (IoT) and the energy efficiency through smart communication, computation and control techniques.

Network configuration   Distributed generation also termed as distributed energy or on-site generation can be defined on the basis of generation of power near to the consumer load.

Demand-side management   The load management based upon the load profile at customers' end for the objective of energy efficiency is termed demand-side management.

Energy efficiency   The utilization of electrical energy in such a way the output and the level of comfort is not compromised but the input energy is minimized for the same operation or process is known as energy efficiency.

Energy efficiency performance   The energy efficiency performance of a distribution system depends on the quantity and quality of supplying power, voltage profile, and number of customers supplied at one time, reliability and energy security, etc. Therefore, energy efficiency performance involves improving several parameters, without compromising any of these, varying their weightage depending upon the operating constraints.

2 Evaluation of Soft Computing Techniques and IEC61850 Protocols for the Development of the Internet of Energy Framework

Anjali Uppal and Pawan Kumar
Thapar Institute of Engineering & Technology, Patiala,
Punjab, India

CONTENTS

2.1 Background 42
2.2 Literature 42
2.3 Soft Computing Methods 45
    2.3.1 Genetic Algorithms 45
    2.3.2 Harmony Search Algorithm 47
    2.3.3 Particle Swarm Optimization 48
    2.3.4 Grey Wolf Optimization 50
    2.3.5 Artificial Neural Networks (ANNs) 53
    2.3.6 Fuzzy Logic Systems 55
    2.3.7 Ant Colony Optimization 57
    2.3.8 Teaching Learning-Based Optimization 58
        2.3.8.1 Teacher Phase 58
        2.3.8.2 Student Phase 59
    2.3.9 Jaya Algorithm 60
2.4 Application of Soft Computing Techniques in Power and Energy Systems .. 62
2.5 Energy Management 63
    2.5.1 Overview of IEC 61850 63
        2.5.1.1 Communication Protocols 64
        2.5.1.2 Distribution Automation System 65
    2.5.2 Building Energy Management System 65
2.6 Future Directions 66
2.7 Conclusions 67

References.. 68
Other Related Readings 70
Keywords and Descriptions 70

2.1   BACKGROUND

The framework of the Internet of Energy (IoE) is the amalgamation of three technologies, namely, communication, computation, and the control system. The concept of smart computing is recent for the analysis of the power system and management of energy. The methods of soft computing techniques are similar to the human brain, which is why it is also known as artificial intelligence. The human brain can provide valid conclusions based on incomplete and partial data obtained from previous research. Soft computing is the approximation of the process at a very low level. There is a lot of difference between soft and hard computing. The former requires just a tolerance of imprecision whereas the latter requires a precisely stated analytical model. Soft computing can solve real-world problems in much less time whereas hard computing requires a lot of computation time. The soft computing techniques are artificial neural networks, fuzzy logic, and have population-based heuristic algorithms, which are categorized into two groups, i.e. evolutionary and swarm intelligence [1]. Some of the evolutionary algorithms are genetic algorithm, evolution programming, differential evolution, and artificial immune algorithm. Some swarm-based algorithms are particle swarm optimization, ant colony optimization, artificial bee colony, firefly optimization, etc. Apart from these algorithms, there are some others that are working on natural phenomena such as harmony search algorithm, gravitational search algorithm, biography-based algorithm, etc. All the above-mentioned techniques require some controlling parameters whereas the teaching learning method proposed [15] has only two phases and it is widely accepted. After its success, a new algorithm with fewer parameters was defined known as the Jaya algorithm. The commonly used soft computing methods discussed in this chapter are,

1. Genetic algorithm (GA)
2. Harmony search algorithm (HAS)
3. Particle swarm optimization (PSO)
4. Grey wolf optimization
5. Artificial neural networks (ANNs),
6. Fuzzy logics (FL)
7. Ant colony optimization (ACO)
8. Teaching learning-based optimization (TLBO)
9. Jaya Algorithm

2.2   LITERATURE

Due to economic reasons and some important factors coming out from operational issues, the modern power system is operating closer to their operating limits. Because of this stressful condition, the transfer capability of power is becoming a major concern in system planning and its operation. Power transfer capacity indicates how much power can be transferred in a particular area without affecting the system security. The power transfer capability of a particular system varies from time to time as the operating conditions of the interconnected power system network vary in real-time. Due to these reasons, the transfer capabilities and voltage calculations need to be updated for their application in the operation of the power system. The most commonly used algorithms are optimal power flow, continuation power flow, and the repeated power flow method for computing power transfer capability. To provide solutions with less time consumption, artificial neural networks can be applied in different areas of research. Neural networks can tackle new problems that are difficult to refine or solve analytically. Moreover, the optimal reactive power dispatch is another important parameter in energy management systems. It protects the power systems. For continuous safety and reliability of the system, the major task is to determine the optimal operating tendency and optimal placement of the shunt devices for minimizing the power losses [1–4]. Due to continued rapid growth in demand for power with the unmatched generation, voltage stability is becoming a new challenge for power system operation and planning. In recent years, many meta-heuristic techniques are implemented to resolve the optimization problem such as PSO, GA, HSA, ACO, TLBO, etc. [1]. GA uses mutation and crossover probabilities, selection operator; PSO is based on inertia weight, cognitive as well as social parameters. ACO is based on pheromone by ants; HSA uses pitch adjustment rate, number of practices, and consideration rate of harmony memory. PSO is analogous to evolutionary algorithms like GA as it is a randomly selected solution, and it continues doing iterations until the optimal solution is not found. However, PSO deals with evolving position particles instead of creating new particles [1]. The prime distinction between HSA and GA is that HSA assembles a new vector from all actual vectors (all memories present in harmony search memory) while GA creates a new vector from only two actual vectors (parents). However, TLBO consists of controlling parameters like the size of population and number of generations whereas Jaya contains no parameters and is like a decision-based algorithm. Apart from this, a distribution automation system (DAS) and energy management system (EMS) are crucial components in power system for controlling load, leveling of load, demand response, and provides a solution to the problems caused by the connection of a large number of DERs in distribution network [2]. Due to its ability to exchange information among various supporting manufactures in inter or intrasubstation communication, the IEC 61850 is gaining wide acceptance in supervisory control communication. If IEC 61850 is implemented in communications in DAS and EMS, it is intended that it will help in reducing the cost of equipment as well as the maintenance cost of each system [2] (Table 2.1).

From the above literature, it can be noticed that the energy efficiency performance of power systems depends upon several parameters. In the past, researchers have developed different soft computing approaches for energy management that are suitable for different objectives under different operating conditions. With the advances in the energy management schemes, the role of IEC 61850 has gained momentum and all the research related to the substation automation has involved IEC61850 protocols for smart energy system development.

TABLE 2.1
Summary of Related Research Work

Ref. No.	Author(s)/*et al.*	Descriptions
[1]	Fernando (2008)	Soft computing techniques in power system
[2]	Senke *et al.* (2012)	Energy management by IEC standard 6185
[3]	Sivanandam & Deepa (2008)	Description of genetic algorithms
[4]	Kumar *et al.* (2020)	Coordinated operation and planning of distribution for configuration management
[5]	Kumar *et al.* (2017)	Imposing voltage security and network radiality for reconfiguration of distribution systems using efficient heuristic and meta-heuristic approach
[6]	Kumar & Surjit (2014)	Reconfiguration of load model for loss minimization
[7]	Marini & Beata (2015)	Particle swarm optimization: A tutorial
[8]	Andervazh *et al.* (2013)	Network reconfiguration using particle swarm optimization
[9]	Azizian & Gevork (2018)	Transformer design using PSO
[10]	Zhang *et al.* (2019)	Optimal power allocation scheme of microgrid using grey wolf optimizer
[11]	Bose (2017)	Artificial intelligence techniques in smart grid and renewable energy systems
[12]	Chin Teng (1996)	Neural fuzzy systems
[13]	Wang & Chanan (2008)	Optimal placement of reclosers and DG using Ant Colony
[14]	Rao (2016)	Teaching learning-based algorithm
[15]	Rao *et al.* (2011)	Teaching learning method for constrained mechanical design optimization
[16]	Rao (2016)	New model Jaya for solving the constrained unconstrained optimization problems
[17]	Jiang *et al.* (2018)	Application of grey wolf optimization for combinatorial problems
[18]	Nagnizahed *et al.* (2018)	Power system stability enhancement using teaching learning optimization
[19]	Bouchekara *et al.* (2014)	Optimal power flow using teaching learning algorithm
[20]	Rao & Vekanta (2019)	Application of Jaya algorithm in engineering and sciences
[21]	Kong *et al.* (2017)	Short-term load forecasting using neural network
[22]	Zhang *et al.* (2019)	Optimal power allocation scheme using grey wolf optimization
[23]	Deshmukh *et al.* (2020)	Fuzzy logics-based supervisory control for power management in microgrid.
[24]	Mmansiri *et al.* (2018)	Fuzzy control algorithm for battery storage and demand side power management for economic operation of smart grid
[25]	Mao *et al.* (2014)	Application of IEC61850 in energy management for microgrids
[26]	Ali *et al.* (2015)	Energy efficient reconfiguration for practical load combinations in distribution system
[27]	IEC standard (2012)	Communication network and systems in substation application
[28]	Mohagheghi *et al.* (2011)	Application of IEC 61850 in distribution
[29]	Ali *et al.* (2015)	Substation communication network architecture for energy efficient system using IEC 61850
[30]	Aftab *et al.* 2018)	IEC61850 and XMPP communication-based energy management in microgrids
[31]	Mohagheghi *et al.* (2009)	Modelling distribution automation system using IEC61850
[32]	Estates, Defence (2001)	Building energy management system
[33]	Kumar *et al.* (2020)	Intensification of energy efficiency in commercial and residential use by imposing social, technical, and environmental constraints.

(Continued)

TABLE 2.1 (Continued)
Summary of Related Research Work

Ref. No.	Author(s)/*et al.*	Descriptions
[34]	Kumar *et al.* (2019)	Perspectives and intensifications of energy efficiency in residential and commercial buildings using demand side management
[35]	Kumar *et al.* (2019)	Energy efficiency evaluation in residential and commercial buildings with demand side management

2.3   SOFT COMPUTING METHODS

The soft computing methods such as genetic algorithms, fuzzy logics, particle swarm optimization, gray wolf optimization, harmony search algorithm, ant colony optimization, artificial neural network, teaching-learning algorithm, and Jaya algorithm are described next in this section.

2.3.1   GENETIC ALGORITHMS

Genetic algorithms work on the principle of genetics and natural selection. They are practiced for calculating optimal and the solution is very near to optimal for solving difficult problems that would otherwise would take a whole life to solve. An optimal solution is that which enhances the fitness function. GAs are a subset of Evolutionary Computation, which is a larger branch of computation. GAs contains a population of all possible solutions to a given problem. Each solution is represented by a chromosome and to code all the possible solutions into the chromosome is the first step of the GA. These solutions undergo recombination and mutation to produce new children and the process is repeated again and again for various generations [3]. Every individual will be assigned a fitness value, which is calculated based on the value of an objective function. The fitter individuals are given a higher chance to yield the fittest individuals. In this way, better solutions are evolved over generations until it fulfills the stopping criteria. GAs tend to provide the best solution at a steady speed. This brings genetic algorithms into picture powerful tools for solving the optimization problems [3].

The basic algorithm for the genetic algorithm is as follows,

Step 1. Find a suitable solution for the problem, i.e. genetic random population of n number of chromosomes [start].

Step 2. Compute fitness function p(x) for every chromosome present in the population [fitness].

Step 3. Repeat the subsequent steps to constitute a new population until and unless it completes [new population].

Step 4. Following the value of fitness select two chromosomes of parents from the pool or population [selection].

Step 5. With the help of the crossover of parents, a new offspring is formed. If the crossover is not performed, then the offspring will be the same copy of its parents [crossover].

Step 6. Mutate new offspring at each location with the help of mutation probability [mutation].

Step 7. Place the newly formed offspring in the new population [accept].

Step 8. For further sum use population is generated newly [replace].

Step 9. If conditions are satisfied, then stop and go back to the best solution in the current population [test].

The flow chart for the genetic algorithm is shown in Figure 2.1

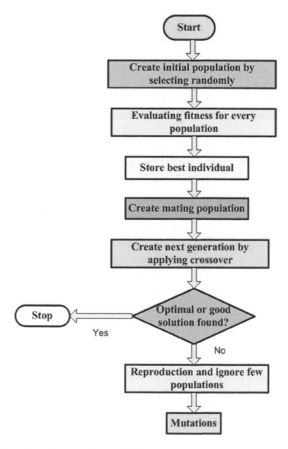

FIGURE 2.1 Flowchart for genetic algorithm.

2.3.2 HARMONY SEARCH ALGORITHM

This is a meta-heuristic approach that tries to cause improvisation of music harmony where the musicians can improve the pitch of their instrument by searching for a pleasant harmony. Harmony is defined as the special relationship between various sound waves having different frequencies. The musician practices for improvement in aesthetic estimation and to find the best harmony. The optimization process and the musician's improvisations have many similarities. Iterations in power system optimizations are referred to as practice or improvisations. Variables and values of variables are analogous to musical instruments and the notes of musical instruments. Every solution represents harmony. The comparison between musical and optimization techniques is shown in Table 2.2, which reveals the various similarities between the two [4].

In optimization problems, a harmony search uses the harmony memory (i.e. HM) to store all the solutions; a feasible solution is known as harmony. Harmony memory size provides all the cache solutions in the harmony memory. To implement the HS algorithm for optimization, the algorithm is as follows [4–6]:

Step 1. Initialize the harmony memory by assigning random values to each design variable.
Step 2. For each harmony, the values of the objective function are calculated based on initial HM and then the harmony with the worst objective function is determined.
Step 3. New harmony is extemporizing in each iteration.
Step 4. The new harmony may be added or excluded in harmony memory based on the objective function value. If it gives better value, it replaces the worst harmony in HM and then HM is updated.
Step 5. Repeat the above procedure until the stopping criteria are not fulfilled. When the terminating criteria have been obtained move to the next step.
Step 6. The good harmony is stored in harmony memory and design performance can be achieved by an optimum solution.

The basic flowchart for the harmony search algorithm is shown in Figure 2.2 [5, 6].

TABLE 2.2
Comparison between harmony search and optimization process

Objective	Musical Process or Harmony Search	Optimization Process
Components	Music instruments	System components that are to be optimized
Type of result	Harmony is determined by artistic estimation	The solution vector is determined by the value of the objective function
Goal	Best harmony	Global optimum
Approximations	Musicians can change the pitch of the instruments	The algorithm adjusts the value of all decision variables
Attempts to get a better result	Represented by practice	By iterations

---

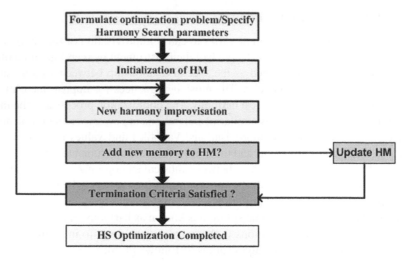

FIGURE 2.2   Flowchart for harmony search algorithm

2.3.3 PARTICLE SWARM OPTIMIZATION

Particle swarm optimization is a population-based search algorithm, and it provides an alternative solution to complex non-linear problems of optimization. It works based on the natural process of bird swarms, fish shoaling or schooling, and so on. This algorithm is influenced by the method of communication and sharing the knowledge among individuals such as the fact that when birds, insects, and animals are searching for food they migrate, although they do not know the best position. But from their social behavior, if any of them finds a desirable path, the rest of the members follow that path quickly [7].

The PSO technique works on animals' activity and their behavior to solve the optimization problem [7, 8]. In PSO, the population is known as a swarm and each member of the population is considered as a particle. It starts with random initialization of the population then each particle starts moving in a random direction and goes through the searching space by remembering its best previous position [8, 9]. PSO comprises the subsequent steps,

Step 1: Initialization of the population of particles with random position and velocity in the 'd' dimensional search space. There are some steps that have to be followed for the initialization of the population.

- Calculate the fitness function for every particle.
- Record and find the non-dominating solutions and save the file in an archive.
- Initialization of memory for each individual where the best position is stored.
- From the archive, choose the global best position.
- After this, increase the generation number.

Step 2: Update the velocity of all the particles at each iteration according to the equation:

$$V_{jd}{}^{n+1} = wV_{jd}{}^{(t)} + k_1 r_1 \left(P^{(t)}{}_{best\ jd} - X_{jd}{}^{(t)} \right) + k_2 r_2 \left(g^{(t)}{}_{best\ d} - X_{jd}{}^{(t)} \right) \qquad (2.1)$$

$V_{jd}{}^{(t)}$ = velocity of particle j, in dimensional state d

$X_{jd}{}^{(t)}$ = position of particle j, in dimensional state d

$P^{(t)}{}_{best\ jd}$ = best position of individual j in dimensional state d

$g^{(t)}{}_{best\ jd}$ = best position in group

k_1 And k_2 = Accelerating constants

w = inertia weight factor

r_1 ,r_2 = random variables on range [0, 1]

Step 2: Upgrade the position of particles in accordance to the equation:

$$X_{jd}{}^{(t+1)} = X_{jd}{}^{(t)} + V_{jd}{}^{(t+1)} \qquad (2.2)$$

$X_{jd}{}^{(t+1)}$ = new position

$X_{jd}{}^{(t)}$ = previous position

$V_{jd}{}^{(t+1)}$ = new velocity

- Check all the constraints for ensuring the feasibility of all generable solutions. The position of the individual is set to maximum and minimum operating points according to equation (2.3):

$$X_{jd}{}^{t+1} = \begin{cases} X_{jd}{}^{(t)} + V_{jd}{}^{(t+1)} \text{if } X_{jd}{}^{min} \le X_{jd}{}^{(t)} + V_{jd}{}^{(t+1)} \le X_{jd}{}^{max} \\ X_{jd}{}^{min} \qquad \text{if } X_{jd}{}^{(t)} + V_{jd}{}^{(t+1)} < X_{jd}{}^{min} \\ X_{jd}{}^{max} \qquad \text{if } X_{jd}{}^{(t)} + V_{jd}{}^{(t+1)} > X_{jd}{}^{max} \end{cases} \qquad (2.3)$$

$X_{jd}{}^{max}$ and $X_{jd}{}^{min}$ are the maximum and minimum position of particles in dimensional space d

- Update the archive that is storing the non-dominating solution.

Step 3: Update the memory with the best position of the particle and the global best position using the equation:

$$\begin{aligned} P^{(t+1)}{}_{best\ jd} &\leftarrow X_{jd}{}^{(t+1)} \text{ if } f\left(X_{jd}{}^{(t+1)}\right) < f\left(P^{(t)}{}_{best\ jd}\right) \\ g^{(t+1)}{}_{best\ d} &\leftarrow X_{jd}{}^{(t+1)} \text{iff } f\left(X_{jd}{}^{(t+1)}\right) < f\left(g^{(t)}{}_{best\ d}\right) \end{aligned} \qquad (2.4)$$

Step 4: When the number of iterations reach their maximum, terminate the process after achieving good fitness (Figure 2.3).

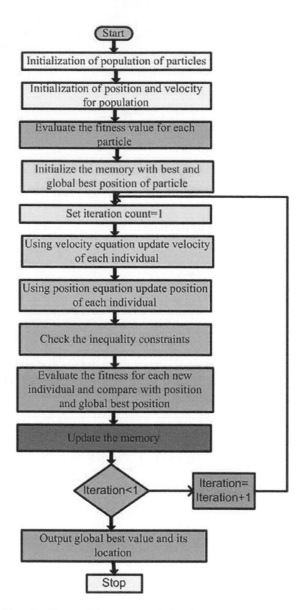

FIGURE 2.3   Flowchart for particle swarm optimization

2.3.4   GREY WOLF OPTIMIZATION

Another meta-heuristic technique inspired by grey wolves is the grey wolf optimization technique. Alpha, beta, gamma, and omega are the commonly used four types of grey wolves wherein the leaders are alphas, which can be either male or female. Alphas have the responsibility of making decisions such as hunting, sleeping, and time to wake up. All the decisions of the alpha are dictated to the pack and they have to follow it at any cost, which is why the alpha wolf is more dominant. However, sometimes a democracy can also be visualized in which the alpha follows the other wolves in the pack [10]. The second level of the hierarchy is beta, which is known as subordinate wolves helping the alpha wolves in decision-making. It commands the other low-level wolves and reinforces the command of the alpha throughout the pack and gives feedback to the alpha. The next category is the low ranking of wolves and they are known as the omega. However, the omega is not an important individual in the pack but in case of losing the omega, the whole pack will face problems and internal fights. In some cases, the omega is also the babysitters in the pack. Apart from alpha, beta, and omega the next subordinate is the delta. Deltas have to submit to the alpha and beta but they dominate the omega. Scouts have the responsibility of watching the boundary of the territory, sentinels protect the pack by providing the guarantee of safety to the same, elders are experienced wolves, and hunters provide food to the pack and come under the category of delta wolves [10]. Three main steps in this approach are hunting the prey – searching, encircling, and attacking the prey are implemented.

In the GWO the algorithm is being guided by α, β, δ and the omega wolves follow these three wolves.

(a) **Encircle the prey:** According to the above discussion, the grey wolf encircles the pray during the hunt. The mathematical model for encircling behavior is given in the following equations as

$$\vec{C} = \left| \vec{D}\vec{Y_p}(t) - \vec{Y}(t) \right| \qquad (2.5)$$

$$\vec{Y}(t+1) = \vec{Y_p}(t) - \vec{B}.\vec{C} \qquad (2.6)$$

t = current iteration
$\vec{B}$ and $\vec{D}$ = coefficient vectors
$\vec{Y_p}$ = position vector of prey
$\vec{Y}$ = position vector of grey

The vectors $\vec{S}$ and $\vec{D}$ are calculated as:

$$\vec{S} = 2\vec{a}.\vec{s_1} - \vec{a} \qquad (2.7)$$

$$\vec{D} = 2.\vec{s_2} \qquad (2.8)$$

Also, s_1 and s_2 are random vectors and components are literarily decreased.

(b) **Hunting:** The gray wolf can encircle and recognize the position of prey. The alpha has a role to guide the hunt. Following the mathematical model, the alpha, beta, and gamma are assumed to have better knowledge about the location of prey. Therefore, save the better solution and oblige the search agents to update the new position. The new positions are updated according to the formula

$$\vec{C_\alpha} = \left| \vec{D_1}.\vec{Y_\alpha} - \vec{Y} \right| \qquad (2.9)$$

$$\vec{C_\beta} = \left| \vec{D_2}.\vec{Y_\beta} - \vec{Y} \right| \tag{2.10}$$

$$\vec{C_\delta} = \left| \vec{D_3}.\vec{X_\delta} - \vec{Y} \right| \tag{2.11}$$

$$\vec{Y_1} = \vec{Y_\alpha} - \vec{B_1}.\left(\vec{C_\alpha} \right) \tag{2.12}$$

$$\vec{Y_2} = \vec{Y_\beta} - \vec{B_2}.\left(\vec{C_\beta} \right) \tag{2.13}$$

$$\vec{Y_3} = \vec{Y_\delta} - \vec{B_3}.(\vec{C_\delta}) \tag{2.14}$$

$$\vec{Y}\left(t+1 \right) = \frac{\vec{Y_1} + \vec{Y_2} + \vec{Y_3}}{3} \tag{2.15}$$

(c) **Attacking prey:** When the prey stops moving, the gray wolves finish the hunt after attacking the prey. In the mathematical model approach, the value of $\vec{a}$ is decreased. With the decrement of $\vec{a}$ there is fluctuation in $\vec{D}$.

(d) **Searching for prey:** The search for grey wolves is according to the position of alpha, beta, and delta. In the search of prey, they diverge from each other and converge to attack prey.

The steps involved in the GWO algorithm are described as follows, and the flow-chart is shown in Figure 2.4.

Step 1: Initialization of the grey wolf population Y_i (I = 1, 2 ... n)

- Then, initialize a, B, and D
- Calculate the fitness of each search agent.
- Y_α = is the best level of search
- Y_β = second best level search
- Y_δ = third best level of search

While (t > Minimum number of iterations)

- For each level of search
- Update the position of the current level of search by the above-mentioned equations
- End for the update of search level
- Update a, B, and D
- Calculate fitness value of all levels of search
- Update Y_α, Y_β, and Y_δ
- t = t+1

  end while
- return Y_α

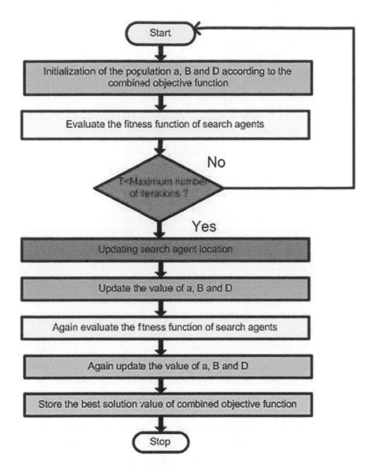

FIGURE 2.4   Flowchart of grey wolf optimization technique

2.3.5 ARTIFICIAL NEURAL NETWORKS (ANNs)

ANNs are the type of systems that are formed to harness a few principal characteristics similar to that of the human brain. They portray the aspiration class of computational systems. ANNs are useful in various kinds of applications such as matching and categorization, estimation, clustering, etc. while such kinds of conventional systems are inefficient in such kinds of applications. However, the conventional systems are highly accurate in arithmetic operations especially. The nature of ANN just like that of the human brain illustrates the ability to adapt and learn from sets of data or information. ANNs in general are based on the concept of representation of clusters of actual neurons in the brain.

ANN involve interconnected nodes that are huge in number and generally operate in the parallel formation and are arranged in structured architecture as shown in Figure 2.5.

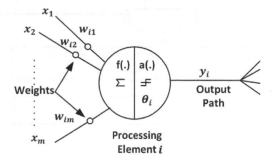

FIGURE 2.5 Concept of neural networks

A basic neuron has three vital components, namely: cell body, dendrites, and axon. An interconnected tree-like network is represented by dendrites, represent a network of various nerves attached to the main body of the cell. An axon is represented by a kind of single, lengthy connection emerging and stretching from the cell body. The end of an axon is divided into various fine strands. Each strand is terminated in a minute bulblike organ known as a synapse, in which the neuron initiates the command for the surrounding neurons. There are tentatively 100,000 synapses for each neuron in the human brain. Synapses are excitatory, which allows the passing of impulses and causes initiation for the neighboring neurons, or inhibitory as they allow the neighboring impulses to block the initiation of the neuron.

The weight w_{ij} symbolizes the strength of the connection link (or the synapse) combining neuron j and neuroni, (connecting source to destination). A positive weight reflects an excitatory response and negative weights correspond to an inhibitory response. $w_{ij} = 0$ indicates the absence of connection between neurons j and i. The common characteristics exhibited by all kind of neural networks are mentioned below:

1. Mathematical model inspired by biological neurons.
2. Highly interconnected system.
3. The weights used in ANN reflect knowledge possessed by the network.
4. It can adapt, recall, and formulate a set of data by assigning and commanding the connecting weights.
5. Computational power is reflected by the combined behavior of the system.

Framework for Artificial Neural Network (ANNs)

Step 1. Initially, random weights are assigned to all the connecting neurons.
Step 2. Using the information from inputs and hidden linkages, the rate of processing of information is finalized.
Step 3. Using the processing rate of hidden nodes and linkages to the output, the rate of activation for output nodes is decided.

Step 4. At output node, an error is calculated and all the linkages between hidden and output nodes are re-initialized again.

Step 5. Using the error observed at the output node and weights cascade down the error to hidden nodes.

Step 6. Now, re-initialization of weights between input and a hidden node is down.

Step 7. The entire process is repeated over and over again until the rate of convergence is achieved.

Step 8. Using the final weights of linkage nodes, score the processing rate of output nodes.

2.3.6 FUZZY LOGIC SYSTEMS [12]

Fuzzy logic is a technique of analyzing that is similar in many ways to the human brain. The approach adopted in fuzzy logic reflects how decision-making is done in the human mind involving all the possibilities existing in the form of digital values between GOOD or BAD. The traditional logic understood by the system takes the exact input and results in a definite output in the form of RIGHT or WRONG, in many ways equivalent to the human brain's Good or Bad. It can also be understood that the decision-making in humans includes a variety of possibilities in-between GOOD or BAD, such as:

- CERTAINLY GOOD
- POSSIBLY GOOD
- CANNOT PREDICT
- POSSIBLY BAD
- CERTAINLY BAD.

Fuzzy logic indicates the level of options that can be understood through the input to target the desired output. It can be adopted in various kinds of systems with different applications ranging from small microcontrollers large and interconnected complex systems, and can also be used in a hybrid combination of both hardware and software. The framework of fuzzy logics is shown in Figure 2.6.

Fuzzy logic is beneficial for various purposes such as

- Control of products
- Acceptable form of reasoning with minor corrections
- Helps in dealing with various forms of uncertainty.

It has mainly four components (or subparts)

- Fuzzification module – It modulates the inputs of the systems, which are categorized into different fuzzy sets. Generally, the input signal is divided into five main parts (given in Table 2.3).
- Knowledge base – IF-THEN rules are included in the knowledge base memory

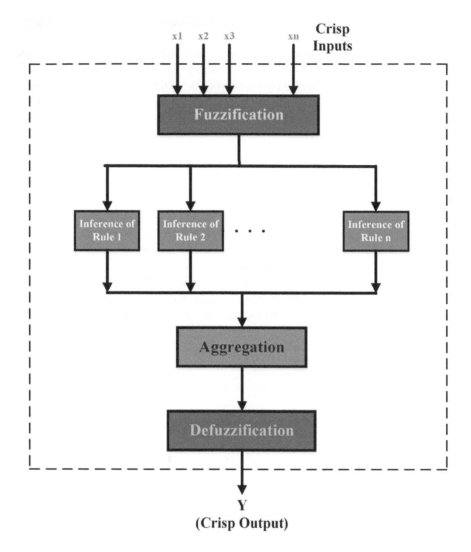

FIGURE 2.6   Framework for fuzzy logic systems

TABLE 2.3
Parts of input signal

C	X has bigger Positive value
DE	X has Medium Positive value
G	X is Small
IJ	X has Medium Negative value
KL	X has Large Negative Value

- Interference engine – It implements the process of understanding by formulating fuzzy inference on the inputs by applying IF-THEN rules.
- Defuzzification module – The fuzzy sets deduced from the interference engine are transformed back into the crisp value.

The membership functions are applied to several variables of fuzzy sets. Basically, the membership functions allow you to quantify the parameters through different terms and represent them graphically.

The algorithm for fuzzy logics is has the following steps:

Step 1. Define variables and different terms.
Step 2. Construct membership functions.
Step 3. Construct knowledge base of rules.
Step 4. Convert crisp data sets into fuzzy data sets using membership functions (**Fuzzification**).
Step 5. Evaluate all the rules (**Inference Engine**).
Step 6. Combine results from each rule (**Inference Engine**).
Step 7. Convert output data into crisp (non-fuzzy) values (**De-Fuzzification**).

2.3.7 Ant Colony Optimization

The ant colony optimization algorithm was first presented in the year 1991. Nowadays, this technique is used for various multi-objective optimization, data clustering, and classification problems, etc. Ant colonies portray very interesting behaviors: even when only a single ant has basic capabilities, the behavior of the entire colony is found to be highly well defined.

To apply ant colony optimization, the issue is converted into a problem of detecting the most suited path on a weighted graph. The artificial ants slowly construct their solutions stepwise by following the graph. The solution formulation process is highly probabilistic and is influenced by the pheromone model, which involves a set of variables associated with graph components whose values are adjusted at runtime by the ants.

During the movement of an ant, it leaves pheromone in its tracks. By employing such pheromones, information is transferred from one ant to another. This process of information transformation can be described in steps such as: (1) Initially, the ant detects the source (F), in a random manner (a), then comes back to its original position by following a trajectory-leaving pheromone (b); (2) Ants randomly follow four possible ways, but the weightage of the path leads it towards the optimized route (weightage is usually decided based upon the deposition of pheromones in a particular path); (3) Ants take the shortest route and it causes the deposition of more pheromones in that path whereas the longest path may lose their pheromones with time or iterations. The flowchart is depicted in Figure 2.7.

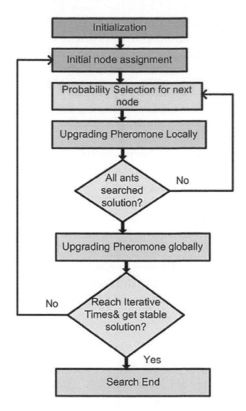

FIGURE 2.7   Flowchart for Ant Colony Method

2.3.8   TEACHING LEARNING-BASED OPTIMIZATION

This is based on the teaching-learning method and is used to resolve the constrained mechanical design optimization problems. It is motivated by the teacher providing a clear understanding to students via mutual interactions. In this algorithm, the population size is represented by the group or class of students. Also, students represent the solution of a problem whereas the subjects offered to them are considered as the various design variables. Therefore, the fitness function is represented with the result of each student [14]. TLBO works in two phases:

   i). Student phase
   ii). Teacher phase.

2.3.8.1   Teacher Phase

Consider 'm' = number of subjects in class (design variables i = 1,2 ... m)
   M_p= number of students having population size, j = 1, 2 ... M_p
   For any teaching-learning cycle (iteration, k = 0, 1, 2... J_n)
   M_i^k = mean value for the result of students in any particular subject 'i'

The teacher is a highly learned, skilled, and knowledgeable person in the community. To replicate this concept, the most possible and reasonable solution is the best student in the entire population. Let

X_n^k = the most possible and reasonable solution among the population at the k_{th} learning cycle.

$X_{n,i}^k$ = best possible and reasonable solution of the population having i^{th} design at k_{th} learning cycle.

The difference between the teacher's result and the average result of a student in a subject 'i' is given by

$$D_i^k = r\left(X_n^k - T_F M_i^k \right) \tag{2.16}$$

T_f = Teaching factor, which determines the value that is to be modified.

All the possible and reasonable solutions are enhanced by shifting their positions towards the best possible solution by taking the present mean value of possible solutions into consideration. To simulate this, the j_{th} solution of the population at k_{th} teaching-learning cycle is revised under the given expression:

$$X^k_{new,j,i} = X^k_{old,j,i} + D^k_i \tag{2.17}$$

2.3.8.2   Student Phase [14,15]

In this phase, students acquire knowledge through mutual interactivity with other students. Student 'v' grasps knowledge from another student 'w' of the class. If student 'w' is better than student 'v,' then student 'v' moves toward 'w.' Two students are randomly selected from class. The two students randomly selected are feasible solutions such as X^k_v and X^k_w where 'v' and 'w' are two integer random numbers belonging to [1, M_p]

The algorithm for teaching-learning optimization technique is as follows and the flowchart is described in Figure 2.8:

Step 1. Initialization of the parameters for optimization such as the size of the population, number of iterations, number of design variables and parameters, and set bounds for design variables.

Step 2. Initialization of the population by generating the random population following its size and the total number of design variables.

Step 3. Compute the fitness of possible solutions in population and systemize the solutions in accordance with fitness value.

Step 4. Adjust the solution by simulating the approach that states that the teacher provides learning to students.

Step 5. Adjust the solution through the concept that students learn through mutual interaction.

Step 6. Repeat step 3 until the maximum iteration is not achieved.

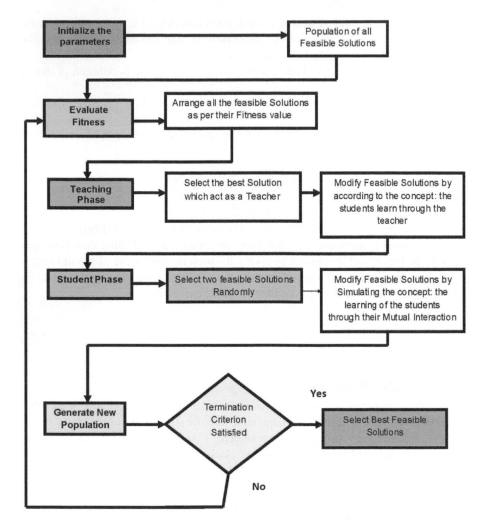

FIGURE 2.8   Flowchart for teaching learning algorithm

2.3.9   JAYA ALGORITHM [16]

This is a very powerful optimization algorithm used to determine constrained and unconstrained optimization problems. It works on the basis of the concept that the solution obtained for a particular problem moves towards the best and avoids the worst solution. It needs only common control parameters and doesn't need any definite parameters for the algorithm.

Consider f(x) to be the objective function that is to be minimized. Assume there are 'm' number of design variables and 'n' number of candidate solutions.

Let the best candidate obtain the best value of f(x) and the worst will obtain the worst value in the entire candidate solution. If $X_{p,q,r}$ is the value of the pth variable for the qth candidate during the rth iteration, then the value is modified as

$$X'_{p,q,r} = X_{p,q,r} + r_{1,p,r} + \left(X_{p,best,r} - \left|X_{j,k,i}\right|\right) - r_{2,p,r}\left(X_{p,worst,r} - \left|X_{p,q,r}\right|\right) \qquad (2.18)$$

Where,

$X_{p,\,best,\,r}$ = variable p for the best candidate

$X_{p,\,wrong,\,r}$ = variable p for worst solution

$X'_{p,q,r}$ = upgraded value of $X_{p,\,q,\,r}$

$s_{1,\,p,\,r}$ And $s_{2,\,p,\,r}$ = random number for the pth variable for the qth candidate during the rth iteration in range varies [0, 1]

$X'_{p,q,r}$ is accepted if it gives a better function value

At the end of iteration, the accepted function values are maintained and it becomes the input for the next iteration. The working of the Jaya algorithm is explained by the flowchart shown in Figure 2.9.

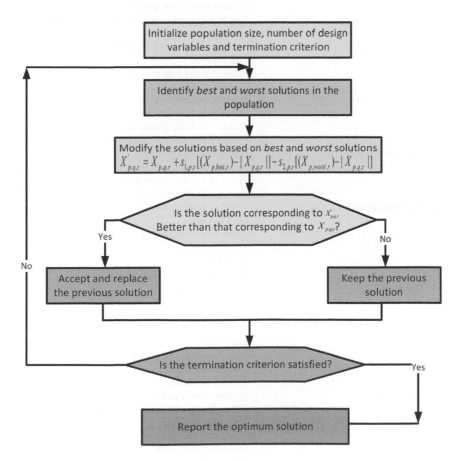

FIGURE 2.9 Flowchart for Jaya algorithm

2.4   APPLICATION OF SOFT COMPUTING TECHNIQUES IN POWER AND ENERGY SYSTEMS

The applications of various soft computing techniques in power and energy systems are summarized in Table 2.4

TABLE 2.4
Applications of soft computing techniques [17–24]

Soft Computing Techniques	Application in Power System
Genetic algorithm	Optimization
	Characterize economic models
	Train neural networks
	Scheduling applications
	Vehicle routing problems
	Multimodel optimization
Harmony search algorithm	Optimal placement of facts devices
	Optimal power flow problems
	Handle non-linear economic dispatch of real-world power system
Particle swarm optimization	Power generation and controlling
	Optimization
	Prediction and forecasting
	Signal processing
Gray wolf optimization	Economic dispatch problem
	Power dispatch problem
	System reliability optimization
	Capacitated vehicle routing problem
Ant colony optimization	Scheduling load problem
	Intelligent testing system
	Power electronic circuit design
	Energy and electricity network design
Artificial neural network	Power system security
	Fault diagnosis
	Power system protection
	Load forecasting
	Unit commitment
	Economic Load dispatch
Fuzzy logics	Contingency analysis
	Distribution planning
	Load frequency control
	Generation dispatch
	Load management
	Reactive power voltage control
	Unit commitment
	Security assessment
Teaching learning	Reactive power planning
	Power system stability enhancement
	Optimal power flow
	Power unit commitment
Jaya algorithm	Optimal coordination of relays in distribution system
	Future energy demand
	Optimization of machining performance characteristics

2.5 ENERGY MANAGEMENT

Energy management is defined as an organized and systematic management of energy in any building or organization to satisfy the economic and environmental requirements. The IEC61850 protocol is useful for the energy management of microgrids and smart grids for achieving coordination among various devices from various manufacturers. Controlling of load, leveling of load and demand response are important parameters to achieve smart grid services by taking energy management system (EMS) and demand-side management into consideration [25,26]. Due to increasing environmental awareness among people, it is becoming common to use the connection of distributed energy resource (DER) systems such as small-scale wind power systems, hydropower systems having a low head, and photovoltaic systems. At the same instant, various utility companies may undergo several issues such as the generation of excessive amounts of electricity, fluctuation in voltage and frequency, a rapid increase in three-phase load unbalancing, and involuntary islanding [25]. To overcome these problems accurately, it is important to consider communication protocols for supervisory control. IEC 61850 [25], an international standard used for communication between the substations, comes into the picture by reducing the cost of equipment as well as maintenance provided by supports of various multi-vendor. The Ethernet is used in it and it represents an object-oriented data model as LNs (logical node) and DOs (data object), this simplifies the system to exchange data and authorize the rising of multi-vendor systems. IEC 61850 can be used as a regulatory control communication protocol in substations.

2.5.1 OVERVIEW OF IEC 61850

This section represents the introduction of the data models and communication protocols that are basic units of the IEC 61850 standard. IEC 61850 class models are shown in Figure 2.10. A substation consists of various types of data related to

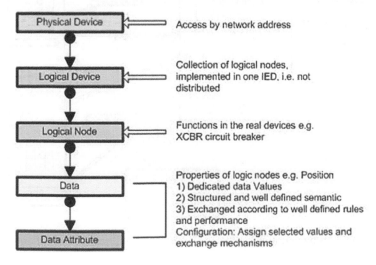

FIGURE 2.10 IEC 61850 class model

equipment, such as the value of current from an instrument transformer, information regarding the event from switchgear, and set or reset value for a protective relay. SAS provides many functions such as monitoring, control, and protection. IEC 61850 contains various types of data and functions, which are split into small and basic elements called 'logical nodes.' The data comprises the logic nodes that are considered as 'data objects' [27, 28, 29]. IEC 61850 uses object-oriented modeling. LNs are described in the IEC 61850-2 as follows: 'the smallest part of a function which exchanges data. A logical node is an object defined by its data and methods.'

Similarly, data objects are defined as 'part of a logical node object that represents the specific information i.e. status or measurement. From an object-oriented point of view, a data object is an instance of a data class.'

2.5.1.1 Communication Protocols

To exchange data between devices, IEC 61850 determines the abstract communication service interfaces (ACSI), and techniques to map the real communication protocols such as manufacturing message specification (MMS) and the Ethernet [28, 29]. It not only includes data, the setting of data, and its control but also consists of events reporting, logging, the transmission of the sampled values, and fast commands such as a trip command. The communication concept is shown in Figure 2.11. The major application of peer-to-peer communication is that it provides brief information that is necessary to be transferred with a low probability of loss within a few milliseconds. It also helps with transmitting the sampled values from the instrumental transformer having a large amount of data within a few milliseconds and its loss can also be detected.

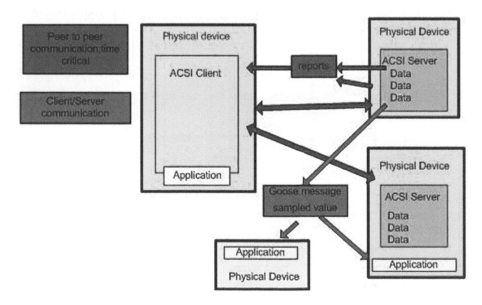

FIGURE 2.11   Communication concept

2.5.1.2 Distribution Automation System

The distribution system means the transfer of power from the distribution substation from the secondary circuit of a transformer and terminates at customer premises. DAS is focused on inspection and controlling the equipment in the field and distribution substation automatically. It reduces the workload of engineers, distribution operators, and field crews. DAS has functions related to the construction, operation, and maintenance of distribution system networks [25]. The various examples of its functions are discussed in the subsequent points:

- For controlling and monitoring the distribution substations and section switches on distribution lines
- To detect and then isolate the fault and its service restoration
- To detect and isolate the disconnected lines of distribution
- Detect and isolate the high-resistance ground faults
- To monitor pole-mounted transformers for detection of earth leakage
- To manage load and voltage for distribution lines having higher values of voltages
- Load management for prediction of life and adjusts the voltage distribution of lines having less voltage for transformer.

2.5.2 BUILDING ENERGY MANAGEMENT SYSTEM

The BEMS enhances the energy efficiencies, brings the buildings into their comfort zone and it lessens the emissions of gas produced by the greenhouse effect by providing a ventilating system, air-conditioning systems, proper lighting, and providing power types of equipment known as DERs, batteries, and TES systems. The BEMS collects the power data and then calculates the optimal values in order to maximize or minimize the value of the objective function. Optimal values are controlled by various above-mentioned optimization techniques. BEMS comprises one or more master stations, that connected through a communication network to the controllers so that it can function separately and handle the plant with which they are connected [41, 42]. Controllers have the ability to control and collect the data from the master station and provide the same to other controllers. In a smart grid, the BEMS is not only limited to optimize the generation and consumption of energy in a particular building, it also has advantages in using these optimizations methods within a community [34, 35]. BEMS has a direct link with the community EMS, which helps in adjusting the supply as well as demand in the community by providing control in DERs, TES systems, batteries, and customer loads through the customer-side EMS. The control messages from the community EMS are transmitted to the customer-side EMS (BEMS in the case of a building) using communication infrastructure [33, 34].

The DAS master station (or community EMS master station) using its discretion issues a control request, which is provided by the BMS master station. Both the BEMS master station and DAS master station are loosely coupled. But, according to its convenience, it can deny the request. (It accepts all the control requests in case of an event, say a major disaster.) An example of a DAS with a distribution system is shown in Figure 2.12

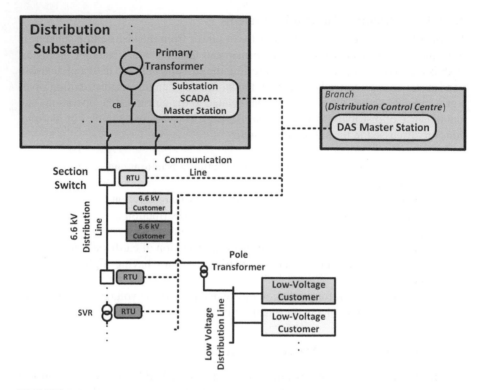

FIGURE 2.12   Example of DAS and the distribution system [2]

The RTU (remote terminal units) and substation SCADA master station communicate with the DAS master station for the distribution automation. The DAS master
station is set in a distribution control center and covers all the areas where customers
are fed by one or more distribution units. The DAS master station uses a communication infrastructure to receive or set the values to and from the equipment. It works on
the basis of communication cables or power line communication. Figure 2.12 shows
the DAS and the distribution system example. The working of the BEMS and DAS
system is described as shown in Figure 2.13 [2, 28, 32].

2.6   FUTURE DIRECTIONS

The application of soft computing techniques has increased its impact in the coming
years. It is playing an important role in both engineering and programming. Soft
computing can be extended from human thinking aspects to bioinformatics aspects.
The artificial neural networks can be extended its role in the development of the
human-like artificial brain. Future work can be extended by adding more intelligent
techniques in virtual power systems. The other issues can also come into the picture
such as the development of a new framework model for scheduling of demand-side
integration, optimization of the size of storage devices, controlling and managing the
forecasting power flow by using stochastic models and algorithms.

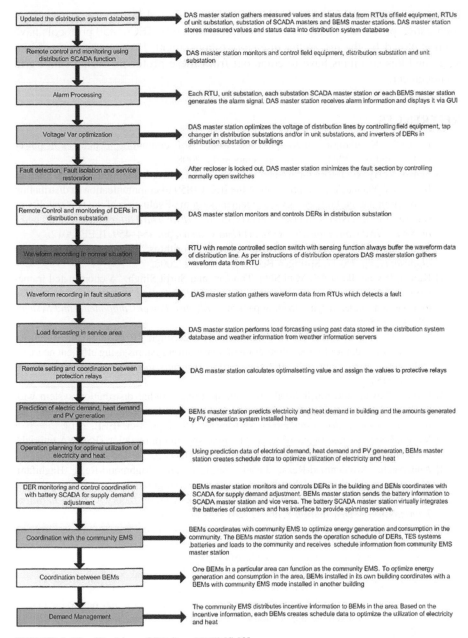

FIGURE 2.13 Working of DAS and BEMS [2]

2.7 CONCLUSIONS

This chapter presented the evaluation of several soft computing techniques and their application in power and energy system optimization and management. The researchers have applied different approaches depending upon the operating constraints and the objective function. Here, it is noticed that the conventional way of energy management has been overlapped with the digital technology where communication protocols have played a vital role. Recently, IEC61850 protocols have been explored by the researcher in energy management. However, it is the initial stage and lots of things have to come out from these protocols during smart grid management.

REFERENCES

[1] Fernando, Kurukulasuriya Joseph Tilak Nihal. "Soft computing techniques in power system analysis" PhD diss., Victoria University, 2008.

[2] Senke, Noriyuki, Tetsuo Otani, Hiroyuki Yusa, Eiji Ohba, Yoshimichi Okuno, Shinjiro Inoue, and Yutaka Arai. Application of the IEC 61850 to communication in distribution automation and building energy management systems-Evaluation of the applicability of standard Logical Nodes and Data Objects. In *2012 IEEE Third International Conference on Smart Grid Communications (Smart Grid Comm)*, pp. 454–459. IEEE, 2012.

[3] Sivanandam, S. N., and S. N. Deepa. "Genetic algorithms." In *Introduction to genetic algorithms*, pp. 15–37. Springer, Berlin, Heidelberg, 2008.

[4] Kumar, Pawan, Ikbal Ali, Mini Shaji Thomas, and Surjit Singh. "A coordinated framework of DG allocation and operating strategy in distribution system for configuration management under varying loading patterns." *Electric Power Components and Systems* (2020): 1–18.

[5] Kumar, Pawan, Ikbal Ali, Mini S. Thomas, and Surjit Singh. "Imposing voltage security and network radiality for reconfiguration of distribution systems using efficient heuristic and meta-heuristic approach." *IET Generation, Transmission & Distribution* 11, no. 10 (2017): 2457–2467.

[6] Kumar, Pawan, and Surjit Singh. Reconfiguration of radial distribution system with static load models for loss minimization In *2014 IEEE international conference on power electronics, drives and energy systems (PEDES)*, pp. 1–5. IEEE, 2014.

[7] Marini, Federico, and Beata Walczak. "Particle swarm optimization (PSO). A tutorial." *Chemometrics and Intelligent Laboratory Systems* 149 (2015): 153–165.

[8] Andervazh, Mohammad-Reza, Javad Olamaei, and Mahmoud-Reza Haghifam. "Adaptive multi-objective distribution network reconfiguration using multi-objective discrete particles swarm optimisation algorithm and graph theory." *IET Generation, Transmission & Distribution* 7, no. 12 (2013): 1367–1382.

[9] Azizian, Davood, and Gevork B. Gharehpetian. "Split-winding transformer design using new hybrid optimisation algorithm based on PSO and I-BB-BC." *IET Science, Measurement & Technology* 12, no. 6 (2018): 712–718

[10] Zhang, Jiancheng, Xinsheng Wang, and Lingyu Ma. "An optimal power allocation scheme of microgrid using Grey Wolf Optimizer." *IEEE Access* 7 (2019): 137608–137619.

[11] Bose, Bimal K. "Artificial intelligence techniques in smart grid and renewable energy systems—Some example applications." *Proceedings of the IEEE* 105, no. 11 (2017): 2262–2273.

[12] Lin, Chin-Teng. *Neural fuzzy systems: a neuro-fuzzy synergism to intelligent systems.* Prentice Hall PTR, 1996.

[13] Wang, Lingfeng, and Chanan Singh. Reliability-constrained optimum placement of reclosers and distributed generators in distribution networks using an ant colony system algorithm *IEEE Transactions on Systems, Man, and Cybernetics, Part C (Applications and Reviews)* 38, no. 6 (2008): 757–764.

[14] Rao, R. Venkata. Teaching-learning-based optimization algorithm In *Teaching learning-based optimization algorithm*, pp. 9–39. Springer, Cham, 2016.

[15] Rao, R. Venkata, Vimal J. Savsani, and D. P. Vakharia. "Teaching–learning-based optimization: a novel method for constrained mechanical design optimization problems *Computer-Aided Design* 43, no. 3 (2011): 303–315.

[16] Rao, R. Jaya: A simple and new optimization algorithm for solving constrained and unconstrained optimization problems *International Journal of Industrial Engineering Computations* 7, no. 1 (2016): 19–34.

[17] Jiang, Tianhua, and Chao Zhang. "Application of grey wolf optimization for solving combinatorial problems: Job shop and flexible job shop scheduling cases." *Ieee Access* 6 (2018): 26231–26240.

[18] Naghizadeh, Ramezan Ali, and Seved Mohammad Azimi. "Power system stability enhancement with teaching-learning-based optimization." In *Electrical Engineering (ICEE), Iranian Conference on*, pp. 1011–1016. IEEE, 2018.

[19] Bouchekara, H. R. E. H., M. A. Abido, and M. Boucherma. "Optimal power flow using teaching-learning-based optimization technique." *Electric Power Systems Research* 114 (2014): 49–59.

[20] Rao, Ravipudi Venkata. Applications of Jaya Algorithm and Its Modified Versions to Different Disciplines of Engineering and Sciences In *Jaya: An Advanced Optimization Algorithm and its Engineering Applications*, pp. 291-310. Springer, Cham, 2019.

[21] Kong, Weicong, Zhao Yang Dong, Youwei Jia, David J. Hill, Yan Xu, and Yuan Zhang. "Short-term residential load forecasting based on LSTM recurrent neural network." *IEEE Transactions on Smart Grid* 10, no. 1, (2017): 841–851.

[22] Zhang, Jiancheng, Xinsheng Wang, and Lingyu Ma. "An optimal power allocation scheme of microgrid using Grey Wolf Optimizer." *IEEE Access* 7 (2019): 137608–137619.

[23] Deshmukh, Rohit R., Makarand S. Ballal, and Hiralal Suryawanshi. "A fuzzy logic based supervisory control for power management in multibus DC microgrid." *IEEE Transactions on Industry Applications* (2020).

[24] Mansiri, Kongrit, Sukruedee Sukchai, and Chatchai Sirisamphan wong. "Fuzzy control algorithm for battery storage and demand side power management for economic operation of the smart grid system at Naresuan University, Thailand." *IEEE Access* 6 (2018): 32440–32449.

[25] Mao, Meiqin, Fengming Mei, Peng Jin, and Liuchen Chang. Application of IEC61850 in energy management system for microgrids In *2014 IEEE 5th International Symposium on Power Electronics for Distributed Generation Systems (PEDG)*, pp. 1-5. IEEE, 2014.

[26] Ali, Ikbal, Mini S. Thomas, and Pawan Kumar. "Energy efficient reconfiguration for practical load combinations in distribution systems." *IET Generation, Transmission & Distribution,* 9, no. 11 (2015): 1051–1060.

[27] IEC: "Communication networks and systems in substations – ALLPARTS", IEC 61850-SER ed1.0, 2012.

[28] Mohagheghi, Salman, Jean-Charles Tournier, James Stoupis, Laurent Guise, Thierry Coste, Claus A. Andersen, and Jacob Dall. Applications of IEC 61850 in distribution automation In *2011 IEEE/PES Power Systems Conference and Exposition*, pp. 1–9. IEEE, 2011.

[29] Ali, Ikbal, Mini S. Thomas, Sunil Gupta, and SM Suhail Hussain. "IEC 61850 substation communication network architecture for efficient energy system automation." *Energy Technology & Policy* 2, no. 1 (2015): 82–91.

[30] Aftab, MohdAsim, SM Suhail Hussain, Ikbal Ali, and Taha Selim Ustun. "IEC 61850 and XMPP communication based energy management in microgrids considering electric vehicles." *IEEE Access* 6 (2018): 35657–35668.

[31] Mohagheghi, Salman, Mirrasoul Mousavi, J. Stoupis, and Z. Wang. Modeling distribution automation system components using IEC 61850 In *2009 IEEE Power & Energy Society General Meeting*, pp. 1–6. IEEE, 2009.

[32] Estates, Defence. "Building energy management systems." In *Her Majesty's Stationery Office, Ministry of Defence.* 2001.

[33] Kumar, Pawan, Dip Vinod Thanki, Surjit Singh, and Srete Nikolovski. "A new framework for intensification of energy efficiency in commercial and residential use by imposing social, technical and environmental constraints." *Sustainable Cities and Society* 62 (2020): 102400.

[34] Kumar, Pawan, Gagandeep Singh Brar, Surjit Singh, Srete Nikolovski, Hamid Reza Baghaee, and Zoran Balkić. Perspectives and intensification of energy efficiency in commercial and residential buildings using strategic auditing and demand-side management *Energies* 12, no. 23 (2019): 4539.

[35] Kumar, Pawan, Gagandeep Singh Brar, and Lovepreet Singh. "Energy efficiency evaluation in commercial and residential buildings with demand side management: A review." In *2019 8th International Conference on Power Systems (ICPS)*, pp. 1–6. IEEE, 2019.

OTHER RELATED READINGS

[36] Pawan Kumar, Ikbal Ali, Taha Selim Ustun and Surjit Singh, *Handbook of research on Power and energy system optimization*. IGI Global, USA, March 2018.

[37] Cao, Bin, Weinan Dong, Zhihan Lv, Yu Gu, Surjit Singh, and Pawan Kumar. "Hybrid microgrid many-objective sizing optimization with fuzzy decision." *IEEE Transactions on Fuzzy Systems* 28, no. 11 (2020): 2702–2710.

KEYWORDS AND DESCRIPTIONS

Internet of Energy   Refers to up-gradation and automation of electricity infrastructures for energy producers and manufacturers. The major benefit is it increases the efficiency, cost-saving, and reduction in wastage

Energy management   The judicious and effective use of energy to maximize the profit and minimize the cost.

Soft-computing techniques or approaches   Deals with approximate models and provide solutions to a real-life problem with easy calculations. Soft computing methods are computational techniques work based on artificial intelligence.

IEC-61850 Protocols   These are Ethernet-based protocols build for electrical substations. It is a regulated method of communication to support integrated systems composed of multiple intelligent electronic devices (IEDs) that are connected to perform monitoring, metering, real-time protection, and control.

Distributed automation system   DAS is a cluster of technologies involving sensors, information and communication networks, processors, through which a utility can optimize and automate the operational efficiency of the distributed power system.

Substation automation system   SAS provides control, automation, protection, monitoring capabilities as part of comprehensive substation control and monitoring solution.

Building energy management system   These are integrated computerized systems for control and monitoring of energy-related building services such as heating, ventilation, and air conditioning (HVAC) systems, lighting, power systems, etc.

3 Internet of Energy for Plug-In Hybrid Electric Vehicle

Arush Singh, Saurabh Ranjan Sharma,
Vivek Kumar Tripathi, Deepanshu Singh Solanki,
and Raj Kumar Jarial
National Institute of Technology, Hamirpur, Himachal
Pradesh, India

CONTENTS

3.1   Background 72
3.2   Literature Review 73
    3.2.1   Historical Background 73
    3.2.2   EVs Vs ICEVs 75
    3.2.3   Types of EVs 75
    3.2.4   HEV Configurations 76
        3.2.4.1   Series HEV (IC Engine Assisted HEV) 77
        3.2.4.2   Parallel HEV 77
        3.2.4.3   Series-Parallel HEV 77
        3.2.4.4   Complex HEV 78
3.3   Plug-in Hybrid Electric Vehicle 79
    3.3.1   Introduction 79
    3.3.2   Grid Applications of PHEV 80
    3.3.3   Battery Performance Assessment 80
        3.3.3.1   State-of-Charge (SoC) 81
        3.3.3.2   State-of-Health (SoH) 81
    3.3.4   EV Charging Schemes 81
        3.3.4.1   AC Charger Level 1 82
        3.3.4.2   AC Charger Level 2 82
        3.3.4.3   DC Fast Charging 82
3.4   Vehicle-to-Grid (V2G) Technology 82
    3.4.1   Introduction 82
    3.4.2   V2G Challenges 84
3.5   Internet of Energy: An Overview 84
    3.5.1   Information Flow in IoE 84
        3.5.1.1   Machine-2-Machine Communication 84
        3.5.1.2   Architecture of M2M Communication 85
        3.5.1.3   Data Logging System 86

        3.5.2   Neighborhood Area Network (NAN)..89
        3.5.3   Wireless Communication...89
3.6   Literature Survey...90
3.7   Proposed Approach 90
        3.7.1   Sample System...91
        3.7.2   Case Study 99
3.8   Future Directions...100
3.9   Conclusions...100
References..101
Related Reading..104
Keywords and Descriptions 105

3.1   BACKGROUND

The electric power system is the largest humanmade network on the planet. Conventionally, bulk power is generated at various generating stations situated in remote locations, and a transmission system then transmits the power to the load centers. Subsequently, a distribution system feeds the power to various loads. Electromechanical generators are driven by a prime mover to produce electrical energy. The prime mover can be driven by heat engines (e.g., thermal power plant, nuclear power plant); by kinetic energy created by wind and water (e.g., wind power plant, hydropower plant), or by other means (e.g., solar power plant, geothermal power plant).

An overhead three-phase high voltage AC supply is typically used for power transmission. High-voltage DC lines are used to either transmit power over long distances or they are used as links for stabilizing power distribution networks where sudden changes in loads or blackouts are likely. Apart from that, microgrids are also developing rapidly, which can operate in grid-connected or islanded modes and have independent controlling capabilities. The integration of renewables with the grid is also a challenge due to their relatively transient/intermittent nature of power generation and its inability to meet load demand without a dedicated electrical energy storage system like pumped-hydro, Li ion or flow battery, etc. [1]. Electrolyzers can also be used to generate hydrogen from surplus electrical energy and use it in turn to supply fuel cells for regeneration [2].

In order to meet load demand from the generated power, demand side management (DSM) techniques are used. DSM techniques are classified as direct DSM (load limiters and direct load control) and indirect DSM (time of use pricing) [3]. Apart from that, peak shaving (minimizing loads during peak hours to mitigate the need of surplus generation through direct control of consumer appliances), energy conservation (optimum power consumption and use of energy-efficient appliances by the customer), and load shifting (operating loads in off-peak hours to minimize the peak demand) are some other practices helpful in DSM [4].

Electric vehicles (EVs) are a very unpredictable and dynamic load for the grid, which may not be a significant challenge for the network to meet their power demand. But it may lead to a varying load curve resulting in problems at the local level and become a problem for the grid at the macro-level in the future [5]. EVs also serve as a distributed storage, which allows the bidirectional flow of power between the network and the EV using vehicle-to-grid (V2G) technology or by other means (e.g., solar power plant, geothermal power plant) [6]. EVs are an integral essential component of the smart grid and can act as a distributed storage unit. Proper energy management of demands of residential and commercial loads along with that of an EV is imperative.

3.2 LITERATURE REVIEW

3.2.1 HISTORICAL BACKGROUND

In 1834, Ányos Jedlik in 1828 and Thomas Davenport developed primordial EV models. Jedlik invented an electric motor and used it in his small model car while Thomas developed a tricycle EV, which used a non-rechargeable battery as its power pack [7]. Subsequently, with invention of rechargeable lead-acid batteries, an EV was developed by David Salomons in 1874 using this battery [8]. In 1900, among the 4200 registered automobiles, EVs formed 38% of the total automobiles sold in USA while only 22% were internal combustion engine vehicles (ICEVs)). By 1912, about 34,000 EVs were registered in USA. Some of the leading EV manufacturers along with their famous EV models developed during 1900–1920 are listed in Table 3.1 [9,10].

However, the popularity of EVs had a steep decline in the period 1920–1960. This was due to multiple reasons. One of them being the development of extensive road networks, which required vehicles capable of travelling longer distances. In addition, mass production of the Ford Model T in 1925 made EVs much more costly than ICEVs. ICEVs suffered from the drawback of having a manual crank, which made it difficult to start. But with the invention of automobile starter motor for electric ignition of ICEVs, this drawback of ICEVs was uprooted and the vehicle became more user friendly. Thus, it can be concluded that, due to a reduced cost, extended range of operation and ease of operation, ICEVs eliminated the EVs from the market [11,12]. This negligence of EVs continued until the 1970s, when the Arab oil embargo (1973) increased demands for alternative energy sources. Apart from that, due to increased air pollution by ICEVs, engineers and scientists started looking back towards electric vehicles. In 1968, the "Great electric car race" was organized to promote EVs in which electric vehicles had to travel a distance of 3,490 miles with 53 recharging stations in between. The EVs travelled from Massachusetts Institute of Technology, Boston, and California Institute of Technology, Pasadena, USA [13,14].

In 1976, under the Public law 94-413, the Electric and Hybrid Vehicle Research, Development and Demonstration Act, congress authorized a program for promotion of EVs. Due to governmental support, automakers in USA (Ford, Chrysler, US electric car, Soelectria, etc.); Japan (Toyota, Nissan, Honda, Mazda, Mitsubishi, Suzuki, etc.) and Europe (PSA Peugeot, Renault, BMW, Mercedes-Benz, Audi, Volvo, Opel, Volkswagen, Fiat, etc.) started taking interest in electric vehicles. Popular EVs developed after the 1990s are listed in Table 3.2.

TABLE 3.1
Leading EV Manufacturers along with Their Famous EV Models

S. no.	Company	EV Model	Year
1	Electric carriage and wagon company (USA)	Electrobat	1894
2	Riker electric motor company (USA)	Victoria	1897
3	Bersey electric cab (UK)	Hummingbirds	1897
4	Pope manufacturing company (USA)	Columbia	1898

TABLE 3.2
Popular EVs developed after the 1990s

S.no.	Model Name	Manufacturer/ Country of Origin	Year	Specifications			
				Motor Spec.	Battery Spec.	Range	Top Speed
1	Impact (concept)	GM, US	1990	102 kW	16.5 kWh, Lead-Acid, 32 × 10V	193 km	161 kmph
2	Reva	Reva, India	1994	13 kW	9.6 kWh, Lead-Acid, 48 V	80 km	65 kmph
3	RAV4	Toyota	1997	50 kW	27 kWh, NiMH, 24 × 12v	150 km	126 kmph
4	Prius Hybrid	Honda	1999	30 kW	1.78 kWh, NiMH, 274V	34 kmpl	160 kmph
5	Model S	Tesla	2009	285 kW	75 kWh, Li-ion,	224 km	180 kmph
6	Leaf	Nissan	2010	80 kW	24 kWh, Li-ion,	117 km	150 kmph
7	Volt	Chevrolet	2010	111 kW	16 kWh, Li-ion,	56 km	160 kmph
8	Model X	Tesla	2012	245 kW	75 kWh, Li-ion,	383 km	210 kmph
9	i3	BMW	2014	125 kW	22 kWh, Li-ion	160 km	150 kmph
10	e-Tron (concept)	Audi	2015	200 kW	90.2 kWh, Li-ion, 385V	450 km	250 kmph
11	Model Y	Tesla	2020	198.5 kW front, 270.5 kW rear	72.5 kWh, Li-ion	425 km	233 kmph
12	Taycan	Porsche	2020	390 kW	93.4 kWh, Li-ion	463 km	250 kmph

3.2.2 EVs Vs ICEVs

In 2000, around 700 million vehicles were operating all around the world and this number is expected to increase to 2.5 billion by 2050. If this many ICEVs starts operation, the global pollution level is expected to rise to intolerable limits. Thus, it is the need of the hour, to look for means of sustainable transport using low or zero emission vehicles. A comparative analysis of EVs with ICEVs is shown in Table 3.3 [15–17].

3.2.3 TYPES OF EVS

EVs may or may not have a multiple energy generation unit to aid the electric motor. Thus, depending upon the type of propulsion system, EVs can be classified as 'Pure' Electric Vehicles (PEVs) or 'Hybrid' [18] Electric Vehicles (HEVs). PEVs have a battery as a common energy source and an electric motor drive connected to its shaft, but they may be coupled with alternative energy source as well. Based on the presence of an alternative source, PEVs have four types, namely, BEV or battery only electric vehicle, FCEV or fuel cell electric vehicle, UCEV or ultra capacitor electric vehicle, and UFEV or ultra flywheel electric vehicle [19].

While the battery is still the best form of energy source for an EV, it suffers from problems such as lower energy density, lower charging speeds, reduced commute range and hence lower efficiency. The fuel cell provides the EV with better energy density and thus improves the commutable range for vehicle on the other hand, ultra-capacitors and ultra-flywheels help boost the battery charging during regenerative braking. On the other hand, HEVs use both the IC (internal combustion) engine and motor for propulsion. HEVs can be classified into five types on the basis of the ratio of power extracted from electric and IC engine. If the power output of the electric

TABLE 3.3
Comparative analysis of EVs with ICEVs

S.no	Basis of Difference	ICEV		EV	
1	Emission of pollutants	CO, CO_2	10.90 gm/km	CO, CO_2	0.08 gm/km
		NOx	0.37 gm/km	NOx	0.07 gm/km
		VOC	0.33 gm/km	VOC	0.01 gm.km
		SOx	0.14 gm/km	SOx	0.08 gm/km
		PMx	0.04 gm/km	PMx	0.03 gm/km
2	Energy diversification	Oil, natural gas		Oil, natural gas, coal, hydro, solar, geothermal, tidal	
3	Efficiency	16% from energy source to wheels		72% from energy source to wheels	
4	Fuel economy	13% to wheels from crude oil		18% to wheels from electricity from thermal plant	
5	Acquisition cost	Low (mass production)		High (initial battery cost, periodic replacement)	
6	Maintenance cost	Low (IC engines are robust)		Low (IM and battery are also robust)	
7	Space requirement	Moderate		High for same amount of power	

motor is very low, it is said to be a **micro hybrid**. As the ratio increases, four other types emerge. These are, **mild hybrid**, **full hybrid**, **plug-in hybrid** (PHEV) and **range extended hybrid** (REV) [20,21] (Table 3.4).

Micro, mild and full hybrid vehicles do not need their batteries to be charged externally, thus these three clubbed together are called **conventional HEVs**. PHEVs and REVs have considerably much higher power output from an electric motor, so they are charged externally. These are said to be **grid connectable** HEVs. A block diagram showing the classification based on propulsion type is shown in Figure 3.1 [22].

3.2.4 HEV Configurations

When compared to the HEV/ICEV, the BEV has greater energy efficiency and offers zero emissions locally. But BEVs have a limited driving range and suffer from frequent charging requirements. This makes hybridization of EVs an interesting prospect. This hybridization can largely increase the range of BEVs and minimize emissions of ICEVs. But as the system involves both a battery and an IC engine, which are to be designed to operate in unison, designing HEVs is a little complicated. Thus, before implementation of the Internet of Energy (IoE) on a HEV, an understanding of HEV configurations is important [23]. The various HEV configurations are as follows:

TABLE 3.4
Different Power Output of Electric Motor

Type	Generator Type	Power Rating	Voltage Rating	Usage
Micro hybrid	ISG	3–5 kW	14–42 V	Start-stop, regenerative breaking
Mild hybrid	ISG	7–15 kW	100–150 V	Start-stop, regenerative breaking, power assist
Full hybrid	EVT	50–60 kW	500–600 V	Start-stop, regenerative breaking, power assist, electronic launch

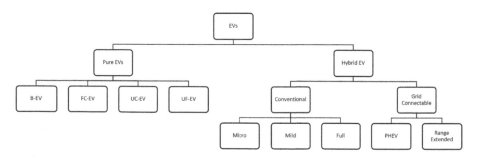

FIGURE 3.1   Classification of EVs on the basis of the type of propulsion system.

3.2.4.1 Series HEV (IC Engine Assisted HEV)

An IC engine-based system is connected to the battery electric system using an electric generator. In this configuration, initially, the IC engine produces mechanical energy by consuming fuel stored in the fuel tank. The mechanical energy generated is used to charge the battery, which in turn drives the vehicle motors for propulsion. This configuration is simple to design, but due to an increased number of mechanical systems (engine, motor, and generator), the reliability and efficiency of the configuration is less compared to other systems. A simple block diagram of a series HEV configuration is shown in Figure 3.2.

3.2.4.2 Parallel HEV

In this configuration, both the IC engine and the battery can be used to drive the vehicle. It has a dual clutch mechanism as it employs a pair of clutches, one for connecting IC engine to transmission system and the other for connecting the battery-driven electric motor to transmission system. A simple block diagram of a parallel HEV configuration is shown in Figure 3.3.

3.2.4.3 Series-Parallel HEV

In this configuration, the IC engine is connected not only to the transmission system but also it is connected to the battery using an electric generator. A simple block diagram of a series-parallel HEV configuration is shown in Figure 3.4.

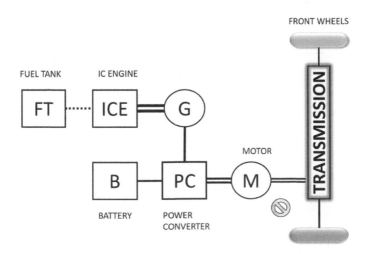

FIGURE 3.2 Series HEV configuration.

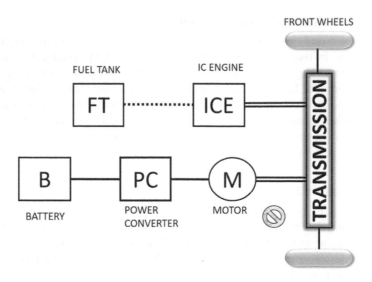

FIGURE 3.3   Parallel HEV configuration.

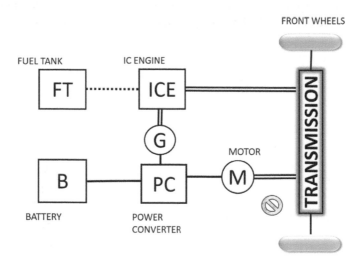

FIGURE 3.4   Series-parallel HEV configuration.

3.2.4.4   Complex HEV

A complex HEV configuration is generally adapted for vehicles with dual axle transmission. A simple block diagram of a complex HEV configuration is shown in Figure 3.5.

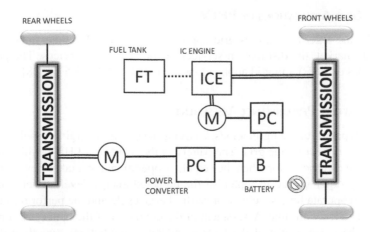

FIGURE 3.5 Complex HEV configuration.

3.3 PLUG-IN HYBRID ELECTRIC VEHICLE

3.3.1 INTRODUCTION

PHEVs bring the best of both worlds. The vehicle can be configured to run mostly on electric power and have an extended range using the IC engine when required or have an alternative configuration where both the engines would aid powertrain demand. PHEVs can be plugged into the grid during offload hours to juice up at lesser costs while still significantly providing a boost in fuel economy; one such example can be seen with the Toyota Prius, where the HEV variant returns 640 miles to a full tank, compared to the PHEV variant that returns 1000 miles for the same conditions, provided owners charge it at night [24–26] (Figure 3.6).

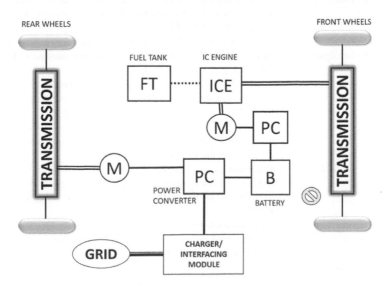

FIGURE 3.6 EV Connected to charger interfacing module to the primary grid.

3.3.2   GRID APPLICATIONS OF PHEV

Primarily, the V2G has various grid applications that can be either related to the wholesale market, the distribution services or the customer services. The potential applications of PHEVs in grid applications are listed in Table 3.5 [27,28].

3.3.3   BATTERY PERFORMANCE ASSESSMENT

Different types of charging methods, charging level, and charging topology of EV have a great impact on the grid. The battery is the heart of a PHEV, which delivers power to the electric motor when the vehicle is operational and takes power from the grid or any other source to replenish the depleted energy levels. Each battery is designed to operate for a specific charge-discharge cycle and the performance of the battery degrades with time. Assessment of the condition of the battery is imperative to assess the performance of the battery and make predictions regarding the estimated range and estimated life of the battery [29]. Primarily, the performance of the battery can be identified by using the following two parameters:

TABLE 3.5
Potential Applications of PHEVs in Grid Applications

S. no.	Application	Description
1.	Frequency regulation	Power interchange flow to match the scheduled interchange flow so as to keep balance in generation and demand avoiding frequency variation within regulation standards.
2.	Spinning, non-spinning and supplemental reserve	Reserves are kept as backup and online to meet excess demand as and when required, response time may take 10 minutes and frequency responsive reserves take 10 seconds to respond.
3.	Load following	Storage provide output variance to dampen the variance in load profile, storage tracking load profiles may change their output to keep balance between generation and load.
4.	Distribution upgrade deferral	Storages extend the useful life of existing infrastructure and avoid expansion and investment costs in infrastructure management to meet adequate capacity to serve loads.
5.	Voltage support	Voltage support is needed to meet voltage excursions by large power loads or distributed generations, storage discharges real power to meet these voltage excursions and provide voltage support.
6.	Power quality	Storage may prevent end-use loads from handling poor power quality through power system by supporting their demands through their discharges for durations of seconds to minutes.
7.	Power reliability	Enhancement of reliability is offered by supporting electricity services during outages either planned or unplanned, storages provide provision of energy backup during such conditions resulting in improved reliability.
8.	Retail energy time-shift	Energy cost reduction by charging discharging time slot allocation, i.e. charging during low cost times and discharging during high-cost times.
9.	Demand charge mitigation	Provides profitable proposition on the basis of demand cost for charging and demand cost at the time of discharging the storage system.

3.3.3.1   State-of-Charge (SoC)

SoC is defined as the level of charge that the battery of a PHEV can hold in relation to its rated capacity. SoC cannot be measured directly but can be estimated using offline techniques (e.g., coulomb counting) and online techniques (e.g., current integration method). SoC is expressed as follows:

$$SoC = \frac{Remaining\ Capacity}{Rated\ Capacity}$$

where, Rated Capacity = battery voltage(Rated) × Ah capacity

3.3.3.2   State-of-Health (SoH)

SoH is a figure of merit in which the current SoH is compared with a threshold value to determine the useful life time and suitability of the battery for a particular application. A battery management system (BMS) is typically used to estimate the SoH of a battery by evaluating a combination of parameters like internal resistance, battery capacity, operating voltage, self-discharge, number of charge–discharge cycles, age of the battery, temperature of battery during its previous uses, etc. Thus, it can be concluded that the performance of battery including safety and durability depends directly or indirectly on charging methods and charging time. Commonly, constant current, constant voltage or a constant current cum constant voltage charging method is used for charging of a PHEV battery.

3.3.4   EV CHARGING SCHEMES

For different circumstances different types of charger are also used. EV owners mainly charge their vehicle while it is parked at their home during early morning or in the night, so they can accordingly decide a charging level for their EV. Generally, there is a user-friendly touchscreen for performing various functions and checking meter reading for SoC of the battery. This kind of EV charging scheme is referred to as a residential charging scheme. The fleet charging scheme involves an outdoor charging scheme in which EVs are connected together as an aggregated fleet and the electrical energy is allowed to transfer between various EVs for optimum demand management of EVs [30]. This type of charging scheme is helpful in peak hours and involves a rigorous use of vehicle-to-grid (V2G) technology (discussed in Section 3.4). Apart from that, there is commercial installment in some areas such as restaurants, hotels, shopping malls, and in some parking areas. AC Level 2 charging is needed in these areas because of lack of available time. EV owners stay for a short time in these areas. The AC Level 1 charging system is installed in the parking areas of airports, railway stations, etc. as it assumes that EV owners are going on a long trip. The AC Level 1 charging system is more economical than the AC Level 2 one in this area because there are time limitations [31]. A brief overview of the various charging levels is given below.

3.3.4.1 AC Charger Level 1

It is the most common and most basic mode of charging as the charging infrastructure for this mode is readily accessible to most people. The typical American voltage level for residential and commercial buildings is between 110 and 120 VAC with a maximum current flow of 16 A, which can solve the purpose for this type of charging. This type of charging uses a three-prong electrical outlet attached to a cord set containing a current-interrupting device in the power supply cable. The design for the vehicle connector at the other end must be approved by the SAE and this connector mates with the vehicle inlet. All the performance-related physical electrical and functional components are specified by the SAE. Most automotive suppliers use the standards for connector designs for AC Level 1 and 2 charging; many companies like Tesla motors have also developed mobile connectors that are compatible with only a few vehicles. Level 1 charging is not a very fast mode of charging as the 1.9 kW maximum charge rate will require over 12 hours to fully charge a 24 kWh pack and over 8 hours to fully charge a 16 kWh pack. It also lacks in control and monitoring capabilities and V2G applications, and due to these limitations of charging time most of vehicle owners prefer Level 2 charging over Level 1.

3.3.4.2 AC Charger Level 2

This is a more preferred and prescribed mode for EVSE by both public and private facilities. A voltage rating of 220 to 240 V with single phase currents are specified by this mode and this higher voltage allows for a charging rate of 19.2 kW, which provides much faster charging in PEVs. AC Level 2 charging is modeled to support refueling modes coincident with destination locations. The connectors are made to support current as high as 80 A but this much high current is very rare so a typical rating would be 40 A, which provides for a maximum current delivered of 32 A. The BMS of the vehicle decides the charge required and draws current accordingly from the EVSE so that an EVSE capable of delivering 30 A would deliver only 20 A as approved by the BMS. The EVSE cannot violate its current rating, i.e. if its rating is 20 A and the BMS demands 30 A, then it won't violate the rating and provide the full current rating of 20 A. AC Level 2 charging is the more popular and preferred mode of vehicle recharging because of its V2G connectivity and easy and faster charging capabilities. It also provides monitoring and control abilities for charging applications. Apart from AC charging, DC fast chargers are also gaining importance for quick charging of EVs. One such example is the supercharging stations offered by Tesla.

3.3.4.3 DC Fast Charging

DC fast chargers (DCFCs) are one of the fastest charging solutions available for energy replenishment in an PHEV. Due to their high initial cost, DCFCs are available only as public charging stations and are preferred as a charging solution for long-distance trips.

3.4 VEHICLE-TO-GRID (V2G) TECHNOLOGY

3.4.1 INTRODUCTION

V2G technology is the technology that allows a grid-able EV to be used as a grid asset. V2G allows bidirectional flow of electrical energy between the vehicle and the grid such that the EV can decide power system dynamics. Information technology has an active role. PHEVs are well suited to act as a grid resource due to their operational flexibility and embedded communications and actuation technology. PHEVs are operationally flexible as they can act as a load (when its battery is charging from the grid) as well as a generating unit (when the battery can deliver power to the grid). Digital and control technologies involved with vehicle safety, navigation, etc. improve the information-sharing capability of the vehicle and make it easier to schedule vehicle charging accordingly [32,33]. The various components of a typical V2G setup are as shown in Figure 3.7. Some other terminologies related with V2G are listed in Table 3.6.

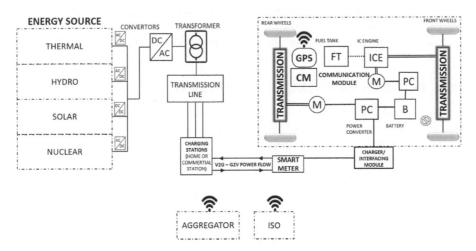

FIGURE 3.7   Various components of a typical V2G setup.

TABLE 3.6

List of Commonly used Terminologies [27–33]

S. no.	Terminology	Description
1	V1G	Unidirectional flow of power from the power grid to a storage device like a battery.
2	V2B (vehicle-to-building) or V2H (vehicle-to-home)	Flow of energy stored in an EV to meet an on-site load demand like a building or home.
3	V2X (vehicle-to-everything)	Flow of energy stored in an EV to meet an on-site load demand without affecting the grid.
4	V2G (vehicle-to-grid)	Flow of energy stored in an EV to meet load demand by injecting power into the grid.
5	ISO (independent system operator)	Helps maintain balance in the grid by controlling the power dispatch to plants and management of system resources.
6	Aggregator	A system that puts together all intelligent systems and uses NAT address to control each connected device separately.
7	G2V (grid-to-vehicle)	Charging the batteries of the vehicle when plugged into power socket connected to the grid.

3.4.2 V2G CHALLENGES

V2G is an excellent approach for saving energy; boosting power system flexibility, reliability, and resiliency; and ancillary services while simultaneously avoiding compliance costs for environmental issues. But it is facing skepticism due to its economic rationale. V2G implementation involves utility costs, administrative costs, interconnection costs, vehicle integration costs [34]. Also, V2G integration increases the uses of a battery and thereby reduces the operational life of an EV battery.

V2G will be justifiable if and only if economic benefits compensate for the battery wear and other costs involved with V2G implementation. Apart from that, experts are dubious about the energy efficiency of the overall V2G process, and comparative studies are often conducted for V2G based battery storage with pumped hydro power plants. EVs like the Hyundai ix35 FCEV, REV 300 ACX, Boulder EV 500/1000 series, Nissan Leaf, Nissan e-NV200, etc. have been modified for V2G compatibility.

3.5 INTERNET OF ENERGY: AN OVERVIEW

Every year, the world population increases and therefore energy consumable machines also increase, which leads to an increase in demand of energy. Currently, a major part of the energy sector depends on fossils fuels, which is already limited. These conditions raise an urgent need for more efficient use of energy and the uses of renewable energy resources. For sustainable development, energy efficiency is an important factor because it offers benefits in economic as well as in another sectors in the long term [35]. In future, there is a need for a proper structure of energy distribution that increases efficiency. In the present situation, increases in energy demand will cause serious network congestion problems and the low quality of transmitted power. Lack of efficient monitoring and inflexibility increases the problem in the energy sector. The smart grid is an intelligent electricity distribution infrastructure that relies heavily on a high-speed communication network for monitoring and control. The IoE can be viewed as an extension of the smart grid concept [36]. The IoE in technological terms refers to the upgrading and automating of electricity infrastructures for producers and manufacturers. The IoE is the implementation of IoT technology into distributed energy system to optimize the efficiency of energy infrastructure and reduces wastage.

3.5.1 INFORMATION FLOW IN IoE

In the IoE there are a lot of machine that have to communicate with each other. Good communication between machines has to be maintained for a coordinated flow of information. Therefore, machine-to-machine (M2M) communication is necessary.

3.5.1.1 Machine-2-Machine Communication

M2M communication is important to manage the energy flow between energy devices and to coordinate with the controller. There is communication between two ends in which one end has embedded devices and the other end is the network server, which connects through a wired or wireless internet network (IoT). In EV, the central data processing unit receives data for decision-making. The central data processing unit acts as a server and the EV acts as client, both linked with each other through a static router. A unique IP address is assigned to the server to operate under the private area network [37].

An EV with an onboard data logging facility can send packets in real time with any defined interval. This packet routes through a data logger to a smart grid for decision-making. The mobility of the EV, speed, position, temperature, SoC, and such types of information are contained in this packet. A 4G modem, Raspberry Pi and programming in Python are used to implement the onboard data logging system in EV [38]. Alternatively, it can be implemented through Bluetooth to EV CAN bus (communication protocol). A type of communication protocol and medium is important between packet sending and receiving. According to the current situation 5G connection is recommended because of the maximum rate density.

3.5.1.2 Architecture of M2M Communication

There are three types of M2M communication categories: Tracking (controllable data sensing), Logging (transfer of data), and Notification (data receiving with decision). The architecture of M2M communication is based on 3GPP (Third Generation Partnership Project). This is the architecture in which the first part represents the communication of an EV through MTC (in which the server is mounted inside the domain) and a dedicated operator controls the EV. These operators offer API on the MTC server. The second part indicates that the MTC server is not controlled by the operator properly. The third part indicates that EV are capable of communication with each other [39,40] (Figure 3.8).

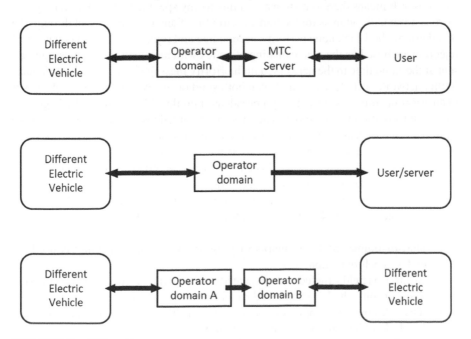

FIGURE 3.8 GPP architecture.

3.5.1.3   Data Logging System

The data logging system acts as an M2M terminal. The logging system is integrated with a radio module. This module enables radio access via a cellular network. LTE EPC (Evolved Packet Core) control application server. Just like the internet, the data logging system uses IP connectivity to communicate with the server using an IP/TCP protocol.

Similar to a cellular network, a M2M terminal is assigned two types of identity by the LTE network operator: IMSI (International Mobile Subscriber Identity) and MSISDN (Mobile Station International Subscriber Directory Number). These two identities ensure EV authentication and allow access to a network. Due to this authentication an IP bearer is established between the PDN-GW (Packet Data Network Gateway) and the vehicle and EV will be ready to exchange data with the application layer service [41].

In EV, different types of component such as electric motor, controller, battery, braking system, sensors, etc. are used. These components need to be monitored periodically. So, there is a need for a system that monitors these components and gives information to the owner. Some information about the battery such as State-of-Charge (SoC) and State-of-Health (SoH) are given to the grid [42].

A real-time monitoring system needs a single board computer with good processing power and RAM. This system can be run by any user-friendly operating system such as Windows, Linux, and Android. Some communication protocols such as I^2C, SPI, UART, CAN bus, and 1-wire can allow different components to communicate with each other to exchanging information [43].

The Electronic Controller Unit uses the CAN bus communication protocol. This protocol uses the broadcast type method for communication between the controller and sensor. It means there is no transfer of bits to any specific node or we can say that there is no specific address for the transmission bit. If any message is sent through the broadcast method each node performs acceptance and rejection. This acceptance and rejection are based on the match making of nodes with messages. If two messages are sent at the same time in the network, a high priority message is accepted by all nodes. In this network each device or node can both send or receive messages. Each sensor in an EV transmits messages through broadcast into the CAN network. ECU gets all type of information from the bus. The message is broadcast from any node in some circumstances such as if any failure is detected by any node, it broadcasts a message or other nodes ask to do broadcast a message to another node. Sometimes nodes continuously broadcast a message. When a message is broadcast into the CAN network, ECU provides assistance after receiving information from the bus. CAN communication uses two-wire data connection, which is CAN high line, CAN low line, and half-duplex system [44]. The frame format of the CAN bus is discussed below.

- Start-of-Frame (SOF) bit marks the beginning of a message and is used for nodes synchronization.
- Arbitration field – Includes a message identifier and RTR (Remote Transmission Request) bit, which distinguish data and remote frames.
- IDE – A dominant single identifier extension (IDE) bit means that a standard CAN identifier with no extension is being transmitted.
- R_0 – Reserved bit (for possible use by future standard amendment).

- DLC – The 4-bit data length code (DLC) contains the number of bytes of data being transmitted.
- Data – Up to 64 bits of application data may be transmitted.
- CRC – Cyclic redundancy check (CRC) is 16-bit checksum.
- EOF – End-of-frame (EOF) marks the end of data and remote frame.
- IFS– This 7-bit inter-frame space (IFS) contains the time required by the controller to move a correctly received frame to its proper position in a message buffer area [45].

SPI is a serial communication protocol that uses three minimum or four maximum wires: SCLK (clock line), MOSI (Master Out Slave In), MISO (Master In Slave Out), and SS (Chip Select) (Figure 3.9).

In this communication protocol, master devices (such as a microcontroller) use chip select or slave select (SS) to communicate with different slave devices (different sensors). Instead of the address method, SPI uses the select line method to communicate with a particular sensor. In SPI, both master and slave are connected with each other's input and output through the MISO and MOSI pin.

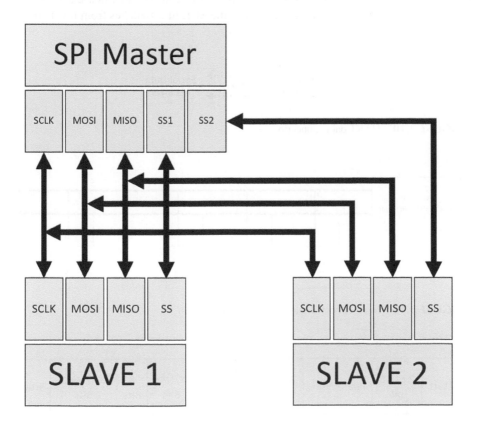

FIGURE 3.9 Master to slave connection.

Universal Asynchronous Serial Receiver and Transmitter (UART) is not a communication protocol like SPI and I2C, but a physical circuit in a microcontroller, or a stand-alone IC. UART has a two-wire data connection for communication: transmission and receiver. A UART's main purpose is to transmit and receive serial data. There is no clock signal, which is why it is asynchronous in nature (Figure 3.10).

An Inter-Integrated Circuit (I^2C) is a two-wire synchronous communication protocol that uses two-wire communication, which is similar to the UART: clock line SCL and data line SDL. Both wires are connected from the master device to different slave devices. Here master devices such as microcontrollers and different types of the sensor are used as slave devices. This master–slave configuration is a feature of SPI. This communication protocol uses the addresses method to send a message to different slave devices. Figure 3.11 shows a basic master–slave interconnected system.

I^2C is a combination of both SPI and UART. SDA is used for transmission and receiving message by master–slave devices and SCL carries a clock signal. The frame format of I^2C is given in Figure 3.12

When the SDA line switches from a high level to low level before the SCL line switches from high to low, this is known as start condition and when the SDA line switches from a low level to high level after the SCL line switches from low to high,

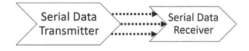

FIGURE 3.10   UART data connection.

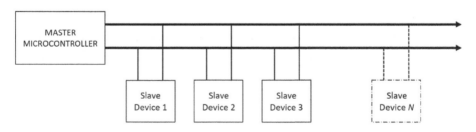

FIGURE 3.11   Interconnected master–slave configuration

Start	7 or 10 bit	Read/Write	ACK/NACK Bits	8 Bits	ACK/NAC K Bits	8 Bits	ACK/NACK Bits	Stop

FIGURE 3.12   Frame format of I^2C

this is known as a stop condition. I²C has four modes: Standard Mode (100 kbps), Fast Mode (400 kbps), High Speed Mode (3.4 Mbps), and Ultra-Fast Mode (5 Mbps).

3.5.2 NEIGHBORHOOD AREA NETWORK (NAN)

This network is important for enabling smart grid applications as it connects the utilities and customers. It basically stores various types of huge amounts of data. It mainly connects to a large number of devices to send important signals that are distributed over large areas. Multi-point-to-point (MP2P) and point-to-multiple-point (P2MP) traffic are supported by this type of network. A wide range of QoS is required in this network. Due to bad weather, power problems, and multipath fading sometimes problems arise in this network. It is location aware, self-configurable, and heterogeneous in nature. This network needs high security and privacy. The connectivity between NAN and HAN is as follows: NAN is connected to s meter and this meter is connected with HAN through Wi-Fi or Zigbee. Two types of communication technologies are used: wireless and wired [46].

3.5.3 WIRELESS COMMUNICATION

There are different types of wireless communication that are used according to their range and data rate. Such different wireless communications are shown in Figure 3.13 [47,48]:

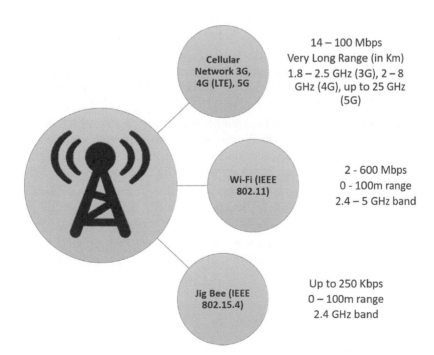

FIGURE 3.13 Wireless communication protocols.

3.6 LITERATURE SURVEY

R. Tull de Salis et al. mention that energy optimization at residential chargers with energy storage control can be a feasible solution to meet EV battery charging solution. A bidirectional energy transfer control by peak shaving in a single building using the building energy monitoring system has been discussed [4].

Zahedi has studied the usage of an EV battery as an energy storage device; its role and potential benefits in the form of grid reliability and a supporting system can be a useful factor for future smart grids. The major benefits of EV integration with conventional grids has been made clear [6].

Massimo Guarnieri has said, with the evolution of electric motors and the introduction of rechargeable batteries, EV came to compete with IC engine vehicles in the automobile industry during the latter half of the nineteenth century [10].

Shen et al. have mentioned that in order to compensate the constraints faced by EVs in the form of initial cost and battery management hybrid electric vehicle (HEV) technology was found as the interim solution [20].

E. Nefedov et al. have said that the Internet of Energy and its application for sustainable utilization of electric vehicle batteries as energy storage is explained with a case study utilizing the vehicle to building technology [40].

Zhilong Lin et al. found that, apart from all the technological and environmental benefits an EV offers, its widescale adoption faces few challenges in the form of large load burdens on the conventional grid. An idea on how to schedule charging and meet load curve is detailed [55].

A. M. Amjad et al. say an energy internet approach by facilitating communication protocols with the aid of optimized energy management within a single house or residential microgrid has been discussed with automated demand side response [56].

M. S. Islam et al. found that load profile and charging patterns become complex with a dense network of charging stations deployed at universities, hospitals, shopping malls, and commercial charging stations. An integrated energy optimized approach to deal with daily EV load profile is shown [57].

Shao et al. say that the customer choice approach to control loads with EV types and charging profile for demand response as a strategy for grid integration of EV has been discussed in their paper [58].

Guan et al. studied the adaptive power management strategy with a smart option for range extension can come in useful and the approach is explained in their paper [59].

3.7 PROPOSED APPROACH

IoE for vehicles provides proper communication channels between vehicles and the grid for proper energy management. In the previous section, an overview of various techniques has been provided for V2G implementation. The proposed approach meets the basic idea of the concept by providing proper communication channels between the generating units through a building energy management system (BEMS) and the EV's battery management system (BMS) through a user interface application in a hypothetical city of the future with a widescale adoption of EV and Smart grids.

The approach mainly focuses on maximizing the energy efficiency of the distributed generation (e.g., PV rooftop generation) and the EVs along with proceeding in maximum energy cost savings through the grid. Future power grids will be composite in nature where all kinds of smart generation, transmission, and distribution systems interact with each other through the aid of communication systems and share energy. Such systems can have a unique model for power transmission among various smart components by considering EVs as a mode of energy carriers. The above system consists of smart residential grids that can meet their own residential demands by their own distributed rooftop generations. Similarly, office microgrids can also handle their power demands for sensitive applications, i.e. these systems have the capability to reduce the energy burden on the main utility grid and thus can make the system cost-efficient in terms of utility expansion and transmission congestion costs. Further, with the large-scale shift for transportation needs towards electric vehicles, EVs can also serve as a storage system and can further have their applications in load balancing, peak shaving, etc. for systems in need considering they have ample energy to spare after meeting their own transportation demands.

The system provides communication devices acting as a medium of interaction between EVs and other system components. Depending on the SOC of the EVs as per their BMS they can charge or discharge their batteries at any node of the considered system. Each EV operator authorizes energy flow between the EV and the system component through a user interface app thus facilitating energy transfer to meet energy demands at distributed components. The above process allows vehicular transportation of electrical energy in a manner that aids the grid components such as storage devices and peak load generators to maximize the system efficiency and also furnish cost effectiveness. An important aspect to consider in the system is provision for interaction between vehicles and other system constituents so as to facilitate smooth communication regarding energy flow. This can be achieved by different communication and networking systems having standards with provision for IoT.

3.7.1 Sample System

The loads are divided into residential and commercial loads. Generally, residential loads have a maximum demand during evening or night time and commercial loads have maximum demand during the day time. Apart from that, separate provisions have been made for residential loads that are not integrated in the smart grid or do not have the ability of becoming a power prosumer. Such residential loads are collectively represented as conventional residential microgrid (CRM). On the other hand, residential loads that are involved with bidirectional energy exchange and EV operation are represented as residential smart grid (RSG). Also, it is assumed that all commercial loads are following the bidirectional power flow approach and are represented collectively as commercial smart grid (CSG). In other words, the city is divided into three microgrids, namely, CRM, RSG and CSG. These grids are assumed to be lumped components in this approach but in a real-life scenario, they may be distributed in nature. CRM is referred to as an aggregated interconnection of residential loads without a smart meter, BEMS, or an EV. On the other hand, houses/offices in residential and commercial microgrids that are incorporated with a proper IOE infrastructure are termed RSG and CSG, respectively. The sample system is shown in Figure 3.14.

With the installation of PV rooftop, the RSG is incorporated with distributed generation capability and it can be assumed that the RSG will draw minimal power from the main grid. Li-ion batteries of the EVs connected to the grid with V2G act as a distributed storage.

Let P_{Hi} be the power consumed by a house in the RSG (excluding the power consumed in charging the EV) and G_{Hi} be the power generated from distributed power generation sources locally at the household. P_{Vi} is the power consumed in charging the EV and S_{Vi} is the power stored in the EV, which can be transferred to the grid for peak shaving.

From a web application, input data is collected for the driving profile of EV owners for the upcoming day and an estimation of idle energy available in the batteries of EVs is computed. This excess energy stored by the batteries after charging through the charging stations also acts as an energy currency. For bilateral power transaction, the houses in RSG and the EVs are integrated with each other using a distributed information processing and power control node (DIPPC). DIPPC is a localized common node that provides a suitable point for data collection using the principles of IoE as discussed in Section 3.5.

A simple system with two houses and an EV connected with a DIPPC is shown in Figures 3.15 and 3.16.

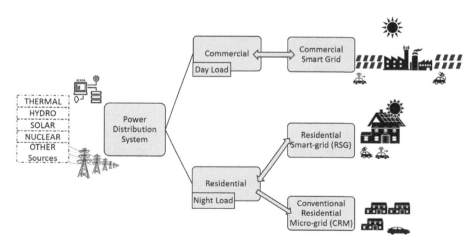

FIGURE 3.14 A sample system.

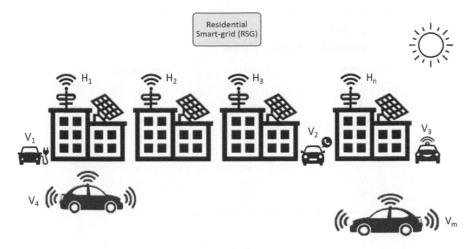

FIGURE 3.15 Distributed information processing and power control node architecture.

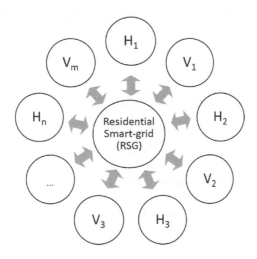

FIGURE 3.16 Residential smart grid mesh.

Consider a system with n houses H_1, H_2, ..., H_n and having m EVs V_1, V_2, ..., V_m connected to a DIPPC with a ring system for bidirectional power flow. It is hypothesized that EVs who are travelling within the city must maintain a minimum SoC of 20% to 50% while for EVs going for an intercity transit, the minimum recommended SoC is between 40% and 80% (Table 3.7).

The power consumed by house (P_H) and vehicles (P_V) is given by

$$P_H = \sum_{i=1}^{n} P_{Hi}$$

TABLE 3.7
House and Vehicle Count

Entity	Count	Gen/Storage
H_1	x_1	g_1
H_2	x_2	g_2
H_3	x_3	g_3
H_n	x_n	g_n
V_1	x_{n+1}	s_1
V_2	x_{n+2}	s_2
V_3	x_{n+3}	s_3
V_m	x_{n+m}	g_m

$$P_V = \sum_{i=1}^{m} P_{Vi}$$

Power generated in houses of distributed residential smart grid (G_H) is given by

$$G_H = \sum_{i=1}^{n} G_{Hi}$$

The power stored in electric vehicles (S_V) is given as

$$S_V \sum_{i=1}^{m} S_{Vi}$$

Hence, the total power demand from the grid per hour can be written as

$$P = P_{Hi} + P_{Vi} - G_{Hi} - S_{Vi}$$

P_{Hi}: power consumed by a house in the RSG

G_{Hi}: power generated from distributed power generation sources locally at the household.

P_{Vi}: power consumed in charging the EV

S_{Vi}: power stored in the EV, which can be transferred to the grid for peak shaving

Test Scenario

Assume a scenario where a domestic household connected to RSG has a daily load requirement of about 21 units and follows the load curve as shown in Figure 3.17 [1,2,3]. If the household has a rooftop solar of 3 kW installed, its generation in a typical summer day is shown in Figure 3.18. It is observed to produce power of about 11 units/day.

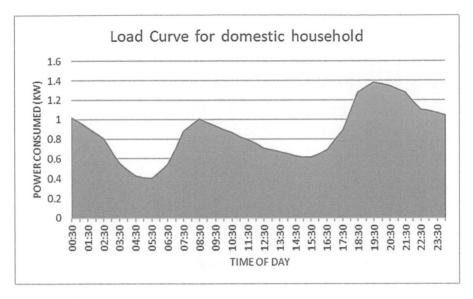

FIGURE 3.17 Load curve for domestic household.

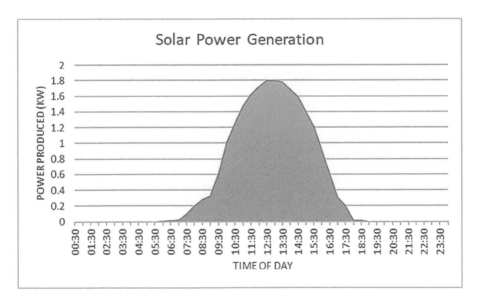

FIGURE 3.18 Solar power generation for a given day.

On any given day, the household is said to own a PHEV with 32 kWhr battery and 40% SoC. The charger for this car is rated 230 V/15 A. To charge the vehicle fully (requiring 19.2 kWhr of energy), it is said to be plugged into charge late into the night to avoid peak time tariff. The battery charging then follows a curve shown in Figure 3.19. Now, the total power demand from grid per hour (P) can be shown as Figure 3.20.

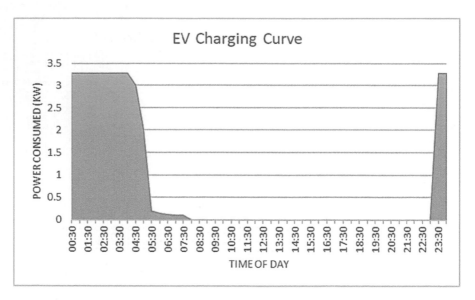

FIGURE 3.19   EV Plugged into the grid for charging for a given day.

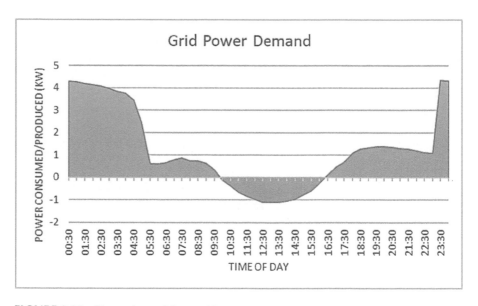

FIGURE 3.20   Power demand from grid.

The negative hump in Figure 3.20 shows solar power being delivered to the grid. The household can also store this energy for later use, for peak shaving or PHEV charging as they see fit. If the household does have a localized energy storage facility available and faces a peak power surcharge from 0730 hrs to 1030 hrs and 1700 hrs to 2200 hrs. In this scenario, the energy stored can be utilized to curb the surcharge. Figure 3.21 shows the load that can be optimized for better energy utilization. The energy requirement from the grid during Peak I is about 3.5 units and during Peak II is about 7 units and about 4 units in between the peaks, i.e. about 15 units of load needs to be supplied by the storage units. If the PHEV docks into the household at 1900 hrs with 40% SoC, it can supply a about 12 units of power and the solar energy about 11 units of power. The graph shown in Figure 3.22, now shows the power consumed from grid if the energy from EV and rooftop solar are efficiently utilized.

Similarly, for CSG that do not allow a bidirectional power flow, a centralized electrical energy storage device like a flow battery is used. A flow battery is the preferred storage due to its almost unlimited longevity and have separate electrolyte

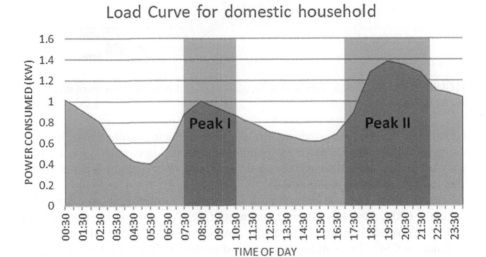

FIGURE 3.21 Domestic load curve with peak period indications.

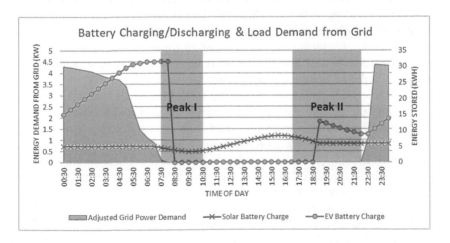

FIGURE 3.22 Power demand from grid.

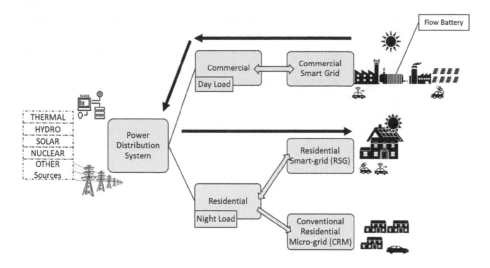

FIGURE 3.23   A sample system with bidirectional power flow with provision of flow batteries for storage.

tanks. Flow batteries are promising but are currently facing challenges of having a comparatively lower peak power and require sophisticated electronics. Flow batteries are used to meet RSG demands during time periods when sunlight is not available. The layout is as shown in Figure 3.23.

This distributed storage helps in peak shaving and co-ordinate power demand of the entire CRM. Also, it is assumed that most of the EVs will undergo transgression from RSG to CSG during daytime and can be connected to the BEMS to meet demands of CSG. This surplus energy stored in the EV, however, may or may not meet the net energy demand of CSG, but it can surely be helpful in functions like peak shaving, load following, voltage support, power quality improvement, etc. V2B is analogous to V2G as it permits communication between vehicles and local distributed generations along with the utility grid. This in turn adds a provision for complete utilization and exploitation of generated energy along with its storage to meet demand in terms of vehicle charging demands or for residential load demands. For CSG, a single commercial load (e.g., a shopping mall) is having a number of EVs that act as distributed storage for the commercial load.

The user interface app is also responsible for collecting all the relevant information regarding the SoC of the batteries through the user and forwarding it to the BEMS for further energy operations. Apart from that, it collects permission data from users so as to get authorization for energy transactions between the vehicle and the residential BEMS. Questions include, "For what approximate duration the owner plans on parking the vehicle," "Whether the owner allows to utilize the battery energy for BEMS," "Whether the owner wants his vehicle to get charged considering there is surplus of energy and if yes then how much in terms of the minimum and maximum SOC values," and the BMS of the vehicle is responsible for providing information about the state of the battery to the owners. So, the approach aims towards a profitable proposition by the efficient utilization of energy through the system combination comprising the EVs, BEMS, charging stations, distributed generation, and the grid.

3.7.2 CASE STUDY

In Denmark, Nissan in collaboration with Enel and Nuvve is experimenting with bidirectional power flow by developing the first commercial V2G Hub. The EV fleet, which comprises ten Nissan e-NV200s, is operated by the utility Frederiksberg Forsyning at its headquarters for maintenance of domestic gas, water, and sewage systems in Greater Copenhagen. Nuvve is the network provider that regulates the flow of power to and from vehicles. Initially developed by the University of Delaware and now funded and sold by Nuvve, the platform ensures that the mileage specifications of the driver are always met and optimizes the power available to the grid. Ten Enel V2G energy transfer units of 10 kW each are used to charge the EVs, which have a battery capacity of 24 kWh. The CHAdeMO DC standard is used for bidirectional energy transfer and is designed to charge/discharge cars up to 100 kW for grid stabilization.

In 2018, V2G integration was accepted for the latest Nissan Leaf model. This is the first EV to have received such approval. Based on our assumption that bi-directional charging equipment will become widely available to interested EV owners in the United States in the near future, we conclude that individual EVs will be a good option between 2020 and 2025 for V2G peak power integration. In addition, with battery capacity growing with each EV announced, individual EVs should have ample SoC during the peak hours of 4 to 9 p.m. to support peak demand integration.

Parker's research in Europe is a further continuation of this work. Four EV models are the key components in Parker, used for the experimental validation: Nissan Leaf, Nissan Evalia, Mitsubishi Outlander PHEV, and Peugeot iON, supported by partners Nissan, Mitsubishi Motors, and PSA for the Parker project. The EVSEs used are supplied by project partner Enel X and are DC CHAdeMO bidirectional chargers with 10 kW. The Enel EVSE is linked to all OEM vehicles and each comprises a "EV / EVSE pair" used for checking. Since the EVSE is focused on DC charging, the power electronics and inverters required to enable V2 G will be included. In particular, for DC charging, the EV cannot be used in isolation, but relies on the EVSE's functionality and efficiency to connect it to the power system. Via an aggregator developed by project partner NUVVE, the bidirectional power flow between EV and EVSE is regulated. The results for active power performance test are shown in Figure 3.24, which highlights that the delivered power followed closely with the request setpoint.

For the vehicles tested (Nissan Leaf, Nissan Evalia, Peugeot iON, Mitsubishi Outlander PHEV), the experimental validation demonstrated good performance and can act as a benchmark for forthcoming car models and specifications. Using an aggregator, the response time was estimated at 5–6 seconds (including contact delays) down to a few seconds when directly operating the charger and vehicle [54].

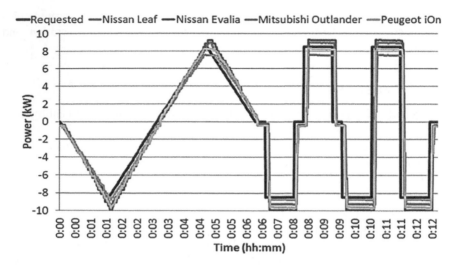

FIGURE 3.24   Graph showing grid requested power and power delivered by each respective car in V2G configuration.

3.8   FUTURE DIRECTIONS

Even though extensive research is going on in the field of IOE and incorporation of V2G into energy management regime, the authors of this chapter strongly believe that IOE has its fair share of challenges. Monitoring and control of electrical loads at residential level is a costly affair and it also involves the development of an extensive V2G infrastructure. Thus, the authors of this chapter recommend the following steps to be taken to improve the concept of IOE for PHEVs:

(a)   Evolution of cheap battery technology with negligible degradation due to successive charging/discharging cycles
(b)   Development of cheap, simple and secure IOE infrastructure
(c)   Aggregation of power management systems on a bulk level
(d)   Optimum utilization of PHEV batteries for supporting the grid without compromising with the life of the battery.

3.9   CONCLUSIONS

The chapter summarizes the application of the IoE for plug-in hybrid EVs. Plug-in hybrid vehicles can be considered both as a challenge and as an opportunity for future grids and proper energy management is the way forward for optimum utilization of the resources available. The chapter starts with a discussion on the fundamentals of power system where the various aspects of power generation, integration of renewable and, demand side management in brief. Subsequently, an exhaustive overview of the evolution, types, configurations, charging schemes, charging options, smart charging software and, plug-in hybrid EVs has been provided. Particular attention has been given to the role of vehicle-to-grid technology and the role of IoE in this field. Afterward, the role of the IoE in plug-in hybrid EVs has been discussed along with a discussion on the process of information flow, data logging, and monitoring systems. Lastly, an approach has been discussed for implementation of the IoE in a hypothetical city of the future having a sizable number of electric vehicles. From the work done in this chapter, it can be concluded that, with an increase in the number of plug-in hybrid electric vehicles, the energy demands and the load forecast for the grid will become quite complex and this problem can be solved to a great extent by optimum usage of technologies like the IoE.

REFERENCES

[1] X. Luo, J. Wang, M. Dooner, and J. Clarke, "Overview of current development in electrical energy storage technologies and the application potential in power system operation." *Applied Energy*, 137, pp. 511–536, 2015, doi: 10.1016/j.apenergy.2014.09.081.

[2] N. A. Kelly, T. L. Gibson, and D. B. Ouwerkerk, "Generation of high-pressure hydrogen for fuel cell electric vehicles using photovoltaic-powered water electrolysis." *International Journal of Hydrogen Energy*, 36, no. 24, pp. 15803–15825, 2011, doi: 10.1016/j.ijhydene.2011.08.058.

[3] M. Ifland, N. Exner, and D. Westermann, "Appliance of direct and indirect demand side management." *IEEE 2011 EnergyTech, ENERGYTECH 2011*, pp. 1–6, 2011, doi: 10.1109/EnergyTech.2011.5948534.

[4] R. T. De Salis, A. Clarke, Z. Wang, J. Moyne, and D. M. Tilbury, "Energy storage control for peak shaving in a single building." *IEEE Power & Energy Society General Meeting*, pp. 1–5, 2014, 10.1109/PESGM.2014.6938948.

[5] M. S. Islam and N. Mithulananthan, "Daily EV load profile of an EV charging station at business premises," in *IEEE PES Innovative Smart Grid Technologies Conference Europe*, 2016, pp. 787–792, doi: 10.1109/ISGT-Asia.2016.7796485.

[6] A. Zahedi, "Electric vehicle as distributed energy storage resource for future smart grid," in *2012 22nd Australasian Universities Power Engineering Conference: "Green Smart Grid Systems"*, *AUPEC 2012*, 2012, pp. 1–3.

[7] Z. Shahan, "Electric car history (in depth)," *Sustainnovate*, 2015. https://cleantechnica.com/2015/04/26/electric-car-history/ (accessed Jul. 09, 2020).

[8] D. Crolla, *Encyclopedia of automotive engineering*. Chichester: Wiley, 2015.

[9] R. Matulka, "*The history of the electric car | department of energy*." U.S. Department of Energy, 2014. www.energy.gov/articles/history-electric-car (accessed Jul. 09, 2020).

[10] M. Guarnieri, "Looking back to electric cars," in *3rd Region-8 IEEE HISTory of Electro - Technology CONference: The Origins of Electrotechnologies, HISTELCON 2012 - Conference Proceedings*, 2012, 10.1109/HISTELCON.2012.6487583.

[11] Ching Chuen Chan, "The rise & fall of electric vehicles in 1828–1930: Lessons learned," in *Proceedings of the IEEE*, 101, no. 1, pp. 206–212, 2013.

[12] Ernest H. Wakefield, *History of the electric automobile: Hybrid electric vehicles*. PA, Warrendale: Society of Automotive Engineers, 1998.

[13] G. Electric and C. Race, "Cambridge or bust." *Engineering and Science*, pp. 9–17, Oct. 1968.

[14] C. W. Beardsley, "Clean air car race-the worcester gremlin kva-sst." *IEEE Transactions on Vehicular Technology*, 20, no. 2, pp. 18–23, 1971, doi: 10.1109/T-VT.1971.23473.

[15] A. Faiz, C. S. Weaver, and M. P. Walsh, *Air pollution from motor vehicles*. The World Bank, 1996.

[16] J. J. Schauer, M. J. Kleeman, G. R. Cass, and B. R. T. Simoneit, "Measurement of emissions from air pollution sources. 5. C1 - C32 organic compounds from gasoline-powered motor vehicles." *Environmental Science & Technology*, 36, no. 6, pp. 1169–1180, 2002, doi: 10.1021/es0108077.

[17] C. Brunel, "Pollution offshoring and emission reductions in EU and US manufacturing." *Environmental and Resource Economics*, 68, no. 3, pp. 621–641, 2017, doi: 10.1007/s10640-016-0035-1.

[18] U. S. D. of Energy, *"Electric vehicle basics | Department of Energy."* Office of Energy Efficiency & Renewable Energy. www.energy.gov/eere/electricvehicles/electric-vehicle-basics (accessed Jul. 13, 2020).

[19] K. V. Singh, H. O. Bansal, and D. Singh, "A comprehensive review on hybrid electric vehicles: architectures and components." *Journal of Modern Transportation*, 27, no. 2, pp. 77–107, 2019, doi: 10.1007/s40534-019-0184-3.

[20] C. Shen, P. Shan, and T. Gao, "A comprehensive overview of hybrid electric vehicles." *International Journal of Vehicular Technology*, 2011, 2011, doi: 10.1155/2011/571683.

[21] B. Wahono, W. B. Santoso, A. Nur, and Amin, "Analysis of range extender electric vehicle performance using vehicle simulator." *Energy Procedia*, Apr., 68, pp. 409–418, 2015 doi: 10.1016/j.egypro.2015.03.272.

[22] L. Guzzella, A. Sciarretta, L. Guzzella, and A. Sciarretta, "Electric and hybrid-electric propulsion systems." *Vehicle Propulsion Systems*, pp. 67–162, 2013, doi: 10.1007/978-3-642-35913-2_4.

[23] G. Rizzoni, "Powertrain control for hybrid-electric and electric vehicles." *Encyclopedia of Systems and Control*, pp. 1–10, 2014 doi: 10.1007/978-1-4471-5102-9.

[24] Article available at : www.researchgate.net/publication/323497072_Overview_of_Electric_and_Hybrid_Vehicles

[25] Article available at : www.academia.edu/Documents/in/Plug_in_Hybrid_Electric_Vehicle_PHEV_

[26] Article available at : www.academia.edu/39517400/PlugIn_Hybrid_Electric_Vehicles_Potential_for_Urban_Transport_in_China_The_Role_of_Energy_Sources_and_Utility_Factors

[27] Article available at : https://docs.cpuc.ca.gov/PublishedDocs/Published/G000/M080/K775/80775679.pdf

[28] M. Yilmaz and P. T. Krein, *"Review of benefits and challenges of vehicle-to-grid technology."* *2012 IEEE Energy Conversion Congress and Exposition (ECCE)*, Raleigh, NC, 2012, pp. 3082–3089.

[29] K. Mahmud, G. E. Town, S. Morsalin, and M. J. Hossain, "Integration of electric vehicles and management in the internet of energy." *Renewable and Sustainable Energy Reviews*, 82, 2017, pp. 4179–4203, 2018.

[30] A. Briones and J. Francfort, *"Power flow regulations and building codes review by the AVTA."* Idaho National Laboratory, Idaho, US, 2012.

[31] G. Saldaña, J. I. S. Martin, I. Zamora, F. J. Asensio, and O. Oñederra, "Electric vehicle into the grid: Charging methodologies aimed at providing ancillary services considering battery degradation." *Energies*, 12, no. 12, 2019.

[32] C. C. Chan and K. T. Chau, "An overview of power electronics in electric vehicles." *IEEE Transactions on Industrial Electronics*, 44, no. 1, pp. 3–13, 1997.

[33] Habib S, Kamran M, Rashid U. Impact analysis of vehicle-to-grid technology andcharging strategies of electric vehicles on distribution networks – a review." *Journal of Power Sources*, 277:205–214, 2015.

[34] F. Mwasilu, J. J. Justo, E. K. Kim, T. D. Do, and J. W. Jung, "Electric vehicles and smart grid interaction: A review on vehicle to grid and renewable energy sources integration." *Renewable and Sustainable Energy Reviews*, 34, pp. 501–516, 2014.

[35] N. H. Motlagh, M. Mohammadrezaei, J. Hunt, and B. Zakeri, "Internet of Things (IoT) and the energy sector." *Energies*, 13, no. 2, pp. 1–27, 2020.

[36] Y. R. Kafle, K. Mahmud, S. Morsalin, and G. E. Town, *"Towards an Internet of Energy." 2016 IEEE International Conference on Power System Technology POWERCON 2016*, 2016.

[37] Stojmenovic, I. Machine-to-machine communications with in-network data aggregation, processing, and actuation for large-scale cyber-physical systems." *IEEE Internet of Things Journal*, 1, 122–128, 2014.

[38] Abdalla I, Venkatesan S. Scalable addressing of M2M terminals in 4G cellular wireless networks. In: *Proceedings of the Wireless Telecommunications Symposium (WTS)*. IEEE, pp. 1–6, 2013.

[39] R. Pratt, F. Tuffner, and K. Gowri, *Electric vehicle communication standards testing and validation – Phase I: SAE J2847/1*. Richland, WA: Pacific Northwest National Laboratory, 2011 [Online].

[40] E. Nefedov, S. Sierla, and V. Vyatkin, "Internet of Energy approach for sustainable use of electric vehicles as energy storage of prosumer buildings." *Energies*, 11, no. 8, 2018.

[41] Y. Kabalci, E. Kabalci, S. Padmanaban, J. B. Holm-Nielsen, and F. Blaabjerg, "Internet of Things applications as energy internet in smart grids and smart environments." *Electronics*, 8, no. 9, pp. 1–16, 2019.

[42] V. C. Güngör et al., "Smart grid technologies: Communication technologies and standards." *IEEE Transactions on Industrial Informatics*, 2011.

[43] Javier Ibáñez Vial, J. W. D., Monitoring battery system for electric vehiclebased on one wire technology. In: *IEEE Vehicular Power & Propulsion*. 2004. Santiago: Vehicle Power and Propulsion Committee.

[44] Electronics Engineering Herald, 2006. Controller area network (CAN) interface in embedded systems.

[45] Mahmud K, and G. E. Town, A review of computer tools for analyzing the impact of electric vehicles on power distribution. In: *Proceedings of the Power Engineering Conference (AUPEC)*, 2015 Australasian Universities, pp. 1–6, 2015.

[46] Lee, J. S., Y. W. Su, and C. C. Shen. A comparative study of wireless protocols: Bluetooth, UWB, ZigBee, and Wi-Fi. In: *Proceedings of the Industrial Electronics Society, IECON 2007 33rd Annual Conference of the IEEE*, pp. 46–51, 2007.

[47] Zhang, X., Q. Wang, G. Xu, and Z. Wu, *A review of plug-in electric vehicles as distributed energy storages insmart grid*. In *Proceedings of the 5th IEEE PES Innovative Smart Grid Technologies (ISGT) European 2014 Conference*, Istanbul, Turkey, 12–15 October 2014.

[48] Mekki, K., E. Bajic, F. Chaxel, and F. Meyer, *Overview of cellular LPWAN technologies for IoT deployment: Sigfox, LoRaWAN, and NB-IoT*. In *Proceedings of the 2018 IEEE International Conference on PervasiveComputing and Communications Workshops (PerCom Workshops)*, Athens, Greece, 19–23 March 2018; pp. 197–202.

[49] M. Jaradat, M. Jarrah, A. Bousselham, Y. Jararweh, and M. Al-Ayyoub, "The Internet of Energy: Smart sensor networks and big data management for smart grid," *Procedia Computer Science*, 56, no. 1, pp. 592–597, 2015.

[50] Garcia, P., P. Arboleya, B. Mohamed, A. A. C. Vega, "Implementation of a hybrid distributed/centralized real-time monitoring system for a DC/AC microgrid with energy storage capabilities," *IEEE Transactions on Industrial Informatics*, 12, 1900–1909, 2016.

[51] R. Yaqub, "Architecture and protocols for toll-free electric vehicle charging," *World Electric Vehicle Journal*, 10, no. 1, 2019.

[52] A. Langton and N. Crisostomo, "Vehicle – Grid integration: A vision for zero-emission transportation interconnected throughout California's electricity system," *California Public Utilities Commission*, 2014.

[53] Halim, F., S. Yussof, and M. E. Rusli, "Cyber security issues in smart meter and their solutions," *International Journal of Computer Science and Network Security*, 18, 99–109, 2018.

[54] Bach Andersen Peter, Seyedmostafa Hashemi, Tiago Sousa, Meier Soerensen Thomas, Lance Noel, and Bjoern Christensen, "The Parker project: Cross-brand service testing using V2G," *World Electric Vehicle Journal*, 10, 2019, www.mdpi.com/2032-6653/10/4/66}

[55] Zhilong Lin, Tongke Zhong, Zhaoxia Jing, and Shan Huang, "*Impact of electric vehicles charging on load curve,*" *9th IET International Conference on Advances in Power System Control, Operation and Management (APSCOM 2012)*, Hong Kong, pp. 1–7, 2012 doi: 10.1049/cp.2012.2123.

[56] A. Anvari-Moghaddam, H. Monsef, A. Rahimi-Kian, J. M. Guerrero and J. C. Vasquez, "*Optimized energy management of a single-house residential micro-grid with automated demand response.*" *2015 IEEE Eindhoven PowerTech*, Eindhoven, pp. 1–6, 2015 doi: 10.1109/PTC.2015.7232243.

[57] M. S. Islam and N. Mithulananthan, "*Daily EV load profile of an EV charging station at business premises,*" *2016 IEEE Innovative Smart Grid Technologies - Asia (ISGT-Asia)*, Melbourne, VIC, pp. 787–792, 2016 doi: 10.1109/ISGT-Asia.2016.7796485.

[58] Shao, Shengnan, Manisa Pipattanasomporn, and Saifur Rahman, Grid integration of electric vehicles and demand response with customer choice. *IEEE Transactions on Smart Grid*, 3, pp. 543–550. 2012 10.1109/TSG.2011.2164949.

[59] Guan, Jen-Chiun, Bo-Chiuan Chen, and Yuh-Yih Wu, "Design of an adaptive power management strategy for range extended electric vehicles," *Energies* 12, 1610, 2019. 10.3390/en12091610.

RELATED READING

[60] Zecchino, A., A. Thingvad, P. B. Andersen, and M. Marinelli, "Test and modelling of commercial V2G CHAdeMO chargers to assess the suitability for grid services." *World Electric Vehicle Journal*, 10, 21, 2019.

[61] Andersen, P. B., S. Hashemi, T. Sousa, T.M. Soerensen, L. Noel, and B. Christensen, *Cross-brand validation of grid services using V2G-enabled vehicles in the Parker project*. In Proceedings of the 31st International Electric Vehicles Symposium & Exhibition & International ElectricVehicle Technology Conference, Kobe, Japan, 3 September–3 October 2018.

[62] Marinelli, M., S. Martinenas, K. Knezovic, and P. B. Andersen, Validating a centralized approach to primary frequency control with series-produced electric vehicles." *Journal of Energy Storage*, 7, 63–73, 2016.

[63] Knezović, K., M. Marinelli, A. Zecchino, P.B. Andersen, and C. Træholt, "Supporting involvement of electric vehicles in distribution grids: Lowering the barriers for a proactive integration." *Energy* 134, pp. 458–468, 2017.

[64] Knezovic, K., S. Martinenas, P.B. Andersen, A. Zecchino and M. Marinelli, Enhancing the role of electric vehicles in the power grid: Field validation of multiple ancillary services." *IEEE Transactions on Transportation Electrification*, 3, 201–209, 2017.

[65] Thingvad, A., C. Ziras, and M. Marinelli, "Economic value of electric vehicle reserve provision in the Nordic countries under driving requirements and charger losses." *Journal of Energy Storage*, 21, pp. 826–834, 2019.

[66] Thingvad, A., L. Calearo, P. B. Andersen, M. Marinelli, M. Neaimeh, K. Suzuki, and K. Murai, *Value of V2G frequency regulation in Great Britain considering real driving data*. In Proceedings of the 2019 IEEE PES International Conference and Exhibition Innovative Smart Grid Technologies (ISGT Europe), Washington, DC, USA, 17–20 February 2019.

[67] Tan, K. M., V. K. Ramachandaramurthy, and J. Y. Yong, Integration of electric vehicles in smart grid: A review on vehicle to grid technologies and optimization techniques." *Renewable and Sustainable Energy Reviews*, 53, 720–732, 2019.

[68] Hashemi, S., N. B. Arias, P. B. Andersen, B. Christensen, and C. Træholt, *Frequency regulation provision using cross-brand bidirectional V2G-enabled electric vehicles*. In Proceedings of the 2018 the 6th IEEE International Conference on Smart Energy Grid Engineering (SEGE 2018), Oshawa, ON, Canada, 12–15 August 2018.

[69] Zecchino, A., A. Thingvad, P. B. Andersen, and M. Marinelli, *Suitability of commercial V2G CHAdeMO chargers for grid services*. In Proceedings of the 31st International Electric Vehicles Symposium & Exhibition & International Electric Vehicle Technology Conference, Kobe, Japan, 30 September–3 October 2018.

KEYWORDS AND DESCRIPTIONS

Internet of energy   It is the process of automation of electrical assets which allows bi-directional flow of information for optimum operation of the power system network.

Software-defined network   It is a networking technology which allows dynamic, programmable and efficient information flow which allows optimal monitoring and control of connected systems.

Demand side management   It is the process of management of energy demand of consumers such that the generating capacity is matched by the load demand in the most economic manner.

Electric vehicle   It is a vehicle that uses one or more electric motor for propulsion and is powered by sources like a battery, ultra-capacitor, ultra-flywheel, etc.

Hybrid electric vehicle   It is a vehicle that generally uses conventional IC engine driven propulsion system along with an electric motor-based propulsion system.

Vehicle-to-grid technology   It allows bidirectional flow of power from vehicle-to-grid and grid-to-vehicle by using embedded communications technology in an electric vehicle and a smart-grid.

Frequency regulation   It is the process of power interchange flow to match the scheduled interchange flow so as to keep balance in generation and demand avoiding frequency variation within regulation standards.

Load following   It is the process to dampen the variance in load profile, storage tracking load profiles may change their output to keep balance between generation and load.

Distribution upgrade deferral   It is the process to extend the useful life of existing infrastructure and avoid expansion and investment costs in infrastructure management to meet adequate capacity to serve loads.

Voltage support   It is the process to meet voltage excursions by large power loads or distributed generations, storage discharges real power to meet these voltage excursions and provide voltage support.

Power reliability   It is the process of supporting electricity services during outages either planned or unplanned, storages provide provision of energy backup during such conditions resulting in improved reliability.

Retail energy time-shift   It is the process to minimize energy cost by charging discharging time slot allocation i.e. charging during low cost times and discharging during high-cost times.

Demand charge mitigation   It is the process of developing a profitable proposition on the basis of demand cost for charging and demand cost at the time of discharging the storage system.

State-of-charge   It is defined as the level of charge which the battery of a PHEV can hold in relation with its rated capacity.

State-of-health   It is defined as a figure of merit in which the current State-of-Health is compared with a threshold value to determine the useful life time and suitability of the battery for a particular application.

V1G   It is the unidirectional flow of power from the power grid to a storage device like a battery.

V2B   It is the process of flow of energy stored in an EV to meet an on-site load demand like a building or home.

V2X   It is the process of flow of energy stored in an EV to meet an on-site load demand without affecting the grid.

G2V   It is the process of charging the batteries of the vehicle when plugged into power socket connected to grid.

4 Assessment of Plug-in Hybrid Electric Vehicle (HEVs) Through Big Data Analysis

Vikas Khare

School of Technology, Management and Engineering, NMIMS, Indore, India

Cheshta J. Khare

Electrical Engineering, Shri G.S. Institute of Technology & Science, Indore, Madhya Pradesh, India

Savita Nema

Electrical Engineering, Maulana Azad National Institute of Technology, Bhopal, Madhya Pradesh, India

Prashant Baredar

Department of Energy, Maulana Azad National Institute of Technology Bhopal, Madhya Pradesh, India

CONTENTS

4.1 Background 108
4.2 Literature Review 108
    4.2.1 Optimum Design of EVs 108
    4.2.2 Thermal Management of Battery 108
    4.2.3 Control System of EVs 109
    4.2.4 Reliability Assessment of EVs 109
4.3 Proposed Approach 110
4.4 Pre-feasibility Assessment of HEVs by Big Data Analysis 112
4.5 Hadoop Distributed HEV System 120
4.6 Modeling of Hybrid Electric Vehicle System 124
4.7 Modeling from MapReduce Algorithm and Development of
    Decision Tree 125
4.8 Hierarchical Data Clustering of Hybrid Electric Vehicle 132
4.9 Future Directions 135
4.10 Conclusions 135
References 135
Keywords and Descriptions 137

4.1   BACKGROUND

Existing vehicles exhaust a large volume of gas, which is harmful to the environment, and an increasing ecological awareness and the shortage of fossil-fuel resources are strong incentives to develop more efficient vehicles, with less fuel consumption but with all driving comfort. One of the major challenges in the global society today is to reduce the negative impacts that road transportation has on the environment due to toxic and green-house-gas emissions. As a consequence, these types of emissions from vehicles are legally regulated on national and sometimes regional levels. To comply with more stringent regulations, vehicle manufacturers are forced to invest in various fuel-saving technologies. In the evaluation of the electric vehicle (EV), it is necessary to assess the huge number of data, for proper decision-making regarding the electric vehicle system. In the recent scenario of the Internet of Energy, big data analysis is a very important tool for the assessment of a huge amount of information. In this chapter, Internet of Energy-based big data analysis provides an assessment of hybrid plug-in electric vehicles.

4.2   LITERATURE REVIEW

This is a time of technological advancement and electric vehicles play an important role in the automobile industry. In the recent scenario the electric vehicle is a very hot topic for research and many researchers have done lots of work in the modeling, controlling, policy issue and economic analysis of electric vehicles.

4.2.1   OPTIMUM DESIGN OF EVs

Chu et al. [23] described the framework of ammonia-based plug-in EVs. To eliminate some limitations of normal EVs, a hydrogen plus fuel cell hybrid vehicle is discussed, where ammonia acts as a source of hydrogen, which increases the range of vehicles. The electric motor, battery, capacitor, and fuel cell were the main components of this dynamic model. Zhang et al. [34] proposed an optimum design and parameter assessment of the novel drive system operated by hybrid green vehicles. The technical assessment is done using a genetic algorithm and the result shows fuel consumption was reduced by nearly 16.32% as compared to the conventional EV drive system. A vehicle framework assessment process, static and dynamic condition, and different modes of drive system are also discussed in this paper. Tanozzi et al. [7] assessed thermal parameters of hybrid EVs. A combination of the gas turbine and fuel cell is used as a range extension technique of EVs, which resulted in an increased life span and coefficient of performance of EVs. The design of the heat exchanger network, optimum sizing of the heat exchange, and optimization of thermal parameters are the three key points of discussion in this paper.

4.2.2   THERMAL MANAGEMENT OF BATTERY

Wiriyasart et al. [30] offer a computational analysis technique to signify the temperature distribution, thermal management, and stress drop using nano-fluids flowing in the corrugated mini-channel of the EV battery cooling module. The EV battery modules encompass 444 cylindrical lithium-ion cell batteries (18650 type). It is found that the temperature distributions change with the flow rate of coolant, mass waft rate, and coolant types. The best cooling performance of the proposed module (Model II) is obtained with nano-fluids as the coolant showed a 28.65% reduction in temperature as compared to a conventional cooling module (Model I). Lyu et al. [15] explained thermal management of the EV battery through the thermal cooling system. Laboratory practice is carried out on an EV battery system, which shows a capable cooling effect with a sensible quantity of power consumption. Further, the test results show that the battery surface temperature decreases from around 54°C to 11°C using a water-cooling system for a single cell with a copper holder when 40 V is supplied to the heater. Behi et al. [10] described the thermal management of Li-ion EV through air cooling and a heat pipe. Air cooling and a heat pipe reduce the temperature by approximately 20%. Results show that the most extreme module temperature for the cooling technique utilizing constrained air cooling, heat funnels, and a heat pipe with copper sheet (HPCS) reaches 41.4°C, 38.5°C, and 38.1°C, which can reduce the module temperature contrasted and normal air cooling by up to 35.5%, 43.1%, and 43.7% individually. Besides, there is 38.2%, 67.5%, and 74.4% improvement in the temperature consistency of the battery module for constrained air cooling, heat funnels, and HPCS individually.

4.2.3 Control System of EVs

The control system is the combination of different elements, which work together for the desired output. The function of the control system used in EVs is to maximize the range and reduce the exhaust emission. Wu et al. [31] described the system control of the fuel cell system operated vehicles by thermo electric surge control and this control system reduces the heat loss and develops saturated characteristics of the vehicle system. The result shows that the surge control system solved the thermo-electric surge problem and improved the efficiency of fuel cell-operated EVs. He et al. [11] explained the concept of the neural network braking control system for the operation of EVs. This control system is used to improve the energy economy and braking stability of EVs and also single pedal regenerative braking is controlled by an adaptive fuzzy controller. A further proper control system is also assessed through the multi-objective neural network

4.2.4 Reliability Assessment of EVs

Reliability is one of the main parameters for assessment of any device as it identifies the fault rate of that device. In the case of EVs, maintainability and validity of different mathematical functions play a key role in the performance assessment of EVs [54]. Dubarry et al. [18] described a reliability and maintainability analysis of an EV battery and assessed the fault rate of the bidirectional charging capability of the battery system. Results show that extra cycling to release vehicle batteries to the power grid, even at consistent force, is impedes cell execution. Extra utilization of the battery packs could shorten the lifetime for vehicle use by five years. On the other hand, the effect of postponing the charge so as to diminish the effect on the power grid is seen as irrelevant at room temperature. Kamruzzaman et al. [12] described a reliability assessment of the hosting capacity of EVs. Their paper proposes a reliability-restricted demand response-based approach to optimize the allowable penetration of EVs on electric power network buses. The persistent rise in EV would affect the efficiency of the power systems if no countermeasures are taken. Implementation of demand response programs can be an effective solution to reduce or even avoid burden reduction. Anand et al. [1] described a probabilistic reliability assessment of the distribution system of EVs. In this paper, a reliability assessment of different technical parameters of EV by the Markov chain process and simulation of travel pattern and charging capacity is assessed by the Monte-Carlo simulation process. The proposed methodology is used to conduct reliability studies on the example test method, and a range of research findings is presented.

4.3 PROPOSED APPROACH

Increasing environmental consciousness and a shortage of fossil fuel supplies are strong reasons to create more reliable cars, with no fuel consumption and all kinds of driving comfort. Hybrid electric vehicles are new developments in the automobile industry, offering a pollution-free atmosphere and protecting the world from a lot of greenhouse gas. Modeling of the electric vehicle system, storage, and management, tracking and forecasting is based on a vast volume of data, which cannot be handled and analyzed without the use of the internet. The general concept of vehicle design includes the basic ideology of physics, particularly Newton's second law of motion. According to Newton's second theorem, the acceleration of an object is proportional to the net force applied to it. Therefore, the mass accelerates when the net force acting on it is not zero. The propulsion unit of the vehicle provides the energy required to drive the vehicle forward. This power of the propulsion unit allows the vehicle to overcome the resistance forces due to gravity, air, and resistance between road and vehicle. A hybrid vehicle blends the two types of electricity. Possible combinations include diesel / electric, petrol / flywheel, and fuel cell / battery. Usually, one energy source is storage and the other is conversion from fuel to electricity. The two power sources can be combined to support two different propulsion systems. In order to be a hybrid, the vehicle must have at least two modes of propulsion [7,14]. For example, a transport bus that uses diesel to drive a generator, which in turn drives many all-wheel electric motors, is not a hybrid. But if the bus has electrical energy storage to provide a second form of electrical assistance, then it is a hybrid vehicle. Such two-power sources may be combined in sequence, which means that the gas engine

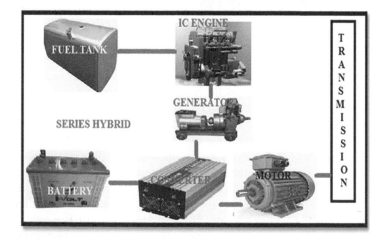

FIGURE 4.1   Series hybrid of electric vehicle system [9].

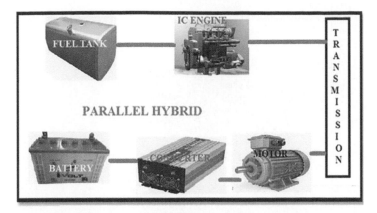

FIGURE 4.2   Parallel hybrid of electric vehicle system [9].

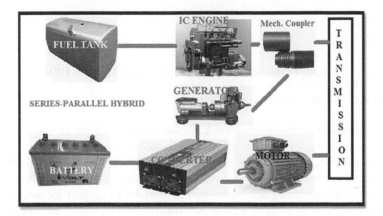

FIGURE 4.3   Series-parallel hybrid of electric vehicle system [9].

charges the batteries of the electric motor that drives the car or, in parallel, either of the two mechanisms can drive the car directly [7,14]. A hybrid electric vehicle incorporates a gasoline engine with an electric motor. Figures 4.1, 4.2, and 4.3 show general block diagrams of hybrid electric vehicles such as series hybrid, parallel hybrid, and series-parallel hybrid electric vehicle systems.

This chapter assesses performance of hybrid electric vehicles with the help of big data analysis, where big data refers to a massive volume of both structured and unstructured data that is too large and difficult to process using conventional database and software techniques. Studying large numbers of cases provides higher statistical strength, whereas cases with higher complexity may lead to higher false discovery rates. Big data issues include data collection, data storage, data processing, search, exchange, upload, visualization, query, update, privacy, and data source. Figure 4.4 shows the big data tool for a hybrid electric vehicle system. A review of datasets will identify new connections to spot industry patterns, disease prevention, and crime prevention and so on. Researchers, corporate leaders, medical professionals, advertisers, and governments alike constantly face difficulties with massive databases in areas such as web search, fintech, urban computing, and industrial computing. Scientists

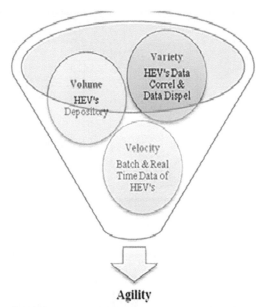

Agility

Effective Utilization of Battery and Electric Motor in HEV's

FIGURE 4.4   Big data tool for hybrid electric vehicles.

experience limitations in e-science work, including meteorology, genomics, and connectomics, and complex physical simulations, biological and environmental research.

The goal of this chapter is to present a web-based technical platform for the management of large quantities, variety, and speed of plug-in electrical vehicle-related information through broad data tools such as Hadoop to support the assessment of plug-in electrical vehicles. The architecture involves device modeling, storage, management, monitoring, and forecasting on the basis of a vast amount of data needed to test the electrical vehicle by means of big data analysis. This chapter also includes the market basket model and the principle of the MapReduce algorithm in the field of electric vehicles. At the end of this chapter, the use of big data in the field of solar-powered hybrid electric vehicles is also discussed [1].

4.4   PRE-FEASIBILITY ASSESSMENT OF HEVs BY BIG DATA ANALYSIS

Pre-feasibility studies are an early study of a possible assessment of different parameters of a project. These are led by a small team and are structured to provide a company's stakeholders with the essential details needed to initiate the project or to choose between possible investments. Usually, these studies provide an overview of the logistics of the different project, capital needs, main problems, and other details. If millions of battery charging and discharging data, power data generated by the propulsion unit, road condition data, and hybrid vehicle aerodynamic data used in hybrid electric vehicles are broken down into batches, interval, and real-time data, then these are the terms of the big data velocity. In view of electric vehicles, big data includes a variety of large volumes of data on battery charging and discharging data, power data provided by the propulsion unit, and road condition data. Hybrid vehicle aerodynamic data include different types of data in the form of 3D data, audio, video, and unstructured text. Storage of data in the hybrid electric vehicle depot is in the form of Kilobytes, Megabytes, Gigabytes, Terabytes, etc. and this is called the data volume of the hybrid electric vehicle network [2,3].

Modus operandi of hybrid electric vehicles: Data reflects the actual time status of the charging and discharging output evaluation of the battery and the loading of hybrid electric vehicle equipment. This is the very basic information on the pre-feasibility evaluation used by the system engineer to test and operate the hybrid electric vehicle power plant.

Non-modus operandi of hybrid electric vehicles: Information file consists of data elements battery charging and discharging, power supplied by propulsion unit, road condition, vehicle aerodynamics, vehicle composite mass, vehicle resistance, tire ground adhesion and maximum traction, and other technological parameters of a hybrid electric vehicle. The NoSQL database environment is capable of ensuring that hybrid electrical vehicle network data continue to function without data loss and acts as a hybrid electric vehicle server.

Figure 4.5 shows the content and capacity of the hybrid electric vehicle depository for prefeasibility analysis. The hybrid electric vehicle depository is divided into four parts for proper pre-feasibility assessment of the hybrid electric vehicle system and these are Enterprise Resource Planning (ERP), Customer Relationship Management (CRM), World Wide Web and big data, and their data range considered from Megabyte to Petabyte. ERP module data are the data that are related to capital, replacement, and

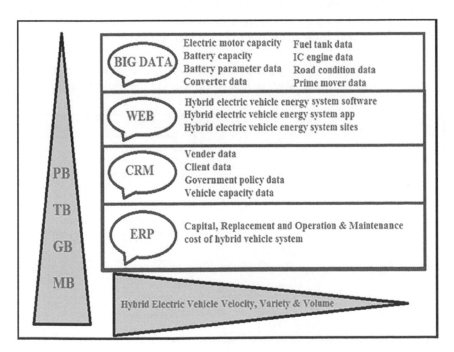

FIGURE 4.5   Layout of hybrid electric vehicle system depository.

operating cost of the battery, gasoline engine, motor, generator, and transmission system. CRM is the collection of non-technical data consisting of vendor information, client data, tender information, different types of hybrid electric vehicle company data, and data related to government policy, government subsidy, government renewable energy framework, which is essential to develop a hybrid electric vehicle system in the study area. The collection of information on all the three modules is contained in one dataset, which is called a big data module of the hybrid electric vehicle depository. It is the brain and heart of hybrid electric vehicle depository because it accumulates all the data that is necessary to develop a hybrid electric vehicle system in an efficient manner. After the creation of a depository, at the level of prefeasibility analysis, it is necessary to develop business understanding, data understanding and data, and preparation of hybrid electric vehicle system [15,18]. Figure 4.6 shows the key points of prefeasibility analysis through big data analysis.

Business understanding: To apply the concept of big data for prefeasibility analysis of a hybrid electric vehicle system, one must understand the electric vehicle project objectives and requirements from a business perspective, and then convert this knowledge into real-time data. The following information needs to be gathered:

- Objective of hybrid electric vehicle project
- Effect of project of the society and environment
- Evaluation of economic, business opportunity of hybrid electric vehicle project
- Evaluation of different technical parameter
- Estimated cost / benefit analysis of hybrid electric vehicle
- Evaluation of environmental and social risks of this project
- Evaluation of funding options for hybrid electric vehicle project
- Start of the permitting phase of electric vehicle project,

A pre-feasibility report is a high-level analysis of the key aspects of the project and the goal is to determine whether it is worth moving the project forwarding and

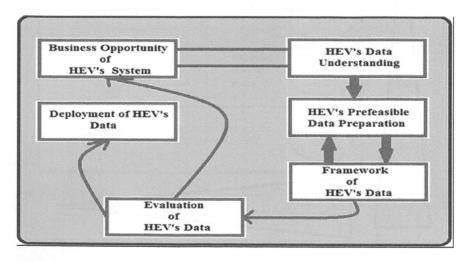

FIGURE 4.6   Prefeasibility analysis through big data analysis.

spending more money and time or not [8,10]. The typical pre-feasibility study may cover the following issues:

- Definition of hybrid electric vehicle, parallel electric vehicle and series electric vehicle, battery, converter, and electric motor
- Project barriers due to technical, political, and financial condition
- Possible technological concepts (several concepts can be described and briefly assessed)
- Estimate of expected energy generation to run the vehicle.

Data understanding: The data comprehension process starts with the initial data collection of the hybrid electric vehicle system and continues with activities to get acquainted with the data, to identify data quality issues, to discover first insights into the data, or to detect interesting subsets to shape hypotheses for hidden information. The following types of evaluation are required in the data-understanding phase:

- Initial evaluation of road condition, rolling resistance, dynamic radius of the tire
- Initial evaluation of charging and discharging capability of the battery
- Initial evaluation of characteristics of different types of electric motor
- Initial evaluation of environmental and social risks and impacts
- Initial evaluation of construction costs (CAPEX) and operating costs (OPEX) of hybrid electric vehicle
- Initial financial and economical assessment
- Initial risk evaluation
- Initial evaluation of necessary permitting and licensing of electric vehicle project
- Planning and project implementation, including tentative time schedule of

Data preparation: The hybrid electric vehicle system data preparation phase comprises the final electric vehicle system dataset from the initial raw data to final assessment. Tasks include table, record, and attribute selection as well as transformation and cleaning of hybrid electric vehicle system data for modeling purposes, which is done by different software. In this phase, if the result of the pre-feasibility study is favorable, a comprehensive feasibility analysis will follow. This feasibility analysis consists of a considerably more detailed evaluation of all facets of the project. The aim of the feasibility study is to discuss the project in sufficient detail so that interested parties and stakeholders can continue with its development. A feasibility study must include an environmental and social impact assessment and a well-comprehensive technical overview, rough layout, key plant details, etc. are required in order to determine the CAPEX / OPEX and to carry out a comprehensive environmental assessment and thus a conceptual design analysis is required [11,12,13].

Prefeasibility analysis is done through regression analysis, a very effective tool of big data analysis, which identifies relationships between different parameter through regression analysis. The coefficient of the road condition for dry roads and wet roads is described by equation [1], which is the very initial level of parameter for the assessment of the hybrid electric vehicle system. Table 4.1 shows the data of the coefficient of road adhesion for dry roads and wet roads.

TABLE 4.1

Data of the Coefficient of Road Adhesion [9]

For Dry Roads	For Wet Roads
0.85	0.67
0.80	0.62
0.75	0.55
0.70	0.45
0.90	0.75
0.65	0.47
0.55	0.35
0.80	0.60

According to the regression analysis, the relationship between two parameters is given by

$$y = AB^x \tag{4.1}$$

In Equation 4.1, where A and B are constants.
Taking log on both sides of the Equation 4.1, we get

$$\log y = \log A + x \log B \tag{4.2}$$

Putting log y = Y, log A = a, log B = b in Equation 4.2, we get

$$Y = a + xb \tag{4.3}$$

From the above equation we get,

$$\sum y = \sum a + \sum bx \tag{4.4}$$

Or

$$\sum y = n \sum a + b \sum x \tag{4.5}$$

$$\sum xy = \sum ax + \sum bx^2 \tag{4.6}$$

$$\sum xy = a \sum x + b \sum x^2 \tag{4.7}$$

Taking x = data of coefficient of road adhesion for dry roads = D and y = data of coefficient of road adhesion for wet roads = W, we get required data for x, y, Y, x^2 and Yx from manual analysis [21]. Table 4.2 shows the logarithmic data of coefficient of road adhesion.

TABLE 4.2

Logarithmic Data of Coefficient of Road Adhesion [21]

Dry Roads [D = x]	Wet Roads [D = y]	$Y = \log_{10}y$	x^2	Yx
0.85	0.67	−0.17393	0.7225	−0.14784
0.80	0.62	−0.20761	0.64	−0.16609
0.75	0.55	−0.25964	0.5625	−0.19473
0.70	0.45	−0.34679	0.49	−0.24275
0.90	0.75	−0.12494	0.81	−0.11244
0.65	0.47	−0.3279	0.4225	−0.21314
0.55	0.35	−0.45593	0.3025	−0.25076
0.80	0.60	−0.22185	0.64	−0.17748
6	4.46	−2.1185	4.59	1.505

Substituting the values from Table 4.2 in Equation, we get

$$-2.1185 = 8a + 6b$$

Substituting the values from Table 4.2 in Equation, we get

$$-1.505 = 6a + 4.59b$$

From equations 4 and 5 we get

$$\text{Then } a = -0.963 \text{ and } b = 0.931$$

$$Y = -0.963 + x(0.931) \tag{4.8}$$

$\log_{10}A = a$
$A = 10^a = 0.1088$
$\log_{10}B = b$
$B = 10^b = 8.53$
We get

$$y = (0.1088)(8.53)^x \tag{4.9}$$

Equations 8 and 9 show the relationship between data of coefficient of road adhesion for wet roads and dry roads. Figures 4.7 and 4.8 show the auto-correlation of the coefficient of road adhesion for wet roads and plot the data of wet roads [9].

For prefeasibility analysis of hybrid electric vehicles mainly two parameters, battery capacity (kwh) and range (km), are assessed through big data analysis by a set

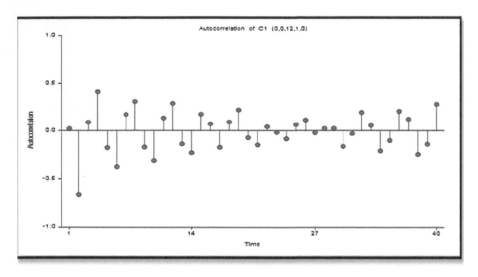

FIGURE 4.7   Auto-correlation of coefficient of road adhesion for wet roads.

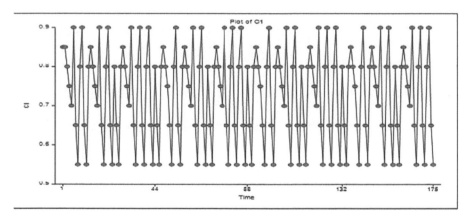

FIGURE 4.8   Data variation of coefficient of road adhesion for wet roads.

of data available from different automobile companies and develop the relationship between parameters (Table 4.3). Figures 4.9–4.13 show cross-correlation of battery capacity (kwh) and range (km), box-cox transformation for simple linear regression for battery capacity and range, Kaplan-Meier survival curve(s) of battery capacity, and density plot of battery capacity and range in km.

Figure 4.13 shows that the discharging and charging time of a battery depends on the distance the vehicle has to cover and is better if the capacity of the battery is more than the required capacity.

TABLE 4.3

Data of Battery Capacity (kWh) and Range (km) [9]

Battery Capacity (kWh)	Range (km)	Battery Capacity (kWh)	Range (km)	Battery Capacity (kWh)	Range (km)	Battery Capacity (kWh)	Range (km)	Battery Capacity (kWh)	Range (km)
42	345	28	136	21	120	30	160	75	496
21	120	60	275	24	135	16	85	20	112
24	135	90	360	20	112	23	110	30	160
20	112	75	496	30	160	17	90	16	85
30	160	20	112	16	85	28	136	23	110
16	85	30	160	23	110	60	275	17	90
23	110	16	85	17	90	17	90	28	136
17	90	21	120	28	136	28	136	60	275
28	136	24	135	60	275	60	275	17	90
60	275	20	112	90	360	90	360	28	136
90	360	30	160	75	496	75	496	60	275
75	496	16	85	20	112	20	112	90	360
20	112	23	110	30	160	30	160	75	496
30	160	17	90	16	85	16	85	20	112
16	85	28	136	23	110	30	160	30	160
23	110	60	275	17	90	16	85	16	85
17	90	90	360	28	136	23	110	21	120
28	136	75	496	60	275	17	90	24	135
60	275	20	112	90	360	28	136	20	112
17	90	30	160	75	496	60	275	30	160

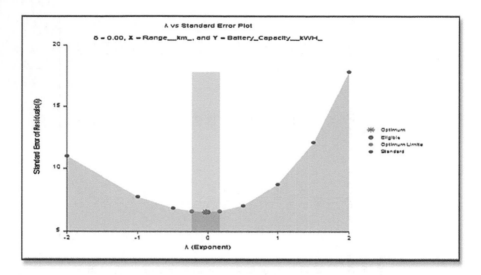

FIGURE 4.9   Box-cox Transformation for simple linear regression for battery capacity and range.

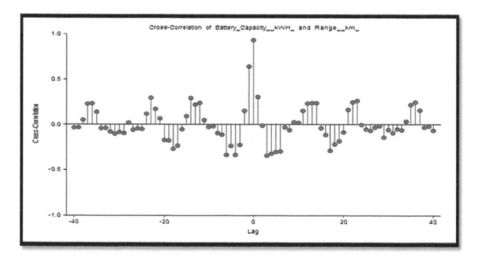

FIGURE 4.10   Cross-correlation of battery capacity and range.

4.5   HADOOP DISTRIBUTED HEVs SYSTEM

The Hadoop ecosystem is a framework of various types of complex evolving tools and components. The MapReduce and Hadoop distributed file system are two core components of the Hadoop ecosystem that provide a great starting point to manage data of the hybrid electric vehicle system. Figure 4.14 depicts the various elements of Hadoop involved at various stages in the hybrid electric vehicle system. Scoop, Zookeeper, and Oozie are used for data exchange, relationships between different

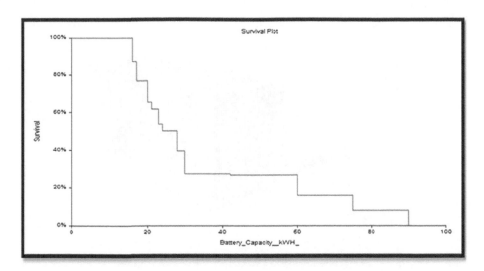

FIGURE 4.11   Kaplan-Meier survival curve(s) of battery capacity.

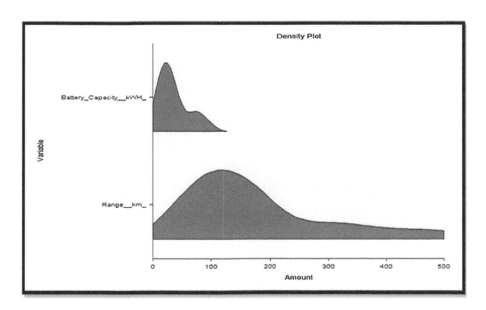

FIGURE 4.12   Density plot of battery capacity and range.

parameter, which can be estimated by regression analysis, and workflow analysis of the hybrid electric vehicle system. Pig and mahout are used for modeling purposes and statistical analysis is done through R-connectors [1,6].

Planning, economics, and resource allocation are the major concerns for any system and they are done through the Hbase and Yarn-based Apache Hadoop ecosystem. In the hybrid electric system, resource allocation is used to find a new type of electric vehicle system and finds a suitable site for the installation of an electric vehicle

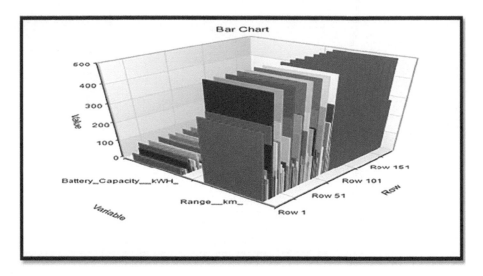

FIGURE 4.13   3D Plot of battery capacity and range in km.

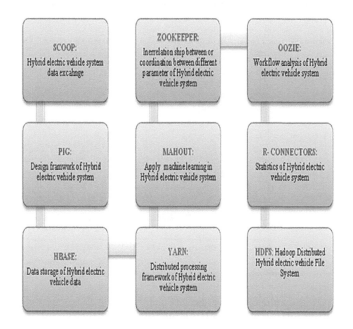

FIGURE 4.14   Apache Hadoop ecosystem [6].

power plant. The hybrid electric vehicle project description, estimation of electric motor speed, result presentation, data analysis of the vehicle, and available and extractable energy from the motor and IC engine are the five main concerns for resource allocation of the hybrid electric vehicle system. The objective and nature of

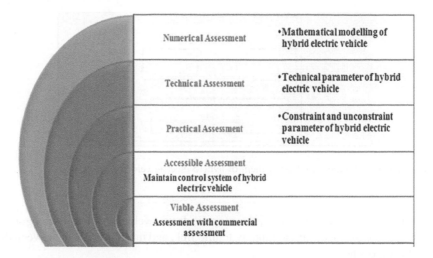

FIGURE 4.15 Hadoop-based resource assessment [6].

the prefeasibility assessment, electric motor conversion characteristics, constraints, and the physical boundary of the assessment are part of the hybrid vehicle prefeasibility assessment [2,3,8,19,20]. Figure 4.15 shows that Hbase and Yarn-based resource allocation is done in the form of numerical, technical, practical, accessible, and viable assessment of the hybrid electric vehicle system.

With the increased use of electric vehicles, it becomes necessary to collect the worldwide hybrid electric vehicle system data and find out the optimum size of an electric vehicle system based on different technical parameters in the environment like Hadoop. In the prefeasibility analysis, a large amount of data on the electric motor and battery is required for analytical processing and resource data is loaded from different sources into the Hadoop system. In hybrid electric vehicle data movement Sqoop and Flume pull the hourly battery charging and discharging data from the source and push it to the Hadoop cluster. Flume is used to collect the resource data of the battery charging and discharging hourly, daily, and yearly, and it collects all the data of the electric vehicle system horizontally and Flume collects large volumes of data. Sqoop is used to move all the data of the hybrid electric vehicle system between Hadoop and the load demand side server of the hybrid electric vehicle system [10,11,12,13]. A description of the Hadoop and Flume based framework on the hybrid electric vehicle system follows:

Flume event: It is used to represent the unit of data, such as battery charging and discharging, motor speed, the mass of the vehicle, road condition and data of aerodynamic drag. The Flume event collects the data in Megabytes, Petabytes and Terabytes, etc. Figure 4.16 shows the Flume-based framework of the ocean energy system.

Flume agent: It contains all the component data that are used in a hybrid electric vehicle system, such as data of the battery, the data of energy conversion through the electric motor system and data gathered from a different measuring unit that is connected in the hybrid electric vehicle system.

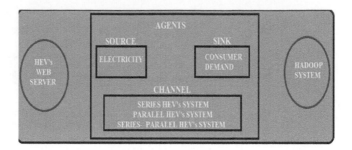

FIGURE 4.16   Flume-based assessment of hybrid electric vehicle system [6].

Flume flow: In the flume flow, the overall electric vehicle system is categorized into three categories: electrical link, hydraulic link, and mechanical link between different components.

Flume client: In the hybrid electric vehicle system flume client means the consumer who purchases an electric vehicle from the distributor.

Channel: Channel is the intermediate function between input and output, and there are three possible types of channel in the hybrid electric vehicle system such as the series hybrid system, parallel hybrid system, and series-parallel hybrid system.

Based on the above discussion, it can be concluded that the Hadoop framework can prove to be an important tool for prefeasibility analysis, modeling, and data storage of the hybrid electric vehicle as it creates an agent and channel in between the source and sink, where the source is related to input parameters and sink is the part of consumer demands.

4.6   MODELING OF HYBRID ELECTRIC VEHICLE SYSTEM

Different modeling techniques are used and technical parameters of EV are calibrated to find the optimal values of performance assessment of a electric vehicle system. At this stage of the vehicle project, one has to develop a model (or models) that appear to be of high quality from a data analysis point of view. By continuing with the final implementation of the model, it is necessary to analyze the model thoroughly and to review the steps taken to create the model, in order to ensure that it achieves the business objectives properly. A draft business case, including cash flow for the project depreciation period, can be planned on the basis of the above information and budgetary estimates for CAPEX and OPEX. International financial institutions usually need a complete feasibility analysis before funding the project [8,10,11]. The conceptual modeling and design typically comprise:

- Analysis of motion and dynamic equation for vehicle
- Evaluation of power delivered by the propulsion unit
- Aerodynamics of the vehicle
- Evaluation of tractive forces, vehicle acceleration and rolling resistance of tires
- Evaluation vehicle power plant and transmission characteristics

- Assessment of torque elasticity and engine speed ratio
- Evaluation of grading resistance, road resistance, resistance to acceleration and total driving resistance
- Development of dynamic equation of vehicle motion
- Evaluation of design parameters of major subsystem such as electric propulsion, energy source and auxiliary system
- Evaluation of design parameter of electric propulsion subsystem comprises electronic controllers, power converter, electric motor, mechanical transmission and driving wheels
- Development of general configuration of electric vehicle.

4.7 MODELING FROM MAPREDUCE ALGORITHM AND DEVELOPMENT OF DECISION TREE

The MapReduce algorithm takes the data of the hybrid electric vehicle system as the input, processes it, generates the output, and returns the required answers. MapReduce is based on the parallel programming framework to process large amounts of data dispersed across different system. When MapReduce is applied in a hybrid electric vehicle, it collects large amounts of data of the past year and processes overall data for the next stage [1,6].

Table 4.4 shows the collected data of 35,040 hybrid electric vehicles for the MapReduce algorithm to develop prototypes of the HEV system.

After the completion of data storage, the data map task is done in three steps: simulation of data, data analysis, and validation of data. On the MapReduce task one year's data of all the parameters of the hybrid electric vehicle systems is reduced to month-wise, then day-wise and hour wise. Figure 4.17 shows the application of the MapReduce algorithm in the field of the hybrid electric vehicle system, where in the first phase three blocks of the electrical propulsion unit, energy source subsystem, and auxiliary sub-system are considered, and different input parameters are used to model the hybrid electric vehicle. In the second stage the electrical and mechanical link is modeled and is connected between different electrical and mechanical devices and in the third stage hydraulic link, is modeled used to in fluid power source, along with a conventional internal combustion engine (ICE), Figure 4.18 shows the final layout of the hybrid electric vehicle system obtained from the MapReduce algorithm [2,3,10,11].

TABLE 4.4
Data Requirement in MapReduce system [6]

IC Engine Data 8760 Hours	Fuel Tank Data 8760 Hours	Motor Speed Data 8760 Hours	Battery Charging Data 8760 Hours	Converter Data 35,040 Hours
Grading resistance Data	Rolling resistance Data	Vehicle acceleration Data	Tractive force Data	Overall hybrid vehicle Data

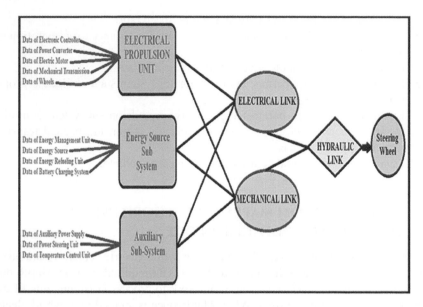

FIGURE 4.17   Framework of HEVs through the MapReduce process [9].

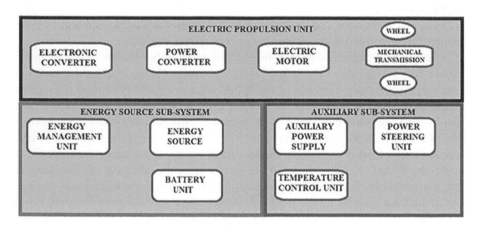

FIGURE 4.18   Final layout of hybrid electric vehicle [9].

A decision tree, of the HEV system is developed using the above model. Another important criteria for HEV is the fulfillment of load demand for which four input parameters, namely (Table 4.5) battery-charging capability, motor speed, electric current, and coefficient of performance of IC engine are considered. All the parameters are worked in the three different modes: minimum value, normal value and maximum value.

In Table 4.5 the possibility of fulfilling the load demand is 9 out of 14.

Entropy H(S) is a measure of the amount of uncertainty in the dataset S,

$$H(S) = \sum_{c \in C} -p(c) \log_2 p(c)$$

TABLE 4.5
Input Parameter of Modeling of Hybrid Electric Vehicle Energy System [9,21]

No. of Days	Battery Charging	Motor Speed	Electrical Current	Coefficient of Performance of IC Engine	Fulfill the Load Demand
1	Normal	Maximum	Maximum	Minimum	No
2	Normal	Maximum	Maximum	Maximum	No
3	Maximum	Maximum	Maximum	Minimum	Yes
4	Minimum	Normal	Maximum	Minimum	Yes
5	Minimum	Minimum	Normal	Minimum	Yes
6	Minimum	Minimum	Normal	Maximum	No
7	Maximum	Minimum	Normal	Maximum	Yes
8	Normal	Normal	Maximum	Minimum	No
9	Normal	Minimum	Normal	Minimum	Yes
10	Minimum	Normal	Normal	Minimum	Yes
11	Normal	Normal	Normal	Maximum	Yes
12	Maximum	Normal	Maximum	Maximum	Yes
13	Maximum	Maximum	Normal	Minimum	Yes
14	Minimum	Normal	Maximum	Maximum	No

Where S = Current dataset for which entropy is being calculated

C = Sets of classes in S and where C = {Yes, No}

P(c) = The proportion of the number of elements in class C to the number of elements in set C.

So, based on the above Equation we can define 9 yes conditions out of 14 and find entropy.

$$= \frac{9}{14} \log 2 \frac{9}{14} + \frac{5}{14} \log 2 \frac{5}{14} = 0.9399$$

So that 0.9399 is the base entropy of the system.

Now we calculate entropy of battery charging. First, we assess while battery charging is at normal condition and Table 4.6 gives the data on a normal battery charging:

TABLE 4.6
Information System of Normal Battery Charging [9,21]

No. of Days	Battery Charging	Motor Speed	Electrical current	Effect of IC engine	Fulfill the Load Demand
1	Normal	Maximum	Maximum	Minimum	No
2	Normal	Maximum	Maximum	Maximum	No
8	Normal	Normal	Maximum	Minimum	Yes
9	Normal	Minimum	Normal	Minimum	Yes
11	Normal	Normal	Normal	Maximum	Yes

Calculation of entropy of normal battery charging, where 3 out of 5 yes conditions and the yes condition represents the normal battery charging also fulfills the load demand in certain circumstances.

Information (battery charging, normal) $= \frac{2}{5}\log 2\frac{2}{5} + \frac{3}{5}\log 2\frac{3}{5} = 0.9699$

The information system of maximum battery charging is shown in Table 4.7.

Information (battery charging, maximum) $= \frac{0}{4}\log 2\frac{0}{4} + \frac{4}{4}\log 2\frac{4}{4} = 0$

The information system for minimum battery charging is shown in Table 4.8.

Information (battery charging, minimum) $= \frac{2}{5}\log 2\frac{2}{5} + \frac{3}{5}\log 2\frac{3}{5} = 0.9699$

The entropy of battery charging is $= \frac{5}{14}\times 0.9699 + \frac{4}{14}\times 0 + \frac{5}{14}\times 0.9699 = 0.6927$

So, the actual entropy of battery charging given by is 0.9399 (base entropy) - 0.6927 = 0.2472

Now to calculate entropy of motor speed, first we assess Mmaximum motor speed and Table 4.9 represents data on maximum motor speed:

Information (motor speed, maximum) $= \frac{2}{4}\log 2\frac{2}{4} + \frac{2}{4}\log 2\frac{2}{2} = 1$

The information system of normal motor speed is shown in Table 4.10.

Information (motor speed, normal) $= \frac{2}{6}\log 2\frac{2}{6} + \frac{4}{6}\log 2\frac{4}{6} = 0.9232$

The information system of minimum motor speed is shown in Table 4.11.

TABLE 4.7
Information System of Maximum Battery Charging [9,21]

No. of Days	Battery Charging	Motor Speed	Electrical Current	Effect of IC Engine	Fulfill the Load Demand
3	Maximum	Maximum	Maximum	Minimum	Yes
7	Maximum	Minimum	Normal	Maximum	Yes
12	Maximum	Normal	Maximum	Maximum	Yes
13	Maximum	Maximum	Normal	Minimum	Yes

TABLE 4.8
Information System of Minimum Battery Charging [9,21]

No. of Days	Solid to Moisture Ratio	Motor Speed	Electrical Current	Effect of IC Engine	Fulfill the Load Demand
4	Minimum	Normal	Maximum	Minimum	Yes
5	Minimum	Minimum	Normal	Minimum	Yes
6	Minimum	Minimum	Normal	Maximum	No
10	Minimum	Normal	Normal	Minimum	Yes
14	Minimum	Normal	Maximum	Maximum	No

TABLE 4.9
Information System of Maximum Motor Speed [9,21]

No. of Days	Battery Charging	Motor Speed	Electrical Current	Effect of IC Engine	Fulfill the Load Demand
1	Normal	Maximum	Maximum	Minimum	No
2	Normal	Maximum	Maximum	Maximum	No
3	Maximum	Maximum	Maximum	Minimum	Yes
13	Maximum	Maximum	Normal	Minimum	Yes

TABLE 4.10
Information System of Normal Motor Speed [9,21]

No. of Days	Battery Charging	Motor Speed	Electrical Current	Effect of IC Engine	Fulfill the Load Demand
4	Minimum	Normal	Maximum	Minimum	Yes
8	Normal	Normal	Maximum	Minimum	No
10	Minimum	Normal	Normal	Minimum	Yes
11	Normal	Normal	Normal	Maximum	Yes
12	Maximum	Normal	Maximum	Maximum	Yes
14	Minimum	Normal	Maximum	Maximum	No

TABLE 4.11
Information System of Minimum Motor Speed [9,21]

No. of Days	Solid to Moisture Ratio	Motor Speed	Electrical Current	Effect of IC Engine	Fulfill the Load Demand
5	Minimum	Minimum	Normal	Minimum	Yes
6	Minimum	Minimum	Normal	Maximum	No
7	Maximum	Minimum	Normal	Maximum	Yes
9	Normal	Minimum	Normal	Minimum	Yes

Information (motor speed, minimum) = 1/4 log 2 1/4 + 3/4 log 2 3/4 = 0.8131

The entropy of motor speed is $= \dfrac{4}{14} \times 1 + \dfrac{6}{14} \times 0.9232 + \dfrac{4}{14} \times 0.8131 = 0.9136$

The entropy of motor speed is 0.9399 (base entropy) - 0.9136 = 0.0263

Now to calculate entropy of electrical current, first we assess maximum electrical current and Table 4.12 represents data on the maximum electrical current.

Information (electrical current, maximum) $= \dfrac{3}{7} \log 2 \dfrac{3}{7} + \dfrac{4}{7} \log 2 \dfrac{4}{7} = 0.9888$

Now similar calculations are done for normal electrical current as in Table 4.13.

Information (electrical current, normal) $= \dfrac{1}{7} \log 2 \dfrac{1}{7} + \dfrac{6}{7} \log 2 \dfrac{6}{7} = 0.5916$

TABLE 4.12
Information System of Maximum Electrical Current [9,21]

No. of Days	Battery Charging	Motor Speed	Electrical Current	Effect of IC Engine	Fulfill the Load Demand
1	Normal	Maximum	Maximum	Minimum	No
2	Normal	Maximum	Maximum	Maximum	No
3	Maximum	Maximum	Maximum	Minimum	Yes
4	Minimum	Normal	Maximum	Minimum	Yes
8	Normal	Normal	Maximum	Minimum	No
12	Maximum	Normal	Maximum	Maximum	Yes
14	Minimum	Normal	Maximum	Maximum	No

TABLE 4.13
Information System of Normal Electrical Current [9,21]

No. of Days	Battery Charging	Motor Speed	Electrical Current	Effect of IC Engine	Fulfill the Load Demand
5	Minimum	Minimum	Normal	Minimum	Yes
6	Minimum	Minimum	Normal	Maximum	No
7	Maximum	Minimum	Normal	Maximum	Yes
9	Normal	Minimum	Normal	Minimum	Yes
10	Minimum	Normal	Normal	Minimum	Yes
11	Normal	Normal	Normal	Maximum	Yes
13	Maximum	Maximum	Normal	Minimum	Yes

The entropy of electrical current is $= \dfrac{7}{14} \times 0.9888 + \dfrac{7}{14} \times 0.5916 = 0.7902$

The entropy of electrical current is 0.9399 (base entropy) - 0.7902 = 0.1497

Now the entropy of coefficient of performance of IC engine is calculated, which needs assessment of the maximum effect of the IC engine as in Table 4.14.

Information (coefficient of performance of IC engine, maximum) = $\dfrac{3}{6}\log 2\dfrac{3}{6} + \dfrac{3}{6}\log 2\dfrac{3}{6} = 1$

The minimum coefficient of performance of IC engine is assessed as in Table 4.15.

Information (coefficient of performance of IC engine, minimum) = $\dfrac{2}{8}\log 2\dfrac{2}{8} + \dfrac{6}{8}\log 2\dfrac{6}{8} = 0.8114$

The entropy of the coefficient of performance of the IC engine is = $\dfrac{6}{14} \times 1 + \dfrac{8}{14} \times 0.8114 = 0.8921$

TABLE 4.14

Information System of Maximum Coefficient of Performance of IC Engine [9,21]

No. of Days	Battery Charging	Motor Speed	Electrical Current	Effect of IC Engine	Fulfill the Load Demand
2	Normal	Maximum	Maximum	Maximum	No
6	Minimum	Minimum	Normal	Maximum	No
7	Maximum	Minimum	Normal	Maximum	Yes
11	Normal	Normal	Normal	Maximum	Yes
12	Maximum	Normal	Maximum	Maximum	Yes
14	Minimum	Normal	Maximum	Maximum	No

TABLE 4.15

Information System of Normal Minimum Coefficient of performance of IC engine

No. of Days	Battery Charging	Motor speed	Electrical Current	Effect of IC Engine	Fulfill the Load Demand
1	Normal	Maximum	Maximum	Minimum	No
3	Maximum	Maximum	Maximum	Minimum	Yes
4	Minimum	Normal	Maximum	Minimum	Yes
5	Minimum	Minimum	Normal	Minimum	Yes
8	Normal	Normal	Maximum	Minimum	No
9	Normal	Minimum	Normal	Minimum	Yes
10	Minimum	Normal	Normal	Minimum	Yes
13	Maximum	Maximum	Normal	Minimum	Yes

The entropy of the coefficient of performance of the IC engine is 0.9399(base entropy) - 0.8921 = 0.0478

This is considered low entropy, a low level of disorder (meaning high level of purity). Entropy is measured between 0 and 1. Depending on the number of classes in your dataset, entropy can be greater than 1 but it means the same thing, a very high level of disorder. According to the above calculation in all the assessments, entropy is lower such as the entropy of battery charging is 0.2472, entropy of speed of motor is 0.0263, entropy of electric current is 0.1497 and the entropy of IC engine is 0.0478 due to the lower entropy meaning high levels of load demand is fulfilled. Figure 4.19 shows a decision tree of modeling of the hybrid electric vehicle system.

The decision tree of the hybrid electric vehicle system represents how load demand can be met. As shown in Figure 4.19 with a normal battery charging level and normal electrical current load demand is met and at minimum battery charging and at the minimum effect of the IC engine the load demand is met if the capacity of the system is low.

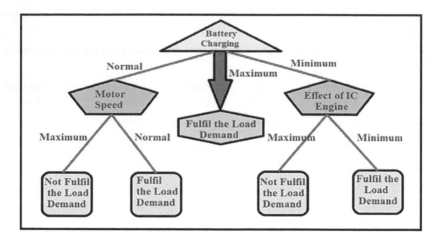

FIGURE 4.19 Decision tree of load frequency control of hybrid electric vehicle system.

4.8 HIERARCHICAL DATA CLUSTERING OF HYBRID ELECTRIC VEHICLE

Hierarchical method of clustering is a step-by-step process of data gathering. In this method data collection and decomposition is done in two ways, (i) agglomerative and (ii) divisive approach. The agglomerative process needs to merge the object and group that are close to one another. In the case of the HEV system, data collection requires the following:

1. Collection of pre-feasibility data of the hybrid electric vehicle system
2. Collection of data for modeling of the hybrid electric vehicle system
3. Collection of data for controlling of the hybrid electric vehicle system
4. Collection of data for reliability assessment of the hybrid electric vehicle system

In divisive approaches, all of the objects are in the same cluster and in the continuous iteration; a cluster is split into smaller clusters [10,11,21]. With the agglomerative approach numbers of clusters are combined into a large cluster (Figure 4.20).

The aerodynamic drag coefficient is an important parameter for any vehicle and is a must to be evaluated before it is brought into operation to see the impact. In Table 4.16, U, V, W, X, Y, and Z are the aerodynamic drag coefficients of different vehicles such as motorcycle with rider, open convertible, limousine, electric car, articulate vehicle, and coach, respectively

After each step, the closest pair of aerodynamic drag coefficients are found and merged. The minimum value is 0.479, and then X and Z are merged (Table 4.17).

Distance evaluation between (XZ) and U = min $[X_{XU}, X_{ZU}]$ = min [3.59, 3.19] = 3.19

Distance evaluation (XZ) and V = min $[X_{XV}, X_{ZV}]$ = min [2.92, 2.48] = 2.47

Distance evaluation (XZ) and W = min $[X_{XW}, X_{ZW}]$ = min [2.22, 2.48] = 2.22

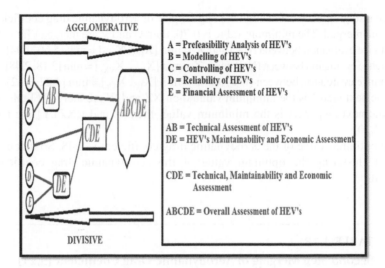

FIGURE 4.20 Agglomerative and divisive approach of hybrid electric vehicle system.

TABLE 4.16
Aerodynamic Drag Coefficient Data Elements [9,21]

Aerodynamic Drag Coefficient	U	V	W	X	Y	Z
U	0					
V	0.71	0				
W	5.66	4.95	0			
X	3.60	2.92	2.22	0		
Y	4.23	3.52	1.39	1	0	
Z	3.19	2.49	2.48	0.479	1.11	0

TABLE 4.17
Merging of Aerodynamic Drag Coefficient [9,21]

Aerodynamic Drag Coefficient	U	V	W	XZ	Y
U	0				
V	0.71	0			
W	5.66	4.95	0		
XZ	3.19	2.46	2.20	0	
Y	4.23	3.52	1.39	1	0

Here also after each calculation the closest pair of aerodynamic drag coefficient sis found and merged. The minimum value is 0.70, then U and V are merged (Table 4.18).

Distance evaluation between (UV) and W = min [X_{UW}, X_{VW}] = min [5.66, 4.94] = 4.94

Distance evaluation between (UV) and XZ = min [X_{UXZ}, X_{VXZ}] = min [3.18, 2.48] = 2.48

Distance evaluation between (UV) and Y = min [X_{UY}, X_{VY}] = min [4.22, 3.52] = 3.52

In the next step 1 is the minimum value then XZ and W are merged (Table 4.19).

In the next step 2.21 is the minimum value, then W and [(XZ),Y] are merged (Table 4.20).

The optimum value of the aerodynamic drag coefficient is 2.48. So that by hierarchical clustering the optimum value of the aerodynamic drag coefficient is obtained.

TABLE 4.18
Second Step Merging of Aerodynamic Drag Coefficient [9,21]

Wave Velocity	(U,V)	W	(X,Z)	Y
(U,V)	0			
W	4.93	0		
(X,Z)	2.47	2.21	0	
Y	3.51	1.38	1	0

TABLE 4.19
Third Step Merging of Aerodynamic Drag Coefficient [9,21]

Wave Velocity	(U,V)	W	[(X,Z),Y]
(U,V)	0		
W	4.94	0	
[(X,Z),Y]	2.48	2.21	0

TABLE 4.20
Second Step Merging of Aerodynamic Drag Coefficient [9,21]

Wave Velocity	(U,V)	[W{(X,Z),Y}]
(U,V)	0	
[W{(X,Z),Y}]	2.48	0

4.9 FUTURE DIRECTIONS

It is at the center of a growing ecosystem of big data technologies that are primarily used to support advanced analytics initiatives, including predictive analytics, data mining, and machine learning applications. The following are the possibilities using big data analysis in the field of electric vehicle systems.

- Create Hadoop Distributed File System (HDFS) for electric motor, battery, and mechanical transmission, which is also used for predictive analysis of hybrid electric vehicle system.
- It is also possible to create a market basket model of reliability analysis of a hybrid electric vehicle system.
- It is also possible to develop a knowledge-based discovery process of data mining of a hybrid electric vehicle system.
- In the near future, the prefeasibility analysis of location assessment for an electric vehicle charging station is also possible through big data analysis, where the unstructured and structured data of a number of parameters of different locations are gathered and then a suitable location identified from the process of data pattern and data visualization.

4.10 CONCLUSIONS

Big data analysis plays an important role in the assessment of the hybrid electric vehicle system and is very useful to predict or forecast the effecting parameters of the hybrid electric vehicle system. The use of big data to model system, storage, management, monitoring and forecasts to assess the performance and reliability of plug-in electric vehicles is discussed. Big data analysis can be effectively used for parameter assessment. This chapter presents an application of big data in the evaluation and assessment of performance of electric vehicles. However, the use of Hadoop, Apache framework, and the MapReduce algorithm can also prove to be very effective in the control, economic and reliability analysis of the hybrid electric vehicle system.

REFERENCES

[1] Anand, M. P. and Bagen, B., "Probabilistic reliability evaluation of distribution systems considering the spatial and temporal distribution of electric vehicles", *International Journal of Electrical Power & Energy Systems* 117 May 2020.
[2] Arghandeh, R. and Zhou, Y, *Big Data Application in Power Systems*, First Edition, Elsevier 2018.
[3] Cox, D. R., "Big data: Some statistical issues", *Statistics & Probability Letters*, 136, pp. 111–115, 2018.
[4] Eckroth, J., "A course on big data analysis", *Journal of Parallel and Distributed Computing*, 118, pp. 166–176, 2018.
[5] Efstathios, E. Michaelides, "Thermodynamics and energy usage of electric vehicles", *Energy Conversion and Management* 203, 1 January 2020.

[6] Ehsani, M., *Modern Electric, Hybrid Electric and Fuel Cell Vehicles: Fundamentals, Theory and Design*, CRC Press, 2005.

[7] Federico, T. and Shivom, S., "3D design and optimization of heat exchanger network for solid oxide fuel cell-gas turbine in hybrid electric vehicles", *Applied Thermal Engineering*, 163, 25 December 2019.

[8] Ganesh, D., Fabian, H., Joule, B., and Marco, P., "A scenario-based study on the impacts of electric vehicles on energy consumption and sustainability in Alberta", *Applied Energy*, 268, 15 June 2020.

[9] Glushkova, D. and Jovanovic, P., "MapReduce performance model for Hadoop 2.x", *Information System* 2017, In Press.

[10] Hamidreza, B. and Danial, K., "A new concept of thermal management system in Li-ion battery using air cooling and heat pipe for electric vehicles", *Applied Thermal Engineering*, 174, 25 June 2020.

[11] Hongwen, H. and Chen W., "An intelligent braking system composed single-pedal and multi-objective optimization neural network braking control strategies for electric vehicle", *Applied Energy*, 259, 1 February 2020.

[12] Kamruzzaman, M. D. and Mohammed B., "A reliability-constrained demand response-based method to increase the hosting capacity of power systems to electric vehicles", *International Journal of Electrical Power & Energy Systems* 121 October 2020.

[13] Lalouni, S., Rekioua, D., Rekioua, T., and Matagne, E.. "Fuzzy Logic Control of Standalone Photovoltaic System with Battery Storage", *Journal of Power System*, 193, 899–907 2009.

[14] Liu, J. and Zhong, C., "An economic evaluation of the coordination between electric vehicle storage and distributed renewable energy", *Energy*, In Press 2019.

[15] Lyu, Y. and Siddique, A. R. M., "Electric vehicle battery thermal management system with thermoelectric cooling", *Energy Reports*, 5, pp. 822–827, November 2019.

[16] Mangu, R., Prayaga, K., Nadimpally, B., and Nicaise, S. 2010. *Design, development and optimization of highly efficient solar cars: Gato Del Sol I-IV. Proceedings of 2010 IEEE Green Technologies Conference*, Grapevine, 15-16 April 2010, 1–6.

[17] Matsumoto, S. 2005. *Advancement of hybrid vehicle technology. Proceedings of IEEE European Conference on Power Electronics and Applications*, Dresden, 11-14 September 2005, 1–7.

[18] Matthieu, D. and Arnaud, D., "Durability and reliability of electric vehicle batteries under electric utility grid operations: Bidirectional charging impact analysis", *Journal of Power Sources*, 358, 1 August 2017, Pages 39–49.

[19] Miller, T. J. E.. *Brushless Permanent Magnet and Reluctance Motor Drive*. Oxford: Clarendon Press, 1989.

[20] Mouli, G. R. C., "System design for a solar powered electric vehicle charging station for workplace", *Applied Energy*, 168, pp. 434–443, 2016.

[21] Oliver, A. G., "Transportation in a 100% renewable energy system", *Energy Conversion and Management*, 158, pp. 266–285 2018.

[22] Shankarmani, R. and Vijayalakshmi, M., *Big Data Analytics*, Second edition, Chennai: Wiley Publication.

[23] Shukai, C., Hua, W., and Qiang, M., "Optimal purchase subsidy design for human-driven electric vehicles and autonomous electric vehicles", *Transportation Research Part C: Emerging Technologies*, 116, July 2020.

[24] Süleyman, Ç., Ahmet, A., and Raif, B., "Real-time range estimation in electric vehicles using fuzzy logic classifier", *Computers & Electrical Engineering*, 83, May 2020.

[25] Torrecilla J. L. and Romo J., "Data learning from big data", *Statistics & Probability Letters*, 136, pp. 15–19, 2018.

[26] Vikas, K. and Aaquil, B., "Design and assessment of solar-powered electric vehicle by different techniques", *International Transaction of Electrical Energy System Wiley*, 30, Dec. 2019.

[27] Vikas, K. and Aaquil, B., "Solar-wind energy assessment by big data analysis", *Innovation in Energy Systems – New Technologies for Changing Paradigms*, Intech Open, 2019.

[28] Vikas, K., Savita, N., and Prashant, B., "Reliability analysis of hybrid renewable energy system by fault tree analysis", *Energy & Environment*, 30, no. 3, pp. 542–555, 2018

[29] Vikas, K., Savita, N.,and Prashant Baredar, *Ocean Energy Modeling and Simulation with Big Data*, 1st Edition, Cambridge: Elsevier Publication 2020.

[30] Wiriyasart, S. and Hommalee, C., "Thermal management system with nanofluids for electric vehicle battery cooling modules", *Case Studies in Thermal Engineering*, 18, pp. 1–20, April 2020.

[31] Xiao-long, W. and Yuan-wu, X., "Extended-range EV-oriented thermoelectric surge control of a solid oxide fuel cell system", *Applied Energy*, 263, 1 April 2020.

[32] Yi, H., Ziyi, W., and Xuerong Li, "Impact of policies on electric vehicle diffusion: An evolutionary game of small world network analysis", *Journal of Cleaner Production*, 265, 20 August 2020.

[33] Yuchu, C. and Yihan, W., "Design of energy and materials for ammonia-based extended-range electric vehicles", *Energy Procedia*, 158, pp. 3064–3069, February 2019.

[34] LiPeng, Z. and Wei, L., "Innovation design and optimization management of a new drive system for plug-in hybrid electric vehicles",*Energy* 186, p. 1 November 2019.

[35] Yujuan, F., Wei, W., Shengwei, M., Laijun, C., and Shaowei, H., "Promoting electric vehicle charging infrastructure considering policy incentives and user preferences: An evolutionary game model in a small-world network", *Journal of Cleaner Production*, 258, 10 June 2020.

KEYWORDS AND DESCRIPTIONS

Electric vehicle   An electric vehicle, also called an EV. Uses one or more electric motors or traction motors for propulsion.

Big data   Big data is a field that treats ways to analyze, systematically extract information from, or otherwise deal with datasets that are too large or complex to be dealt with by traditional data-processing application software.

Hadoop   Hadoop is an open-source software framework for storing data and running applications on clusters of commodity hardware.

Regression analysis   A statistical method that is used to identify the relationship between two or more than two parameters by single and multilevel regression analysis.

MapReduce technique   A technique that converts a set of information to another set of information.

Decision tree   A flow chart-like structure of events.

5 Estimation of Fault Location Using Cyber Physical System in WAMCP

Ankur Singh Rana

National Institute of Technology, Tiruchirappalli,
Tamil Nadu, India

Shufali Ashraf Wani

National Institute of Technology, Srinagar,
Jammu & Kashmir, India

Nisha Parveen

Indian Institute of Technology, Delhi, India

Mini Shaji Thomas

National Institute of Technology, Tiruchirappalli,
Tamil Nadu, India

CONTENTS

5.1 Background 140
5.2 Literature Review 141
5.3 Methodology of Fault Distance Calculation Using IoE under
Different Fault Types 143
    5.3.1 Modelling Transmission Line Network 144
    5.3.2 Phasor Extraction for Faulty Network 145
    5.3.3 Calculation of Sequence Network Components from
the Extracted Phasor Values 145
    5.3.4 Calculation of Fault Location Using Equations for the
Respective Type of Fault 146
        5.3.4.1 Asymmetrical Fault Solution 146
        5.3.4.2 Symmetrical Fault Solution 148
    5.3.5 Simulation and Result 149
    5.3.6 Asymmetrical Fault Solution 151
        5.3.6.1 Error in Fault Location Estimation Using the
Rockefeller and Udren Algorithm 151

          5.3.6.2 Error in Fault Location Estimation Using FFT
                     Algorithm 152
          5.3.7 Symmetrical Fault Solution 153
5.4 Future Directions 154
5.5 Conclusions 154
References 154
Keywords and Descriptions 157

5.1 BACKGROUND

Electricity demand is increasing at a rapid pace, as it is essential for operation of various entities in different industries [11]. With ever-increasing demand, power systems are facing much more competitive environment compared to the early days and are forced to function at the verge of their operating limits [12]. One of the main concerns for the electricity market is to cope with the increased usage of electrical energy especially during fault scenarios (in transmission and distribution systems) [32,33]. In the case of transmission lines, accurate fault location and identification becomes more crucial as they are deployed over long distances. This makes it easy for maintenance engineers to manage customer complaints and outage time. Besides crew repair expense, loss of revenue could be reduced by fast restoration of electrical power system thereby improving its reliability [31]. Hence, implementation of smart initiatives such as Wide-Area Monitoring Control and Protection (WAMCP) supported by optimized energy usage can bring significant potential for improved operation of modern power systems.

With recent advances in *communications and information technology (ICT)*, WAMCP-based intelligent protection systems are gaining popularity. WAMCP are the pre-requisites of the smart grids and support remote data transfer. The cutting-edge technology in communication networks allows wireless exchange of information through an IoT infrastructure. This information can be used to detect and counteract instabilities of the grid. Hence, extension of IoT to WAMCP are potential future trends of power system protection [4,14]. The main components of IoE-based WAMCP include: PMUs, Phasor Data Concentrators (PDCs), an IoT-enabled communicating network and its application software [29]. A typical architecture based on synchrophasor technology for WAMCP is shown in Figure 5.1.

The PMUs act as sensors of phasor data, which is then transmitted to local PDCs via communication media, the edifice of Cyber Physical System (CPS). The number of PMUs installed and the PDCs can vary depending on the requirement. The field information is collected wirelessly by PMUs installed at various locations. The wireless communication medium supports huge information transmission using ICT. The selected information from local PDCs is forwarded to the super PDC wirelessly, which is connected to main control centers [22]. The data archiving and the required application can be directly run at the control center level. It can also be carried out at any level of the synchronized measurement system hierarchy. The archived data can be used for several power system protection and control applications. Fault location is one of the important applications of power system protection. Various types of faults that can arise are symmetrical faults or asymmetrical faults. In symmetrical faults, variation occurs in all three phases of voltage and current waveforms whereas in asymmetrical faults variation occurs in one or two phases of voltage and current waveforms. Depending upon the

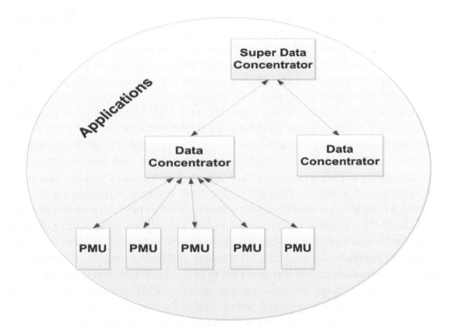

FIGURE 5.1   WAMCP architecture [24].

number of phases involved asymmetrical faults can be divided into line to ground (LG) fault, double line (LL) fault, and double line to ground (LLG) fault.

This chapter is devoted to developing an algorithm for estimating the fault distance on the transmission lines using synchrophasors backed by reliable ICT. The resulting IoE based WAMCP serve as energy efficient monitoring and controlling protection system. One of protection functions of IoT-enabled WAMCP is location of faults at transmission level. Initially, basic types of faults, i.e. symmetrical/ asymmetrical, in the power system networks are discussed. Two phasor measurement methods, the Rockefeller and Udren and the Fast Fourier Transform are used for data extraction from phasors obtained from PMUs at both the terminals of the faulted line. These estimated phasor values are then wirelessly collected at central control level with the help of CPS for calculating the fault location. The algorithm provides separate solution for both the symmetrical and asymmetrical fault. The solution uses the sequence components of both the current and voltage for giving the fault distance and it does not utilize line parameters. Also, the effect of fault resistance is considered in the estimation of fault location accuracy.

The chapter is organized as follows: background is given in Section 5.1 followed by Section 5.2 providing a literature review. Section 5.3 discusses IoE-based fault location estimation with synchronized measurement technology, its simulation and results. Future directions are discussed in Section 5.4 followed by the conclusion in Section 5.5.

5.2   LITERATURE REVIEW

The emerging WAMCP is the direct outcome of developing synchrophasor and is nowadays the focal point in improved operation of modern power systems [6]. The heart and soul of WAMCP technology is synchrophasors or Phasor Measurement Unit (PMU) [19]. Basics of synchrophasor technology for various applications in power systems are provided in [6]. Initially, the information from PMUs was used for post-fault analysis. As ICT technology matured with time to cope with the data frame format of synchrophasors, PMU data was used for real-time applications. This improved the protection and control functions that indirectly improve the utilization of electrical energy. Among various applications of PMUs, estimation of fault location is essential for continuous availability of power at customer level [25]. Various algorithms based on synchrophasor technology are proposed for fault location in the past literature [1,20,30]. These algorithms mainly differ in fault detection principles using data from the PMUs installed either at one or both ends of transmission line.

In order to get a better estimation of the fault distance depending on the data extracted, a fault location algorithm which gets updated as per fault scenario irrespective of the PMU placement was presented in [3]. This algorithm uses three different sets of synchronized pre-fault voltages and currents to determine Thevenin's equivalent and line parameters. Fault location on transposed and/or untransposed lines irrespective of parameters of line was provided in [5]. A fault detection technique for an Extra/Ultra High Voltage transmission line utilizing PMU data was given in [9]. Clarke components of synchronized current and voltage phasors were used for estimating location of fault. An approach for faults location in case of double circuit transmission lines using data from one terminal was presented in [10]. Synchronized measurement in obtaining line parameters and line protection using novel current differential protection scheme was suggested in [27]. Taking into account the unavailability of line parameters, a flexible numerical fault location algorithm for transmission lines was also developed and presented in [28]. A method for faulted line detection to apply protection technique effectively in an interconnected transmission system was proposed in [7] while [15] presented a comparison between detection of fault by only voltage phasors and by using both current and voltage phasors acquired from two ends of the faulted line. Another interesting method for estimating the fault location via two-end measurement of voltage and current was provided in [1] . With the help of these measurements a voltage-current locus was formulated to continuously monitor the condition of the state at every power frequency cycle.

Comprehensive literature for the fault classification and fault detection techniques was provided in [20,21,30]. A deep survey on fault classification methods using basic artificial intelligence techniques was provided in [21]. These classification methods were divided into two parts, viz (i) Standalone techniques, which include: wavelet, artificial neural network, fuzzy logic, and (ii) Hybrid techniques, which cover: neuro-fuzzy technique, wavelet-ANN technique, wavelet-fuzzy-logic technique, wavelet-neuro-fuzzy technique. The survey of modern techniques for the classification of faults such as support vector machine, genetic algorithm, DWT-ELM approach, theory and FPGA-based implementation, GSM technique, PMU-based protection scheme, decision tree-based method, and multi-information measurements was provided in [20]. The improvement in suitable techniques for the fault detection and classification in transmission system was discussed in [30], and the broad classification was done based on either signal analysis or artificial intelligence and also a hybrid of both. All the above discussed literature requires the reliable and fast ICT infrastructure and hence [23] focused on the reliability of communication architecture of WAMCP based on the reliability level. The communication architecture supported by internet connectivity ensures wireless communication for transmission of remotely available massive data [4,13]. Such a smart communication technology is possible due to the advent of IoT. With the application of IoT in different areas, the need of smart devices is increasing, which have high energy demands [26]. To overcome the energy surge, renewable energy sources are integrated making tradition power grid smarter [2,14]. The smart grids enabled with wireless communication infrastructure along with optimal energy usage leads to evolution of IoE [24].

5.3 METHODOLOGY OF FAULT DISTANCE CALCULATION USING IOE UNDER DIFFERENT FAULT TYPES

Usually, the algorithms for estimation of fault location use the concept of one-terminal, two-terminal data from PMUs, i.e. PMUs installed at either on one side of the line or both side of the faulted line. Figure 5.2 depicts a general π model diagram of a transmission line, and the synchronized measurements are taken with the help of PMUs installed at both terminals of the line. E_A and E_B are the equivalent emf at terminal A and B of the line, Z_{SA} and Z_{SB} are the impedance of the power system corresponding to E_A and E_B terminals. Compared to one terminal, information extracted from PMUs installed two terminals is more accurate and impact of fault resistance on estimation of fault location is also less. However, the disadvantage is that gathering information from two terminals is time-consuming but for fault location accuracy is preferred over speed.

PMUs are synchronized with the Global Positioning System (GPS) satellite to get accurate time stamping. PMUs sense the phasor data of faulted line located at a remote distance. The data is transmitted via IoT-based communication infrastructure, which is the direct result of advancing ICT. The use of IoT in a WAMCP system is state-of-the-art technology for monitoring and protection of smart grids. Since smart grids along with use of IoT facilitates the vision of IoE, hence IoE based WAMCP can be used for locating the fault supported by better utilization of electrical energy [16,24]. The flow chart of IoE for fault location estimation as an application of WAMCP is given in Figure 5.3.

In this chapter, the methodology used to estimate the fault location consists of a four-step method:

(i) Modelling transmission line network,
(ii) Phasor extraction for a faulty network supported by ICT,

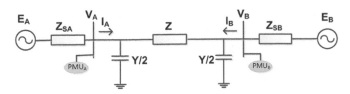

FIGURE 5.2   Schematic diagram of two-end synchronized fault location [18].

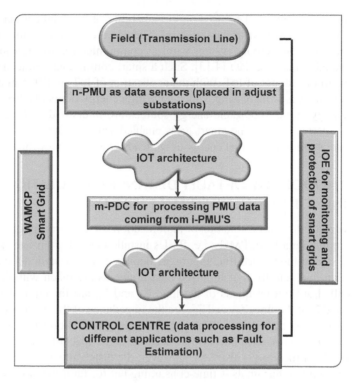

FIGURE 5.3 Use of IoE for estimating faults in transmission lines.

(iii) Calculation of sequence network components (positive and negative) from the extracted phasor values,

(iv) Calculation of fault location using equations defining the type of fault (i.e. symmetrical or asymmetrical).

If a fault occurs anywhere over the transmission line, the distance to fault can be computed in terms of the sequence components of the currents and voltages.

In this chapter, the sequence components are obtained at control centers with the help of fast and reliable ICT architecture, from the current and voltage phasors by the measurement units present at both the ends of the faulted line.

5.3.1 MODELLING TRANSMISSION LINE NETWORK

For the fast restoration of a faulty line, it is necessary to detect the proper distance of the fault location, which is possible with synchronized PMU data as the transmission lines spread over long distances. It is assumed in this chapter that the PMUs are installed at both ends of a faulty transmission line. PMUs at both ends are synchronized with the help of GPS. Consider a transmission line with two terminals denoted as 'A' and 'B'. Now, let a fault occur at the position 'x' units from the terminal 'A' side, as shown in Figure 5.4, where 'F' denotes the fault and

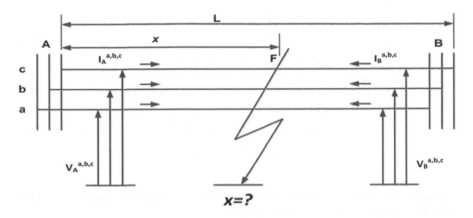

FIGURE 5.4   Three-phase representation of a faulty line.

'L' stands for length of the transmission line. The main focus of this chapter is to calculate the location of fault. During fault a wide variation takes place in voltage, and current values and proper extraction of values is essential for locating the exact location of fault.

5.3.2   Phasor Extraction for Faulty Network

PMUs at both ends will provide the data on a continuous basis, irrespective of fault (occurring or not). When a fault occurs, values from both PMUs are considered, and then phasor extraction is done using two most promising data extraction techniques, i.e. the Rockefeller and Udren algorithm [34] and Fast Fourier Transform (FFT). These phasor measurement algorithms are utilized to extract information in terms of amplitudes and phase angles of voltages and current samples.

The Rockefeller and Udren algorithm is among the easiest methods and uses only three samples: pre-fault, during fault, and post fault value for phasor extraction. It computes the derivative of the samples for proper phasor extraction. The information extracted from phasors using this method sometimes faces problems because of a different sampling rate or delayed signal, etc. Also, the information from a phasor extraction is best when the waveform approaches pure sinusoid. To avoid the errors due to signal delays and random sampling, FFT, which requires a higher number of samples, is used for extraction of the amplitude and phase angle of the fault signal [19].

5.3.3   Calculation of Sequence Network Components from the Extracted Phasor Values

During a fault condition, a system will not remain in a balanced condition (balanced means the magnitude is the same in each phase with a phase difference of 120 among them) [8]. To use the faulty values the unbalanced phasors need to be converted into balanced phasors using the sequence components technique. Sequence components of voltage and current phasors are calculated with the help of Equations (5.1) and (5.2).

$$\begin{bmatrix} V_A^o \\ V_A^p \\ V_A^n \end{bmatrix} = \frac{1}{3} \begin{bmatrix} 1 & 1 & 1 \\ 1 & \alpha & \alpha^2 \\ 1 & \alpha^2 & \alpha \end{bmatrix} \begin{bmatrix} V_a \\ V_b \\ V_c \end{bmatrix} \tag{5.1}$$

$$\begin{bmatrix} I_A^o \\ I_A^p \\ I_A^n \end{bmatrix} = \frac{1}{3} \begin{bmatrix} 1 & 1 & 1 \\ 1 & \alpha & \alpha^2 \\ 1 & \alpha^2 & \alpha \end{bmatrix} \begin{bmatrix} I_a \\ I_b \\ I_c \end{bmatrix} \tag{5.2}$$

Where, $V_A^{o,p,n}$ and $I_A^{o,p,n}$ denote the zero, positive and negative sequence voltages and currents respectively at the line terminals.

5.3.4 Calculation of Fault Location Using Equations for the Respective Type of Fault

In this chapter, various scenarios representing different fault types such as asymmetrical and symmetrical are created, and exhaustive testing is performed to verify the application of this method for all fault types. Straightforward solutions of fault locations for both the asymmetrical and three-phase (symmetrical) faults are presented as under:

5.3.4.1 Asymmetrical Fault Solution

Consider a fault of asymmetrical nature on a transmission line located at 'x' units from A in Figure 5.4. The sequence components of current and voltage, which include positive, negative, and zero can be calculated using the technique of sequence components. These components are gathered from both the ends of line. Only the positive and negative sequence components are considered in the proposed technique as the effect of zero-sequence coupling is not observed. The equivalent sequence circuits, both positive and negative, of the faulty line are shown in Figure 5.5a and b.

From these figures we have:

$$V_A^p - zxI_A^p = V_B^p - z\left(L - x\right)I_B^p \tag{5.3}$$

$$V_A^n - zxI_A^n = V_B^n - z\left(L - x\right)I_B^n \tag{5.4}$$

Where, $V_A^{p,n}, V_B^{p,n}, I_A^{p,n},$ and $I_B^{p,n}$ denote the positive and negative sequence voltages and currents respectively at the line terminals, and z being line sequence impedances [28].

After solving Equations (5.3) and (5.4), we get:

$$zx = \frac{\left(V_A^p - V_B^p\right)I_B^n - \left(V_A^n - V_B^n\right)I_B^p}{I_A^p I_B^n - I_A^n I_B^p} \tag{5.5}$$

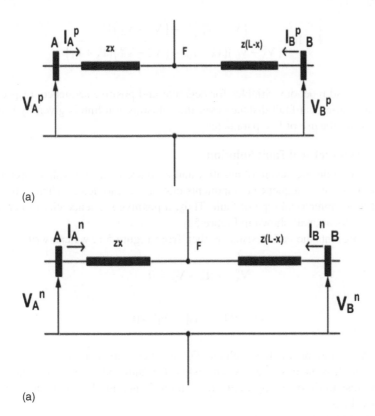

FIGURE 5.5   (a) and (b) Equivalent positive and negative sequence circuit of the faulty line.

$$z(L-x) = \frac{\left(V_A^p - V_B^p\right)I_A^n - \left(V_A^n - V_B^n\right)I_A^p}{I_A^p I_B^n - I_A^n I_B^p}$$ (5.6)

The distance to fault is denoted by x, and it can be expressed in terms of percentage with respect to line length, L

$$x\% = \frac{x}{L}100$$ (5.7)

The above equation can further be written as

$$x\% = \frac{zx}{zx + z(L-x)}100$$ (5.8)

Further simplification of the Equations (5.3), (5.4) and (5.6) give the distance to fault

$$x\% = 100\frac{\left(V_A^p - V_B^p\right)I_B^n - \left(V_A^n - V_B^n\right)I_B^p}{\left(V_A^p - V_B^p\right)\left(I_A^n + I_B^n\right) - \left(V_A^n - V_B^n\right)\left(I_A^p + I_B^p\right)} \tag{5.9}$$

Where n and p denote variables for negative and positive sequence, respectively. Finally, asymmetrical fault distance over the transmission line is given by Equation (5.9) forgoing the use of line parameters.

5.3.4.2 Symmetrical Fault Solution

Symmetrical faults are devoid of negative and zero-sequence equivalent circuits. The presence of negative sequence components can be used to detect whether it is symmetrical or asymmetrical type of fault. Thus, a positive sequence circuit is required for the fault location as shown in Figure 5.6.

If R_F represents the fault resistance, then from Figure 5.6, we can write

$$V_A^p - zxI_A^p - V_F^p = 0 \tag{5.10}$$

$$V_B^p - z\left(L - x\right)I_B^p - V_F^p = 0 \tag{5.11}$$

Here V_F^p represents the fault voltage. For short circuits that are purely metallic in nature the fault voltage is taken as zero, while for faults other than short, i.e. involving some resistance or arcing fault, the voltage is negligible in comparison to the terminal voltage.

After simplification, we get

$$x\% = 100\left(1 + \frac{V_B^p I_A^p}{V_A^p I_B^p}\right)^{-1} \tag{5.12}$$

From these equations, it becomes necessary to have measurements from both the line terminals.

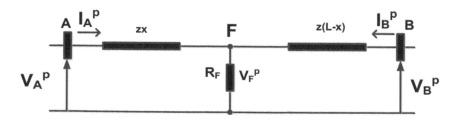

FIGURE 5.6 Equivalent circuit for symmetrical fault location.

5.3.5 Simulation and Result

For validation of the proposed fault location algorithm, a 500 kV, 60 Hz, 200-mile transmission line is chosen for simulation [17]. PSCAD is used for simulation of transmission line. The simulation model of the line is shown in Figure 5.7. The transmission line is divided into five sections of equal length, and then the fault is simulated at different locations to validate the results for estimating the fault location.

The phasor data for different types of faults represented in terms of voltage and current have been extracted using FFT and the Rockefeller and Udren algorithm. This data obtained from both the ends of faulty transmission enables the calculation of the sequence components, which in turn can be used for locating faults using simple mathematical equations. After this, MATLAB code of the proposed fault estimation algorithm is written. Various asymmetrical (L-G, L-L, and L-L-G) and symmetrical faults were simulated at different points i.e. 40%, 60%, and 100% of the line length to estimate their location as per the given method. Figures 5.8, 5.9, and 5.10 show the current and voltage phasors at terminals A and B during the existence of following faults in the line: single line to ground, double line to ground and symmetrical faults. The distortions in phasors occur due to the existing faults.

In Figure 5.8, the distortion can be observed in one phase (B) in the case of both voltage and current phasors, hence the distortion indicates a L-G fault. Similarly, in Figure 5.9 distortions can be observed in two phases (BG) and in Figure 5.10 waveforms of all three phases (BGR) are distorted and hence distortions indicate L-L-G and symmetrical faults, respectively. In all three faults, distortion represents decrease in amplitude in the case of voltage waveform and increase in amplitude in the case of current waveform.

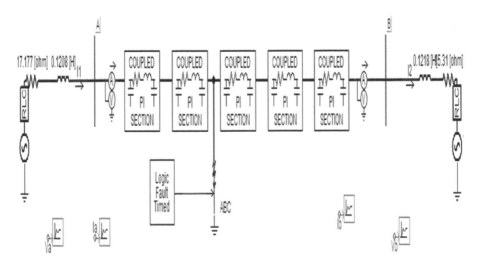

FIGURE 5.7 PSCAD model of 500 kV transmission line.

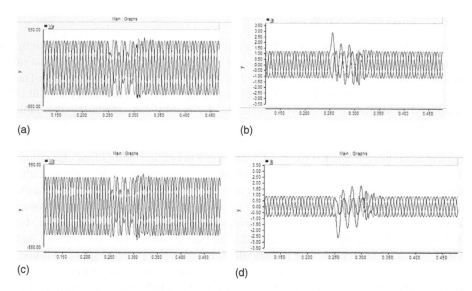

FIGURE 5.8   Phase voltages and currents; (a and c) at terminal A, (b and d) at terminal B for single line to ground (LG) fault.

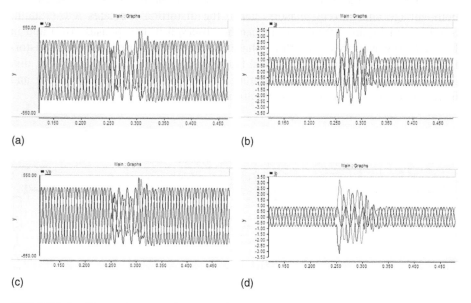

FIGURE 5.9   Phase voltages and currents; (a and c) at terminal A, (b and d) at terminal B for double line to ground (LLG) fault.

Rigorous testing establishes the promising efficiency of the method. The location of the fault for asymmetrical and symmetrical faults is determined by using Equations (5.9) and (5.11). Error in locating the fault was calculated in respect to the length of transmission line as per Equation (5.13).

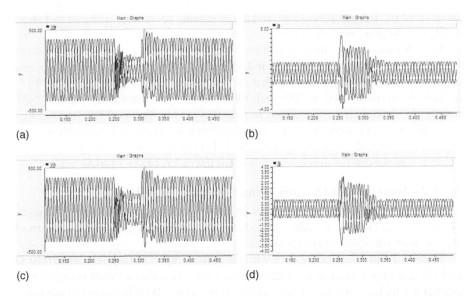

FIGURE 5.10 Phase voltages and currents; (a and c) at terminal A, (b and d) at terminal B for symmetrical fault.

$$\text{Error}\left(\%\right) = \frac{\left|x_{actual} - x_{estimated}\right|}{L}.100\% \qquad (5.13)$$

Where $x_{estimated}$ is the estimated distance of fault on the transmission line and x_{actual} is the actual fault distance, and L is the line length.

5.3.6 Asymmetrical Fault Solution

5.3.6.1 Error in Fault Location Estimation Using the Rockefeller and Udren Algorithm

Table 5.1 presents the percentage error in locating different fault types such as LG faults, LL faults, and LLG faults at the three different locations of the line using the phasor data obtained from the Rockefeller and Udren algorithm. In comparison to other asymmetrical faults, the L-L-G fault is most severe, followed by L-L and L-G. However, their probability of occurrences is in reverse order of severity, i.e. L-G fault

TABLE 5.1
Errors in Fault Distance Calculations

xactual (%)	%Error (L-G)	%Error (L-L)	%Error (L-L-G)
40	0.3445	2.4858	5.8398
60	0.4868	1.5970	3.6872
100	0.9680	0.080	1.9870
Avg error	0.5997	1.3876	3.838

(80%–85%), L-L fault (10%–12%), and the remaining percentage is shared by L-L-G and L-L-L (symmetrical) fault [25].

Table 5.1 shows that errors in fault location identification are calculated for 40%, 60% and 100% of line length (200 miles) for different asymmetrical faults using Equation (5.13).The analysis shows that the percentage of error is maximum for LLG at fault positions located at 40% and 100% length of transmission line. At 60% length, the maximum error is found in L-L faults using the Rockfeller and Udren algorithm. Also, it is found that for L-G faults error percentage increases with increasing distance of fault position, for L-L and L-L-G fault error percentage decreases. Table 5.1 shows that the average error follows the order, LLG> LL>LG.

5.3.6.2   Error in Fault Location Estimation Using FFT Algorithm

Tables 5.2 and 5.3 represent the errors in fault location estimates from FFT techniques for L-G faults, L-L faults, and L-L-G faults at the three different locations of the line with variation in fault resistance.

Tables 5.2 and 5.3 calculate error with the consideration of fault resistance 0.01 Ω and 10 Ω during a fault in the transmission line. The effect of fault resistance on estimating the fault distance is depicted in above tables. With increase in fault resistance the percentage of error is reduced in most of the cases. When phasors are extracted using FFT, percentage of error increases in case of LLG faults with increasing distance of fault location, irrespective of variation in fault resistance. The percentage of error does not follow any pattern in case of LG and LL faults even when resistance is increased thousand times from 0.01 Ω to 10 Ω. For 0.01 Ω resistance, the average percentage of error is found to be maximum in case of L-L-G faults followed by L-G faults and least in case of L-L faults. However, with the increase in Rf value, the trend of average error is L-L-G>L-L>L-G.

TABLE 5.2
Errors in Asymmetrical Fault Distance Calculations ($R_F = 0.01\Omega$)

xactual (%)	%Error (L-G)	%Error (L-L)	%Error (L-L-G)
40	1.0438	0.4669	0.1629
60	0.2745	0.3250	0.9445
100	1.4611	1.0594	1.8091
Avg Error (%)	0.9264	0.6171	0.9721

TABLE 5.3
Errors in Asymmetrical Fault Distance Calculations ($R_F = 100\Omega$)

xactual (%)	%Error (L-G)	%Error (L-L)	%Error (L-L-G)
40	0.6881	1.9013	1.8331
60	0.0063	1.2997	1.7248
100	0.8115	1.750	1.6300
Avg error	0.5019	1.6503	1.7293

The average value of percentage of error is least in case of L-G faults and also decreases with an increase in R_f value, so the Rockfeller and Udren algorithm is best suited for locating L-G faults among asymmetrical fault type. However, in the case of L-L faults the error value increases almost ten times and similarly for L-L-G faults it approximately doubles with an increase in value of arc resistance.

From the above-described results, it is clear that the variation in estimating the fault distance is more in the case of the Rockefeller and Udren algorithm compared to the FFT technique. The reason for this variation is the dependency of phasor extraction in this technique. This technique has great accuracy if the waveform is purely sinusoidal, but in case of fault the waveform may have sinusoidal as well as harmonic components (mostly the waveform is of distorted nature during a fault). Results for FFT have variation because of the consideration of DC components in the fault waveforms.

5.3.7 SYMMETRICAL FAULT SOLUTION

Symmetrical faults were also simulated at the same three points with different fault resistance values using FFT. Three-phase faults use only positive sequence components of the two-line terminals for fault location calculation. Equation (5.12) is used to calculate the fault distance for three-phase faults. The calculation error determined in each case is shown in Table 5.4.

It can be observed from Table 5.4, the percentage of error follows a symmetric pattern and decreases with the increase in distance of fault position for all the variations of arc resistances. Further, the symmetricity is also observed in case of average value of percentage of error. It is found that for all the considered fault positions, average percentage of error increases with increase in resistance. In other words, the accuracy of the algorithm decreases as the arc resistance increases. This trend is not observed in case of asymmetrical faults. It is due to the existence of fault voltage across the fault impedance that cannot be measured.

On comparing the two extraction methods, it can also be clearly observed from the results that when phasor extraction is done using FFT, the fault location algorithm provides comparatively more accurate results. It is because the Rockefeller and Udren method for phasor measurements utilizes three samples and therefore is highly sensitive towards the deviation of the sampling rate. For compensating the issues of sensitivity, the number of samples extracted is increased. In that case, FFT comes to the rescue. Its wide usage in protection relays can be owed to its stability. The convergence rate of algorithm is proportional to time required for extraction of phasors.

TABLE 5.4
Errors in symmetrical fault distance calculations (in %)

xactual (%)	%Error ($R_F = 0.01\Omega$)	%Error ($R_F = 1\Omega$)	%Error ($R_F = 2\Omega$)
40	0.4017	0.9462	2.8458
60	0.5170	0.8928	1.0098
100	0.2639	0.5079	0.5081
Avg error	0.3942	0.7823	1.4545

5.4 FUTURE DIRECTIONS

The future scope of the approach includes the following aspects:

    a. Implementation of methodology on lab based practical transmission line.
    b. Estimation of power swings in adjacent lines due to the fault in some other lines (power swing problems due to opening of circuit breakers in other nearby lines).
    c. Adaptive relaying effects due to inclusion of distributed recourses in a microgrid environment.

5.5 CONCLUSIONS

The chapter proposes an easy-to use four-step fault locating method using synchrophasor measurements from both the ends of the faulted transmission line. The proposed method shows the use of IoE for monitoring and protection of smart grids by estimating fault distance using WAMCP backed by IoT-based communication architecture. The method can be applied to both the asymmetrical faults as well as symmetrical faults. It provides a simple solution, and doesn't require any iterative process for locating fault distance. Various types of faults scenarios were created by simulating the line model. The currents and voltages at both the line terminals in each case were observed, and phasor data was extracted using two phasor measurement methods, the Rockefellr and Udren algorithm and Fast Fourier Transform. From these phasors, sequence components were calculated and the fault was located using a set of mathematical equations.

The average error in determining location of a LLG asymmetrical fault is more in comparison to LG and LL faults using both the Rockefeller and Udren algorithm and FFT. However, the fault location determined using the Rockefeller and Udren method provides a more than acceptable error in some cases. The method utilizes three samples; hence, it suffers from the problem of extreme sensitivity towards the deviation of the sampling rate. The fault location using FFT for phasor extraction uses a number of samples. Hence, it is not sensitive to deviation of the sampling rate. Therefore, fault location can be determined comparatively accurately when phasor extraction is done using FFT. In the case of three-phase faults, results are shown for different values of fault resistance, and from the results it is clear that the accuracy decreases with increase in fault resistance, while the method is independent of line parameters.

REFERENCES

[1] Abu-Siada, A., and Mir, S. (2019). A new on-line technique to identify fault location within long transmission lines. *Engineering Failure Analysis*, 105, 52–64. 10.1016/j.engfailanal.2019.06.071
[2] Ahuja, H., and Kumar, P. (2019). A novel approach for coordinated operation of variable speed wind energy conversion in smart grid applications. *Computers and Electrical Engineering*, 77, 72–87. 10.1016/j.compeleceng.2019.05.004
[3] Al-Mohammed, A. H., and Abido, M. A. (2014). An adaptive fault location algorithm for power system networks based on synchrophasor measurements. *Electric Power Systems Research*, 108, 153–163. 10.1016/j.epsr.2013.10.013

[4] Ansere, J. A., Han, G., Bonsu, K. A., and Peng, Y. (2020). Energy efficient joint power allocation and user selection algorithm for data transmission in internet of things networks. *IEEE Internet of Things Journal*, 4662(c), 1–1. 10.1109/jiot.2020.2995387

[5] Apostolopoulos, C. A., and Korres, G. N. (2010). A novel algorithm for locating faults on transposed/untransposed transmission lines without utilizing line parameters. *IEEE Transactions on Power Delivery*, 25(4), 2328–2338. 10.1109/TPWRD.2010.2053223

[6] De La Ree, J., Centeno, V., Thorp, J. S., and Phadke, A. G. (2010). Synchronized phasor measurement applications in power systems. *IEEE Transactions on Smart Grid*, 1(1), 20–27. 10.1109/TSG.2010.2044815

[7] Eissa, M. M., Masoud, M. E., and Elanwar, M. M. M. (2010). A novel back up wide area protection technique for power transmission grids using phasor measurement unit. *IEEE Transactions on Power Delivery*, 25(1), 270–278. 10.1109/TPWRD. 2009.2035394

[8] Grainger, J., and Stevenson, W. (1994). *Power System Analysis*. McGraw-Hill Education. Retrieved from https://books.google.co.in/books?id=NBIoAQAAMAAJ

[9] Joe-Air Jiang, Jun-Zhe Yang, Ying-Hong Lin, Chih-Wen Liu, and Jih-Chen Ma. (2000). An adaptive PMU based fault detection/location technique for transmission lines. I. Theory and algorithms. *IEEE Transactions on Power Delivery*, 15(2), 486–493. 10.1109/61.852973

[10] Kawady, T., and Stenzel, J. (2003). A practical fault location approach for double circuit transmission lines using single end data. *IEEE Transactions on Power Delivery*, 18(4), 1166–1173. 10.1109/TPWRD.2003.817503

[11] Kumar, P., Ali, I., Thomas, M. S., and Singh, S. (2017). Imposing voltage security and network radiality for reconfiguration of distribution systems using efficient heuristic and meta-heuristic approach. *IET Generation, Transmission and Distribution*, 11(10), 2457–2467. 10.1049/iet-gtd.2016.0935

[12] Kumar, P., Ali, I., Thomas, M. S., and Singh, S. (2020). A coordinated framework of dg allocation and operating strategy in distribution system for configuration management under varying loading patterns. *Electric Power Components and Systems*, 48(1–2), 12–29. 10.1080/15325008.2020.1732501

[13] Li, L. S. (1989). An overview of nephrology in China. *Chinese Medical Journal*, 102(7), 488–48895.

[14] Mahmud, K., Khan, B., Ravishankar, J., Ahmadi, A., and Siano, P. (2020). An internet of energy framework with distributed energy resources, prosumers and small-scale virtual power plants: An overview. *Renewable and Sustainable Energy Reviews*, 127(March). 10.1016/j.rser.2020.109840

[15] Mekhamer, S. F., Abdelaziz, A. Y., Ezzat, M., and Abdel-Salam, T. S. (2012). Fault location in long transmission lines using synchronized phasor measurements from both ends. *Electric Power Components and Systems*, 40(7), 759–776. 10.1080/15325008.2012.658599

[16] Nguyen, V. T., Luan Vu, T., Le, N. T., and Min Jang, Y. (2018). An overview of Internet of Energy (IoE) based building energy management system. *9th International Conference on Information and Communication Technology Convergence: ICT Convergence Powered by Smart Intelligence, ICTC 2018*, 852–855. 10.1109/ICTC.2018.8539513

[17] Novosel, D., Hart, D. G., Udren, E., and Garitty, J. (1996). Unsynchronized two-terminal fault location estimation. *IEEE Transactions on Power Delivery*, 11(1), 130–138. 10.1109/61.484009

[18] Parveen, N., Rana, A. S., and Thomas, M. S. (2016). A practical approach for locating faults for overhead transmission lines using synchronized measurements from PMUs. In *2016 IEEE 1st International Conference on Power Electronics, Intelligent Control and Energy Systems (ICPEICES)* (pp. 1–5). 10.1109/ICPEICES.2016.7853651

[19] Phadke, A. G., and Thorp, J. S. (2008). *Synchronized Phasor Measurements and Their Applications* (Vol. 1). Springer.

[20] Prasad, A, Belwin Edward, J., and Ravi, K. (2018a). A review on fault classification methodologies in power transmission systems: Part—II. *Journal of Electrical Systems and Information Technology*, 5(1), 61–67. 10.1016/j.jesit.2016.10.003

[21] Prasad, Avagaddi, Belwin Edward, J., and Ravi, K. (2018b). A review on fault classification methodologies in power transmission systems: Part—I. *Journal of Electrical Systems and Information Technology*, 5(1), 48–60. 10.1016/j.jesit.2017.01.004

[22] Rana, A. S., Thomas, M. S., and Senroy, N. (2015). Wide area measurement system performance based on latency and link utilization. *2015 Annual IEEE India Conference (INDICON)*. 10.1109/INDICON.2015.7443663

[23] Rana, A. S., Thomas, M. S., and Senroy, N. (2017). Reliability evaluation of WAMS using Markov-based graph theory approach. *IET Generation, Transmission Distribution*, 11(11), 2930–2937. 10.1049/iet-gtd.2016.0848

[24] Rana, M. (2017). Architecture of the internet of energy network: An application to smart grid communications. *IEEE Access*, 5, 4704–4710. 10.1109/ACCESS.2017.2683503

[25] Saha, M. M., Izykowski, J. J., and Rosolowski, E. (2009). *Fault Location on Power Networks*. Springer London. Retrieved from https://books.google.co.in/books?id=CCE8Bm5kpKIC

[26] Shahzad, Y., Javed, H., Farman, H., Ahmad, J., Jan, B., and Zubair, M. (2020). Internet of Energy: Opportunities, applications, architectures and challenges in smart industries. *Computers and Electrical Engineering*, 86 10.1016/j.compeleceng.2020.106739

[27] Sivanagaraju, G., Chakrabarti, S., and Srivastava, S. C. (2014). Uncertainty in transmission line parameters: estimation and impact on linc current differential protection. *IEEE Transactions on Instrumentation and Measurement*, 63(6), 1496–1504. 10.1109/TIM.2013.2292276

[28] Terzija, V., Radojević, Z. M., and Preston, G. (2015). Flexible synchronized measurement technology-based fault locator. *IEEE Transactions on Smart Grid*, 6(2), 866–873. 10.1109/TSG.2014.2367820

[29] Thomas, M. S., Senroy, N., and Rana, A. S. (2014). Analysis of time delay in a wide-area communication network. *Power India International Conference (PIICON), 2014 6th IEEE*. 10.1109/POWERI.2014.7117643

[30] Tîrnovan, R., and Cristea, M. (2019). Advanced techniques for fault detection and classification in electrical power transmission systems: An overview. In *2019 8th International Conference on Modern Power Systems (MPS)* (pp. 1–10). 10.1109/MPS.2019.8759695

[31] Wani, Shufali A, Khan, S. A., Gupta, D., and Nezami, M. M. (2017). Diagnosis of incipient dominant and boundary faults using composite DGA method. *International Transactions on Electrical Energy Systems*, 27(11), 1–12. 10.1002/etep.2421

[32] Wani, Shufali Ashraf, Gupta, D., Farooque, M. U., and Khan, S. A. (2019). Multiple incipient fault classification approach for enhancing the accuracy of dissolved gas analysis (DGA). *IET Science, Measurement and Technology*, 13(7), 959–967. 10.1049/iet-smt.2018.5135

[33] Wani, Shufali Ashraf, Khan, S. A., Prashal, G., and Gupta, D. (2019). Smart Diagnosis of incipient faults using dissolved gas analysis-based Fault Interpretation Matrix (FIM). *Arabian Journal for Science and Engineering*, 44(8), 6977–6985. 10.1007/s13369-019-03739-4

[34] Wu, Q. H., Lu, Z., and Ji, T. (2009). *Protective Relaying of Power Systems Using Mathematical Morphology*. Springer London. Retrieved from https://books.google.co.in/books?id=cse0v8rMfyMC

KEYWORDS AND DESCRIPTIONS

Fault Location Identification   This term is related to locating the fault, i.e. generation level, transmission level or at distribution level.

PMU   PMU stands for phasor measurement unit. It is a GPS-enabled relay structure. PMUs are enabled to sense the disturbance in real time environment because of its high data capturing functionalities.

PDC   PDC stands for Phasor Data Concentrator. It collects the information from various PMUs connected to it through a Cyber Physical System, and then process the collected information to the control center for various application.

CPS   CPS stands for Cyber Physical System. A CPS is used to collect the information and will provide the communication among different stages of data collection.

IoT   IoT stands for Internet of Things. It provides processing of various controlling device without human intervention.

IoE   IoE stands for Internet of Energy. It will use an IoT infrastructure to optimize the energy usage.

6 The Role of Blockchain and IoT in Modern Energy Systems

Wesley Doorsamy and Babu Sena Paul
University of Johannesburg, Johannesburg, South Africa

CONTENTS

6.1 Background 159
6.2 Literature Review 161
6.3 Architectures and Fusion.. 163
    6.3.1 Evolving Energy Systems Architecture 163
    6.3.2 Blockchain and IoT Architectures 163
    6.3.3 Functional Perspectives... 164
    6.3.4 Physical Perspectives 165
    6.3.5 Towards Blockchain- and IoT-based Energy Frameworks 167
6.4 Security 168
    6.4.1 Secure and Trustless Platforms in Modern Energy Systems.............. 168
    6.4.2 Authentication, Permission and Tokenization.................................... 168
    6.4.3 Public and Private Protocols 169
    6.4.4 Smart Contracts.. 170
6.5 Future Directions... 170
6.6 Conclusion... 171
References.. 171
Keywords and Descriptions 174

6.1 BACKGROUND

The energy sector has undergone a tremendous shift over past several decades, with the inherent accompaniment of revolutionary technologies. Some 60 years ago, supervisory control and data acquisition (SCADA) systems emerged and subsequently began widespread deployment in power utilities. The ability to automate supervisory control with remote monitoring and other expanded functionality rapidly extended to generation, transmission and distribution systems with noteworthy improvements in efficiency, security and reliability of operations [1]. The potential applications of SCADA systems in power systems to enhance flexibility and reliability continued to grow for decades after its initial developments [2]. The developments in technologies intertwining information systems in power systems are still continuously evolving.

With the increase in open transmission access [3], need for more resilient and efficient infrastructure [4,5], and subsequent higher levels of penetration of distributed generation/storage [6,7], the emergence of the smart grid was inevitable. The most recent shift is towards the Internet of Energy (IoE) paradigm whereby the energy network is managed and optimized through various edge devices [8]. The need for this paradigm shift still follows on from the increased rate of penetration of renewable energy sources; movement towards decentralized and distributed structures with interest in improved reliability, accessibility, and flexibility; and the advent of smart grid technology together with increased provision for EVs, DC loads, and storage technology; in addition to the overwhelming need for increased security, trust and privacy.

The IoE itself is evolving into a complex multi-layered system comprising power system, information system, and intelligent management system components. The shift in decentralization is no longer confined just to the power system components and sources, and now the management thereof as well as the market is undergoing decentralization. This has created a significant technological gap, which suits the application of blockchain technology in emerging instances of supply, trading and management in the energy sector [9].

Over the years, there have been multiple novel architectures for power systems to ensure reliable monitoring and protection. In [10], an intelligent self-evolving architecture is proposed that employs intelligent agents in a multi-agent type voting framework to alleviate malfunction in the face of an attack on network ports. Security strategies – i.e. authentication, encryption, and access control – in demand response management are also becoming more pertinent in the IoE whereby new technological approaches such consensus algorithms are being recognized as a means of servicing the decentralized energy supply paradigm [11]. Blockchain – together with IoT – can drive these types of intelligent multi-agent frameworks and security strategies with its immutable consensus mechanism. The integration of blockchain into the IoE paradigm is especially necessary, as the growth in privately owned and controlled, distributed energy resources as well as IoT devices on the grid pose security vulnerabilities [12] (Figure 6.1).

The IoE is seen to be the next stage in the evolution of smart grids whereby there is flexible and efficient energy sharing on the grid. However, the subsystems of the

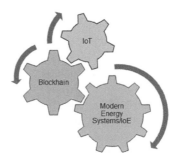

FIGURE 6.1   Blockchain and IoT are critical in driving modern energy systems.

grid require high performance protection communications in a risk-aware network setup to ensure highly coordinated operation with low latency [13,14]. The use of Distributed Applications (DApps) in the blockchain environment is proving to be excellent in providing such high levels of coordination in risk-aware networks together with low latency in various other applications. This level of reliable coordination is particularly desirable in situations employing decentralized control for multiple microgrid systems as presented in [15]. The utilization of distributed computing frameworks to perform modern power system security analysis – for impact prediction and assessment as well as mitigating risk of failure – has long since been a desirable proposition [16]. The emergence of blockchain and IoT fortuitously coincides with these past propositions as ideal candidates to realize such frameworks in a practicable and sustainable manner. Although there have been several proposals for functional schemes that seemingly meet the security demands of the modern information systems management in the new IoE paradigm, such as presented in [17], these still do not offer the flexibility, reliability, and trustlessness that blockchain configurations could offer. A core characteristic of the IoE paradigm is the provision of flexible energy trading platforms for end-users [12]. Dynamic energy management – with measures such as dynamic pricing models – also features in IoE [18]. However, these particular aspects of IoE certainly do suffer in terms of security and privacy, flexibility, and interoperability, especially when it comes to the significantly larger-scale implementations at the different levels of the grid.

The roles of blockchain and IoT in meeting the demands of the next generation of energy system is becoming more evident. This chapter focuses on the features of these particular technologies pertaining to their envisaged role in modern energy systems. The rest of chapter is organized as follows. In the next section, the most recent advances of IoT and blockchain in the energy sector are briefly discussed. Section 6.3 explores the role of these technologies in modern energy architectures through analyzing the evolution of energy architectures themselves, and then discusses the details of the how the functional and physical implementations of IoT and blockchain may be fused within these architectures in a framework that fulfills the demands of the modern energy system. Thereafter, security in modern energy systems is discussed in Section 6.4 and the features of the IoT and blockchain in this context are analyzed – including protocols, permissions, tokenization, smart contracts, etc. Section 6.5 then discusses the critical issue of policy, standards and regulations relating to deployment of IoT and blockchain in modern energy systems before a brief summary of the chapter is provided in Section 6.6.

6.2 LITERATURE REVIEW

IoT has been immensely successful as an enabler in the energy sector for optimization of energy and integration of distributed energy resources, which is a key factor in transition into a more sustainable, flexible, and decentralized modern energy system. However, the widespread deployment of IoT in the energy sector has created security and privacy vulnerabilities arising from the connected, centralized, client-server nature of these systems [19]. Blockchain is considered as the leading candidate and future trend in solving these vulnerabilities through its features as a decentralized, trustless platform [20]. While the argument for suitability of blockchain principles in the evolving energy sector is very compelling, the precise usability and practicability of these principles in achieving the goals of energy utilities are still under research and development [21].

The energy demands of the blockchain platforms in the energy environment – particularly in the face of the ubiquity brought about by modern IoT – is a pertinent focal point of current and future research, such as presented in [22], which proposes an on-demand energy supply scheme for optimizing energy benefit and supporting consensus protocols.

Several blockchain developmental projects in the energy domain are underway inter alia *Power Ledger*, *Share&Charge*, *NRGcoin*, *GrunStromJeton*, *SolarCoin*, *Grid Singularity*, and *Electron*, whereby many demonstrate a great deal of promise in terms of promoting transparency, trust, efficiency, security in the energy domain, with some having drawbacks in terms of scalability, maturity, interoperability and stability [23].

Although blockchain provides for the enhancement of the security, privacy autonomy, governance and integrity of IoT-based systems, another ongoing research challenge is the data flow from an architectural perspective [24]. As the suitability of the blockchain architecture in its principal format is largely deemed incompatible for integration and application in the IoT environment, there have been innovative proposals to augment architectures and alleviate limitations such as presented by the on-chain data allocation mechanism in [24], periodic updating data aggregation mechanisms with lightweight blockchain protocol in [25], and sliding window blockchain architecture in [26]. In [27], a multi-layered/tiered system architecture is proposed to service the new transactive energy paradigm in which blockchain plays a fundamental role.

Of course, a key feature of the modern energy system is the liberalization of the energy markets whereby there is collaborative energy production and consumption together with trading amongst prosumers and between prosumers and operators [28]. Although blockchain and IoT are believed to be inherently part of the solution to achieving this feature in new energy systems, there is still a lack of clarity on the operational models that could realize this feature. Thus, the research and development of operational frameworks for blockchain in energy trading systems is very much ongoing with crowdsourcing models and implementation schemes (including smart contracts and incentives mechanisms) being proposed [29]. In many newly proposed frameworks, smart contracts features as a key enabler of modern energy trading mechanisms for demand response, scheduling and energy auctioning through providing execution autonomy together with secure and transparent transactions [30].

Ultimately, in moving towards a modern energy system or IoE, IoT together with blockchain in particular is expected to have far reaching impacts on multiple aspects of the energy business and operation including billing and metering; sales and marketing; market regulation and trading; automation; grid management; security, identity and privacy management; competition; and resource sharing [31].

6.3 ARCHITECTURES AND FUSION

6.3.1 EVOLVING ENERGY SYSTEMS ARCHITECTURE

The emergence of SCADA had immense impact on power systems and revolutionized energy management system (EMS) architectures [32]. SCADA – through its continuous development of the years – brought modularity to the fore of EMSs and thus provided a growth path for more flexibility and scalable architectures to the extent of an "open architecture" idealization. More recently, the sustainability thrust with development and deployment of decentralized renewable energy sources (DRESs) has brought about a paradigm shift in energy systems architecture by bringing generation closer to where it consumed – i.e. true decentralization [33]. This together with the rapid advancement of electric vehicles, mixed AC/DC loads, battery storage systems, etc. prompted the emergence of the smart grid notion and its encompassing architectures and platforms to service the need of the then future electricity system. This most recent paradigm shift in architecture brings about obvious benefits in terms of resilience, scalability, efficiency and flexibility, whereby the concept and trend of microgrids were established as building blocks of a smart grid [34].

The ongoing development of the factors that prompted the emergence of the smart grid, such as active distribution networks, decentralized sources, and advanced loads, together with emerging requirements needs of the future electricity grid relating to the prosumer concept, liberalization of energy markets, added autonomy, and decentralized control place emphasis on trust, security, and resilience. As with the aforementioned technological advancements that have played key roles in the evolution of power systems, blockchain and IoT are similarly expected to have great impact. Both blockchain and IoT lend themselves to the concepts of truly decentralized architectures and framework by providing the security, trustlessness, and levels of autonomy and resilience that are demanded by the modern power system. In order to investigate and better understand how these technologies may suitably infuse the modern power system architecture with what is needed, we delve deeper into the working principles of blockchain and IoT architectures.

6.3.2 BLOCKCHAIN AND IoT ARCHITECTURES

The emergence of cryptocurrencies has seen the application of Distributed Ledger Technology (DLT) together with blockchain technology. This fundamental link is rooted in the underlying technology of Bitcoin, which was first introduced by Satoshi Nakamoto in the white paper that revealed the cryptocurrency [35]. While DLT and blockchain are not the same, it is envisaged that, like in cryptocurrencies, DLT will certainly have a role to play in modern energy systems in close relation to blockchain. According to the World Bank Group [36], "DLT refers to a novel and fast-evolving approach to recording and sharing data across multiple data stores (or ledgers)". This technology allows for transactions and data to be recorded, shared, and synchronized across a distributed network of different network participants".

Blockchain gives life to DLT in some applications by enabling decentralized storage, transmission, recording, and synchronizing of data in the distributed ledgers.

In this way, blockchain can be thought of as a type of implementation of DLT, as the DLT itself represents the transition from the centralized paradigm and puts forward the principles of decentralization of data. DLT itself is the founding ideology and blockchain is the breakthrough implementation of that ideology. Thus, the DLT ideology itself is critical to the evolution of modern energy systems architecture, as the principles of a decentralized paradigm commonly flows from this ideology. In other words, the combination of advancements of networking, cryptography, and computing enable realization of the DLT ideology, blockchain, and IoT can promulgate this ideology into modern energy systems.

The major principles of anonymity (or privacy) and trustlessness are rooted in DLT, which naturally arise from the decentralized architectural frameworks. Therefore, focus is placed here on the basic architectures arising from DLT ideology and fundamental characteristics thereof. In terms of the approach to architectural principles, there are both physical and functional perspectives when it comes to blockchain and IoT. Here, both perspectives are considered.

6.3.3 FUNCTIONAL PERSPECTIVES

A basic DLT framework consists of three core layers. These are the protocol, network, and data layers [37]. The protocol layer determines how the system interacts externally through specific rules. The network layer actually implements the protocol and connects various actors. The communications, transactions processing, and validation components are found in the network layer. The actual information flow through the system is represented by the data layer. This layer determines usage of data – i.e. creation, storage, modification, referencing, etc. The three layers of the framework are interdependent, but also have a hierarchal relationship – e.g. protocol determines data layer actions and not vice versa (Figure 6.2).

The generalized functional architecture for IoT-based systems can be simplified into three main layers – i.e. server/network, application/middleware and sensing/actuation layers. The sensing or actuation layer is the environmental or device interaction layer and consists of transducers and/or actuators. These could be the current

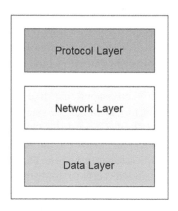

FIGURE 6.2   DLT functional architecture principle.

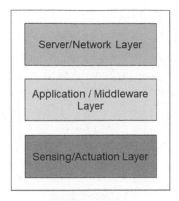

FIGURE 6.3 IoT functional architecture principle.

and voltage transducers on smart meters, as well as limit or isolation switches. In the case of the transducers, measurement data are transferred to the application or middleware layer. In the case of actuators, the control signal for actuation is received from the application of the middleware layer.

The communications between the sensing/actuation layer and application layer occurs over a variety of different platforms such as Bluetooth, Radio Frequency, integrated circuits, and other standard protocols, and is largely dependent on the range of distance between layers, cost, available energy, required data amounts and rates at which data is to be transferred.

The application layer serves as an interface to the server layer and carries out temporary data storage as well as low-level processing. The application layer may communicate to the network or server layer through WiFi, GSM, or wired network. Processing and storage of data occurs in the server/network layer (Figure 6.3).

6.3.4 PHYSICAL PERSPECTIVES

The traditional centralized architecture is well known by now and has been found to have many drawbacks over the years with respect to limitations on reliability, scalability, flexibility etc. The decentralized principle architecture is now making its way into various systems to alleviate the limitations posed by the traditional centralized principle. It should be noted that a key aspect of the centralized principle is controllability. However, as the need to overcome the aforementioned limitations has grown in specific settings, as well as the opportunity to secure decentralized nodes, the centralized architecture becomes more irrelevant in those settings. It is also important to note that although the term decentralized is often used interchangeably with distributed, these two concepts do differ. In general, distributed refers more to the spread of effort, while decentralized refers more to the control or instructions. For instance, in computing distributed would refer to the spread of computational effort amongst nodes, while decentralized would refer to the fact that no one node is instructing another. This simply means that centralized and distributed systems can and do exist – i.e. where control is centralized in one node but computing is distributed amongst many nodes (Figure 6.4).

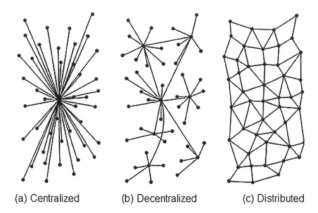

(a) Centralized   (b) Decentralized   (c) Distributed

FIGURE 6.4   (a) Centralized, (b) decentralized and (c) distributed principle architectures.

From a physical network perspective, computing generally follows from two of the most popular network architectures – i.e. the client–server architecture and the peer-to-peer (P2P) architecture [38].

The client–server architecture traditionally consists of a server, with high computational and storage capabilities, and the clients, which exist in a different hierarchal tier and request resources from the server. The server manages the allocation of these resources. This traditional approach offers the benefits of easier securing of data and management of resources but poses limitations on scalability and cost of the server, not to mention the high risk associated with the dependency of the network's reliability on the server [38]. On the other hand, the P2P architecture generally puts forward an anti-hierarchy concept whereby nodes can act as a client or server. This does resolve some of the cost, scalability, flexibility, and reliability challenges posed by the client-server architecture, but does introduce security vulnerabilities. Blockchain does work on the P2P architecture, but employs concepts from Game Theory to resolve the inherent security vulnerabilities by the architecture [39].

One such concept is derived from the Byzantine Generals' Problem, and relates to the core characteristic of consensus [40,41]. To illustrate this concept, the problem is briefly described here. Suppose the Byzantine Army wished to capture a city. Say that the army is divided into four groups, with each group assigned a leader – i.e. a commanding general, and three lieutenants. Hierarchically, the general gives orders to the lieutenants, and all can communicate among themselves about their attack plans using a messenger. Additionally, it should be noted here that the lieutenants or general may be a traitor and the city can only be taken over if most of the leaders attack in synchronism. If all leaders must issue the coordinated message between themselves then this provides a mechanism to overcome the risk of failure if a traitor is in the ranks. Take, for instance, one lieutenant is a traitor and the order from the commander to all lieutenants is to attack. Thereafter, each of the lieutenants, except the traitor, now relay the same attack message to each other. Each of the leaders will have received two attack messages and one retreat message, except for the traitor who would have received three attack messages. The city will still be captured as most of the army would attack. The same outcome is found if the commander is

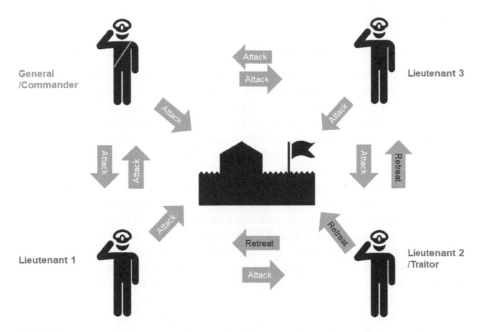

FIGURE 6.5 Byzantine Generals Problem concept from Game Theory analogous to consensus.

instead a traitor, and issues a different message to a lieutenant than to other lieutenants. This algorithm still functions as long as the number of traitors or rogue agents are less than one third. This basic concept in Game Theory is employed for the basis of a consensus algorithm, and similarly strategic decision-making over a blockchain network employs the concept analogous to that as demonstrated from the Prisoner Dilemma [42] (Figure 6.5).

6.3.5 TOWARDS BLOCKCHAIN- AND IOT-BASED ENERGY FRAMEWORKS

Blockchain and IoT are set to change architectures of future energy systems from both functional and physical perspectives. IoT is already being widely deployed by consumers and independent power producers. Many of these users deploy IoT for monitoring and controlling their consumption and production independently of centralized power networks, similarly to the vast upscaling that was experienced during the early evolution of the internet. Thus, liberalizing energy markets implies a technological opening up of networks for interfacing of private and public networks. This means that we are now witnessing a vast array of privately managed energy networks interfacing with public networks, with the need to have open architectures coupled with the appropriate security, trust, and resilience measures. Blockchain has emerged as a solution to providing a trustless and secure platform for transactions across these interfaces that does not require centralized control or intermediaries. While the technological advancements of IoT are already revolutionizing the modern energy system, it is only through the fusion or integration of blockchain within a new energy framework that will truly realize the envisaged future Internet of Energy

6.4   SECURITY

6.4.1   SECURE AND TRUSTLESS PLATFORMS IN MODERN ENERGY SYSTEMS

IoT has played a major role in steps towards the adoption of the IoE paradigm with seamless integration of the different domains and stakeholders, yet the smart grid has seemingly become more vulnerable with increased security attacks [21]. Blockchain is earning the reputation in several use cases across different industries as a means of establishing a secure and trustless platform upon which to transact. As mentioned, the underlying DLT system of blockchain realizes these features at the very foundations of implementable blockchain technology.

DLT is rooted in the evolution of ledgers themselves, which stemmed from the need to create, store and secure digital records of transactions. DLT meets this need through providing a 'ledger' that is not created or stored by one node or agent but is instead stored, appended, and validated by multiple nodes or agents across the network through consensus. This system has been a breakthrough in the evolution of digital trust because transactions can validated without the need for a central authority, and stored as an immutable recorded. Taking the concept of DLT into the realm of energy systems, it can be seen as fit for the purpose of establishing security and trustlessness with the liberalizing of energy systems and integration of open architectures. Thus, all manner and types of transactions across modern energy systems that require authentication, validation, immutable recording and storage, consensus etc. can be accommodated within DLT and, by extension, blockchain-based platforms. Blockchain implementations go beyond just the aforementioned DLT provisions – in relation to security and trustlessness – which enhances their suitability for modern energy systems – i.e. authentications and permissions features, smart contracts and tokenization. These extensions of the blockchain environment are briefly discussed here as they pertain to modern energy systems.

6.4.2   AUTHENTICATION, PERMISSION AND TOKENIZATION

In general, DLT systems and blockchain implementations make provisions for different user types by cryptographically securing access and permissions. Although there are broad categories of permissioned and permissionless systems, whereby all nodes can either participate openly or participate according to restrictions governed by an administrator, the protocols can be defined upon establishment of the blockchain and thus different levels of restrictions and privileges can be specified according to the nature and purpose of the application platform.

In a modern energy system, this protocol can vary as there are a several different instances whereby either permissioned, permissionless or combination thereof can apply to transaction platforms ranging from state and city levels to residential levels within housing clusters or apartment buildings, to charging stations for EVs etc.

Besides the advantages of disintermediation and decentralized offered by such a blockchain platform in the energy sector, there are the benefits of transparency and auditability which reduces the risk of fraud and enables reconciliation. Transactions basically constitute an exchange of value, and in the case of the aforementioned examples in the energy sector, this ultimately means energy trading. Blockchain implementations may rely upon tokens which are cryptographically secured digital objects that can represent access rights or value. The idea of credits or tokens are already widely used in energy trading which may be used by consumers in smart meters. Blockchain takes the concept of a token much further by enabling more flexibility and scalability in its application by providing different types such as utility, access, and payment tokens, as well as incorporating different value trading functionalities. This technological extension of blockchain creates the potential for individuals to exchange the same tokens in different regions whether he/she is charging their EV at a public facility or supplying excess PV generation from their home.

6.4.3 PUBLIC AND PRIVATE PROTOCOLS

Blockchain implementations to date can be broadly classified into private and public according to the access protocols. Private blockchains are restrictive in terms new nodes joining the chain whereas public blockchains are not. Therefore, the rules of interaction vary according to these different types of blockchain which essentially constitute the blockchain's governance. As this coincides with permissioned and permissionless systems, which refers to participation of nodes or agents in transaction processing, four broad categories of blockchain systems are applicable – i.e. permissioned private, permissionless private, permissioned public, and permissionless public blockchains. It is interesting to note that with the wide range of use cases within the energy sector, any of these categories are potentially applicable (Figure 6.6).

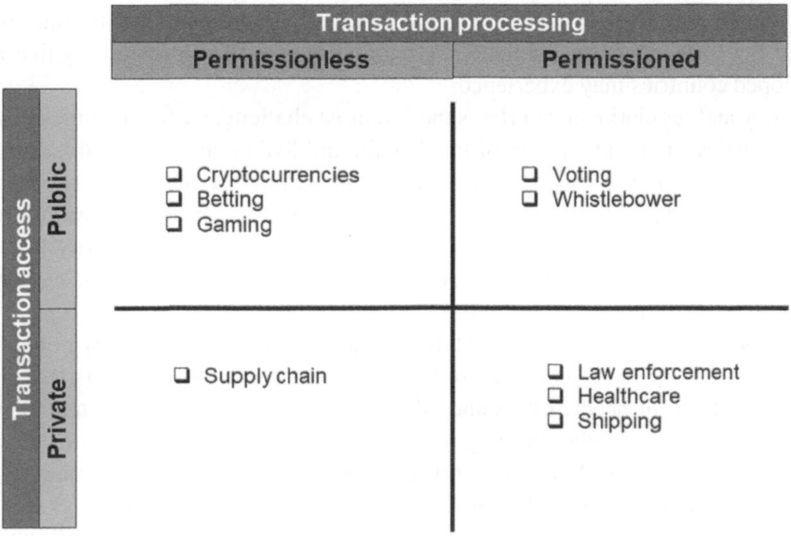

FIGURE 6.6 Types and use-cases of blockchain categories according to access and transaction processing.

6.4.4 SMART CONTRACTS

The various categories of transactions that could occur on the blockchain platforms in the energy sector are inherently linked with a range of actions. For example, the transaction whereby a large factory trades with the city would mean an exchange of money for a certain amount of energy. Before the execution of various actions relating to the transaction, there are various predetermined conditions and terms that need to be validated and adhered to, such as stipulated in the contract entered into between the parties. This transaction necessitates seamless and secure execution of related actions according to the predetermined conditions and terms. Similarly, different types of transactions would have associated executable actions. Smart contracts are scripts in the execution layer of the blockchain that enable execution of these actions, in a deterministic, consistent, stable, and seamless manner. The blockchain provides for these kinds of energy-sector use cases across the different nodes as a distributed application.

6.5 FUTURE DIRECTIONS

Although the energy sector has been relatively conservative in past with narrow focus in line with the aims of utilities in general, there have been gradual shifts in transition to new paradigms urged onwards by climate change and depletion of natural resources. The operational standards, policies and regulations have also been evolving in more recent times with a shift towards liberalization of energy markets and transition away from the modern centralized power system ideology. In fact, due to the rapid nature of this transition, many developing countries are yet to join this transition in the energy sector. On the other hand, since standard operating practices, policies, and regulations are also slow to meet the technological disruption, developing countries have the opportunity to leapfrog transition schemes into more modern formats as they would not suffer from the cumbersome regulatory and infrastructural lag that many developed countries may experience.

Policy and regulation are perhaps the foremost challenges when it comes to widespread deployment and take-up of blockchain and IoT in energy systems. Although blockchain was first conceived within the confines of the payment industry, there are still no clear legal rules and regulations in the sector [23]. This is somewhat justified as the technological development and implementation still lacks maturity in certain instances. Perhaps compounding this uncertainty, is the complexity of the technology that adds to the doubt of its usability [21].

For these reasons, more work that incorporates regulatory and energy policy players is needed [27]. Rules and regulations relating to the actual blockchain technology and its application need to be standardized in order to further its potential in the energy sector [8]. Furthermore, governmental policies relating to subsidies and incentive schemes will have to be reframed to recognize and incorporate the new trading mechanisms offered by blockchain and smart contracts for better transparency and auditability [9]. Additionally, the need for secure operation of IoT enhanced grids must lead to the creation of related policy and regulation, which is in turn expected to see the increased uptake of blockchain.

6.6 CONCLUSION

The evolution of the energy systems has experienced relatively rapid movement in recent years with the transition into more liberalized energy markets with increased penetration of distributed renewable energy resources and further decentralization. IoT has been immensely successful as an enabler in this paradigm shift of the energy sector by providing energy management with extended functionality, efficiency, flexibility, and resilience. However, the widespread deployment of IoT in the energy sector introduces security and privacy vulnerabilities arising from the connected, centralized, client–server nature of these systems. As a decentralized and trustless platform, blockchain is emerging as the foremost candidate in addressing these vulnerabilities.

In this chapter, we begin by examining how the trajectory of the aforementioned evolution of energy systems have come to intersect with blockchain and IoT technologies and examine the implications of their widespread deployment. We then analyze the state-of-the-art and ongoing research and development of blockchain and IoT applications in the energy domain, and extricate key aspects relating to their future development. Thereafter, the working principles of blockchain – as they pertain to the needs of the modern energy system – are described. Finally, the policy and regulatory shortfalls when it comes to blockchain and IoT in the energy sector are briefly described.

As the research and development into blockchain and IoT in modern energy systems is ongoing, there are several key future considerations that arise. While there has been much work on blockchain-secured trading, networks, information flow, etc. within different facets of the energy sector, the major challenge in achieving substantive progress is at the architectural level and how the combination of blockchain and IoT will practicably enhance energy management from remote localities in a trustless, stable, secure, and reliable manner. Furthermore, future development of such models needs to incorporate regulatory and energy policy players to mitigate uncertainties relating to the usability and sustainability of blockchain technology – in cohesion with IoT – in the energy environment.

REFERENCES

[1] Fiedler, H. J., and R. W. Swarthout. "Exploration of utility automation applications through supervisory control." *IEEE Transactions on Industrial Electronics and Control Instrumentation* 1 (1973): 12–20.

[2] Bruce, A. G. Reliability analysis of electric utility SCADA systems In *Proceedings of the 20th International Conference on Power Industry Computer Applications*, pp. 200–205. IEEE, 1997.

[3] Vu, Khoi, M. M. Begouic, and Damir Novosel. "Grids get smart protection and control." *IEEE Computer Applications in Power* 10, no. 4 (1997): 40–44.

[4] Hauser, Carl H., David E. Bakken, and Anjan Bose. "A failure to communicate: Next generation communication requirements, technologies, and architecture for the electric power grid." *IEEE Power and Energy Magazine* 3, no. 2 (2005): 47–55.

[5] Amin, S. Massoud, and Bruce F. Wollenberg. "Toward a smart grid: Power delivery for the 21st century." *IEEE Power and Energy Magazine* 3, no. 5 (2005): 34–41.

[6] Sheble, Gerald B. Smart grid millionaire *IEEE Power and Energy Magazine* 6, no. 1 (2007): 22–28.

[7] Garrity, Thomas F. "Getting smart." *IEEE Power and Energy Magazine* 6, no. 2 (2008): 38–45.

[8] Miglani, Arzoo, Neeraj Kumar, Vinay Chamola, and Sherali Zeadally. "Blockchain for Internet of Energy management: Review, solutions, and challenges." *Computer Communications* 151 (2020): 395–418.

[9] Zhu, Xingxiong. "Application of Blockchain technology in energy internet market and transaction." In *IOP Conference Series: Materials Science and Engineering*, vol. 592, no. 1, p. 012159. IOP Publishing, 2019.

[10] Manickam, A., Kamalasadan, S., Edwards, D. and Simmons, S., 2013. A novel self-evolving intelligent multiagent framework for power system control and protection. *IEEE Systems Journal*, 8(4): 1086–1095.

[11] Li, Gaolei, Jun Wu, Jianhua Li, Zhitao Guan, and Longhua Guo. "Fog computing-enabled secure demand response for Internet of energy against collusion attacks using consensus and ACE." *IEEE Access* 6 (2018): 11278–11288.

[12] Lin, Chun-Cheng, Der-Jiunn Deng, Wan-Yu Liu, and Linnan Chen. "Peak load shifting in the internet of energy with energy trading among end-users." *IEEE Access* 5 (2017): 1967–1976.

[13] Liu, Baoju, Peng Yu, Xue Song Qiu, and Lei Shi. "Risk-aware service routes planning for system protection communication networks of software-defined networking in energy internet." *IEEE Access* 8 (2020): 91005–91019.

[14] Cui, Hantao, Fangxing Li, and Kevin Tomsovic. "Cyber-physical system testbed for power system monitoring and wide-area control verification." *IET Energy Systems Integration* 2, no. 1 (2019): 32–39.

[15] Zhao, Bo, Xiangjin Wang, Da Lin, Madison M. Calvin, Julia C. Morgan, Ruwen Qin, and Caisheng Wang. "Energy management of multiple microgrids based on a system of systems architecture." *IEEE Transactions on Power Systems* 33, no. 6 (2018): 6410–6421.

[16] Di Santo, Michele, Alfredo Vaccaro, Domenico Villacci, and Eugenio Zimeo. A distributed architecture for online power systems security analysis *IEEE Transactions on Industrial Electronics* 51, no. 6 (2004): 1238–1248.

[17] Zhu, Daohua, Yajuan Guo, Jinming Chen, Yan Li, and Haitao Jiang. "Architecture and security protection scheme for distributed new energy public service platform with hybrid cloud system." *The Journal of Engineering*, no. 13 (2017): 2203–2206.

[18] Khan, Sarmadullah, Rafiullah Khan, and Ali Hilal Al-Bayatti. "Secure communication architecture for dynamic energy management in smart grid." *IEEE Power and Energy Technology Systems Journal* 6, no. 1 (2019): 47–58.

[19] Cardenas, D. Jonathan Sebastian, Adam Hahn, and Chen-Ching Liu. "Assessing cyber-physical risks of IoT-based energy devices in grid operations." *IEEE Access* 8 (2020): 61161–61173.

[20] Hossein Motlagh, Naser, Mahsa Mohammadrezaei, Julian Hunt, and Behnam Zakeri. "Internet of Things (IoT) and the energy sector." *Energies* 13, no. 2 (2020): 494.

[21] Kafol, C., Bregar, A. and Trilar, J. "Chapter 15: Blockchain for energy utilities." *DAAAM International Scientific Book*, (2018): 159–174.

[22] Li, Jianan, Zhenyu Zhou, Jun Wu, Jianhua Li, Shahid Mumtaz, Xi Lin, Haris Gacanin, and Sattam Alotaibi. "Decentralized on-demand energy supply for blockchain in Internet of Things: A microgrids approach." *IEEE Transactions on Computational Social Systems* 6, no. 6 (2019): 1395–1406.

[23] Bodkhe, Umesh, Sudeep Tanwar, Karan Parekh, Pimal Khanpara, Sudhanshu Tyagi, Neeraj Kumar, and Mamoun Alazab. "Blockchain for Industry 4.0: A comprehensive review." *IEEE Access* (2020): 1–37.

[24] Yánez, Wendy, Redowan Mahmud, Rami Bahsoon, Yuqun Zhang, and Rajkumar Buyya. "Data allocation mechanism for internet-of-things systems with Blockchain." *IEEE Internet of Things Journal* 7, no. 4 (2020): 3509–3522.

[25] Danzi, Pietro, Anders E. Kalør, Čedomir Stefanović, and Petar Popovski. "Delay and communication tradeoffs for blockchain systems with lightweight IoT clients." *IEEE Internet of Things Journal* 6, no. 2 (2019): 2354–2365.

[26] Koshy, Prescilla, Sarath Babu, and B. S. Manoj. "Sliding window Blockchain architecture for internet of things." *IEEE Internet of Things Journal* 7, no. 4 (2020): 3338–3348.

[27] Zia, Muhammad F., Mohamed Benbouzid, Elhoussin Elbouchikhi, S. M. Muyeen, Kuaanan Techato, and Josep M. Guerrero. "Microgrid transactive energy: Review, architectures, distributed ledger technologies, and market analysis." *IEEE Access* 8 (2020): 19410–19432.

[28] Park, Chankook, and Taeseok Yong. "Comparative review and discussion on P2P electricity trading." *Energy Procedia* 128 (2017): 3–9.

[29] Wang, Shen, Ahmad F. Taha, Jianhui Wang, Karla Kvaternik, and Adam Hahn. Energy crowdsourcing and peer-to-peer energy trading in blockchain-enabled smart grids *IEEE Transactions on Systems, Man, and Cybernetics: Systems* 49, no. 8 (2019): 1612–1623.

[30] Wang, Xiaonan, Wentao Yang, Sana Noor, Chang Chen, Miao Guo, and Koen H. van Dam. "Blockchain-based smart contract for energy demand management." *Energy Procedia* 158 (2019): 2719–2724.

[31] Andoni, Merlinda, Valentin Robu, David Flynn, Simone Abram, Dale Geach, David Jenkins, Peter McCallum, and Andrew Peacock. "Blockchain technology in the energy sector: A systematic review of challenges and opportunities." *Renewable and Sustainable Energy Reviews* 100 (2019): 143–174.

[32] Ockwell, Gary, and R. Kreger. The impact of hardware on open architecture on power systems *IEEE Transactions on Power Systems* 9, no. 1 (1994): 1–5.

[33] Doorsamy, Wesley, and Willem A. Cronje. Sustainability of decentralized renewable energy systems in Sub-Saharan Africa In *Proceedings of 2015 International Conference on Renewable Energy Research and Applications (ICRERA)*, pp. 644–648. IEEE, 2015.

[34] Hatziargyriou, Nikos, ed. *Microgrids: architectures and control.* Chichester: John Wiley & Sons, 2014.

[35] Nakamoto, Satoshi. *"Bitcoin: A peer-to-peer electronic cash system."* (2008).

[36] Natarajan, Harish, Solvej Karla Krause, and Helen Luskin Gradstein. *Distributed Ledger Technology (DLT) and blockchain.* FinTech note; no. 1., World Bank Group, Washington, DC, 2019.

[37] Rauchs, Michel, Andrew Glidden, Brian Gordon, Gina C. Pieters, Martino Recanatini, Francois Rostand, Kathryn Vagneur, and Bryan Zheng Zhang. Distributed ledger technology systems: A conceptual framework Available at SSRN 3230013, 2018.

[38] Liu, Lu, and Nick Antonopoulos. From client-server to p2p networking In *Handbook of Peer-to-Peer Networking*, pp. 71–89. Springer, Boston, MA, 2010.

[39] Bambara, Joseph J., Paul R. Allen, Kedar Iyer, Rene Madsen, Solomon Lederer, and Michael Wuehler. *Blockchain: A practical guide to developing business, law, and technology solutions.* McGraw Hill Professional, 2018.

[40] Dhillon, Vikram, David Metcalf, and Max Hooper. *Blockchain enabled applications: understand the blockchain ecosystem and how to make it work for you.* New York: New Apress, 2017.

[41] Hu, Wei, Yawei Hu, Wenhui Yao, and Huanhao Li. "A blockchain-based Byzantine consensus algorithm for information authentication of the Internet of vehicles." *IEEE Access* 7 (2019): 139703–139711.

[42] Singhal, Bikramaditya, Gautam Dhameja, and Priyansu Sekhar Panda. *Beginning Blockchain: A Beginner's Guide to Building Blockchain Solutions.* New York: Apress, 2018.

KEYWORDS AND DESCRIPTIONS

Blockchain   A cryptographically secured system for recording information.

Internet of Things (IoT)   A network of interrelated physical-objects (computing devices, sensors etc.) connected over the internet.

Internet of Energy (IoE)   Energy network management and optimization through various edge devices.

Distributed   Architectural principle referring to the spread of computational effort amongst nodes of a network.

Decentralized   Architectural principle whereby no one node in a network is instructing another.

7 Solar Energy Generation and Internet of Energy (IoE)
Challenges and Purview

Sanghita Baidya and Champa Nandi

Tripura University, Agartala, Tripura, India

CONTENTS

7.1　Background 175
　　　7.1.1　Introduction 176
7.2　Literature Review 178
7.3　Solar Energy Generation 180
7.4　IOE Scenario 181
　　　7.4.1　IOE for Solar Power Generation 181
　　　7.4.2　IoE and Energy Management 183
7.5　Role of IOE in Solar Industry 184
7.6　Role of IOE in Protection of Integrated Grid 184
7.7　Role of IOE in Automation of Power System Network 185
7.8　Role of IOE on Security Planning in Power System Network 185
7.9　Challenges 186
7.10　Advantages and Opportunities 186
7.11　Future Directions 187
7.12　Conclusions 187
References 187
Keywords and Descriptions 191

7.1 BACKGROUND

The consumption of electricity has drastically increased due to the modernization of societies and the development of industries. Population growth has also been increasing the consumption level of electricity recently. As the main source of power generation all over the world is fossil fuel, excessive growth of electricity consumption increases the diminishing rate of fossil fuel reserves. The limitless use of fossil fuel for energy generation also has a bad effect on the environment, which causes global warming, climate change, etc. Thus, researchers focus on Renewable Energy Sources (RES) for power generation. It is a clean and green energy that means power generation using renewable energy is environment friendly. The use of renewable energy plays a crucial role in increasing global public awareness for protecting the environment. The most abundantly available renewable energy is solar energy. In addition, wind energy, hydro energy, and tidal energy are also used for electricity production. RES are integrated into the existing power grids to make a decentralized power network. Smart grids and microgrids are recent developments in the energy sector. They use distributed renewable energy sources for electricity generation and the bidirectional flow of energy can be seen here. But to manage all the complexity of the power network integrated with RES required a better performance analysis tool. The Internet of Energy (IoE) or Energy Internet is proving this facility to the energy system. It is the bigger concept of the Internet of Things (IoT). To make an automated power network IoE offers an imperative point. For making a real-time protection system in the power grids IoE provides a better communication network with a secure transformation of data and information. The bidirectional flow of energy is more secure while implemented with IoE technology.

7.1.1 INTRODUCTION

To mitigate the excessive growth of greenhouse gases, different control strategies are being implemented. Focusing on renewable energy generation provides a better scope on that matter because energy generation using renewable sources is an eco-friendly phenomenon. The target of greenhouse gas alleviation with the implementation of renewable energy has a positive impact on the industrial and commercial sectors. It is an important and optimistic fact to set the mitigation target on both the possibility of investing the amount of renewable energy and the investment of renewable energy [1]. India has a huge scope to generate electricity using solar energy, as about 5,000 trillion kWh solar radiations in each year are incident over the landmass of India, and they have $0.25kWh/m2$ solar power potential on an average of daily basis [2]. The most interesting thing about solar power generation is that the power plant is independent of any raw material as it is abundantly available by nature. There is also a possibility of the replacement of conventional energy sources to renewable energy sources. The solar energy prospective of India can meet the demand for electricity that may provide energy consumption of per capita base at par with Japan or the USA at the time of peak inhabitants in its demographic transition [2,15,51]. For the last two decades, the rising growth of renewable energy sources along with distributed energy source use in power grids has produced fresh challenges towards the conventional power supply with efficient quality of voltage stabilization. The utilization of renewable energy sources is increased in a rapid manner. Many power electronic devices like power converters are used to combine the solar PV based microgrids with the utility grids. Smart buildings also use those devices for making connections to transmission and distribution systems. Hence the power quality gets affected by the deterioration and harmonics in the general coupling point. The issues regarding power quality and its mitigation are facing electric utility companies [3]. The price of solar panels is gradually decreasing with the advancement of technology. Thus, the installation of the solar PV system is increasing rapidly [4,5]. The existence of arcing faults in the solar system, as well as the energy system, leads to a higher risk of human safety not only in industrial or commercial areas but also in residential means. As the risk is increased day by day, it is a great matter of concern to supply safe and reliable solar energy worldwide. Thus, the detection of an arc fault is extremely important so that a requirement for high penetration of PV can be balanced. The most important task is to detect the arc flash, as it remains for a very short period of time and may lead to a huge fire if not detected properly in due time. It also breaks down the insolation level of the conductors. In the PV array, the flow of current due to arc flash has a very short period of time in the ion path or ionized path [6]. In North America, 600 V DC and in Europe 1000 V DC power is generated from large solar PV installations. The increasing demand to use solar DC voltage levels also has led to the development of PV systems, which also increases the risk of DC arc faults. When the flow of current from one conductor to another is disturbed due to gaping or breakage of the conductors, an electrical arc fault is generated between them. This arc produces heat and thus causes a fire. The risk of DC arcs is developing due to conductors or insulation deterioration, damage on connectors and cables, components aging, etc. Hence, arc faults are considered a common fault event in PV systems. The generation of electrical arc faults on the PV system causes significant damage along with consequent losses. Power generation from the PV system is very sensitive towards the developed arc fault in the system. Thus, to prevent the hazardous situation of different types of faults some safety standards are specified by technical societies [7].

Presently, the Internet of Energy (IoE) technology is becoming a research hotspot and front line in the energy meadow. It is also important for future energy systems [16,17]. Limitations on the use of fossil energy including the worse effects on the environment (climate change, global warming, etc.), enhance the interest of using renewable energy to endorse the transformation of the energy market. Thus, the focus of energy flow structure in the power system is shifted on the use of IoE for better economic operation. The IoE [18] is an absolute energy ecosystem. In the conventional models of energy interconnection in the power network production side and demand side are subverted. But with the implementation of the energy internet each participant will become a community of energy generation and consumption [19]. IoE provides a smart distributed energy system that is able to organize, optimize, collect, and manage the information of energy networks from a variety of edge devices [20].

Though a number of studies based on the IoE domain have already been conducted, this chapter is a separate attempt to overview the ongoing challenges and possibilities of IoE technology in the power network. This chapter also implies the benefits of the use of IoE concept in different fields such as microgrids, smart-grids, smart homes, etc. for maintaining superior communication, power transfer, privacy concerns, and many more including future research interest. The remaining parts of the chapter are organized as follows; Section 7.5 discusses the key factors relating to the generation of solar energy as an alternative of conventional energy. The Internet of Energy (IoE) is described in Section 7.6. The other sections i.e. Section 7.7; Section 7.8 and Section 7.9 give an idea about some important areas of IoE application respectively. The existing challenges and possibilities of IoE technology are identified in Section 7.10 and Section 7.11 respectively. Finally, the conclusion and upcoming possible trends are provided in Section 7.12.

7.2 LITERATURE REVIEW

To deliver a reliable, eco-friendly, and efficient power supply in the power network along with the consumer side Internet of Renewable Energy (IoRE), technology plays a vital role. It is a green energy platform that can offer pollution-free power generation grids. In [15] renewable energy source based eco-friendly electricity grid architecture is designed with the IoRE platform. Controllers and different types of sensors are used to maintain the operation of the IoRE system. For testing the feasibility of this approach, the experimental setup and the simulation model are targeted in future work.

With the idea of energy interconnection within the modern grid, an in-depth analysis is carried out in [19] based on the uniqueness of the IoE technology on the distribution side. A new evaluation index model based on a fuzzy comprehensive evaluation method is established here that enhances the economic operation of the distribution side with interfacing energy internet. It is observed that the index method satisfies thermal demand, information sharing, transportation demand, the requirement of energy storage, the demand for natural gas, and the requirement of coordination deployment. The main purpose of this approach is to minimize the consumption of energy and reduce the electrical loss in the network thus improving its economic efficiency. In addition, static security anxiety and planning to reconstruct the power grid for implementing energy internet to get multi-energy flows are the concerning matter for the future [19].

In [21] a new learning tool is demonstrated to train professional images, like engineers, technicians, and entrepreneurs those who required better skills in the meadow of Energy Internet. The aim of this proposed tool is to overcome the need for experimental knowledge to deal with the challenges incorporated with the smart grids for implementing IoE technology. To improve the skill of implementing the IoE in the power grids and to manage the complex distributed configuration of the power network, advanced tools are very crucial. This proposed tool is designed for smart rural houses embedded with measuring and controlling units based on a small-scale laboratory demonstrator. The demonstrator can access remotely through web server applications with a minimum cost affected single-board computer and it is also able to replicate the actual performance of a smart microgrid connected with several subsystems such as storage of energy, charging of power stations, and generation of electricity from renewable energy. The tested results (in reduced scale) using this demonstrator provided a close output with the real operating conditions in power grids.

The aim in [22] is to integrate the distributed prosumers and the small-scale virtual power plants (VPP) through the IoE network. The advanced features of IoE technology are suitable for managing a better control over the prosumers, VPPs, and distributed energy resources (DERs) along with effective optimization strategies. Transaction of energy by the prosumers in a bidirectional way is a vital element of IoE. The energy management and control strategies, infrastructure, and functions of DERs and VPP of the prosumer side are reviewed and systematically summarized in [22]. A comparative analysis with a traditional grid based on the characteristics of IoE is also given in this study. Basically, an overview of present trends of optimization along with the mathematical formulation types and behaviors are presented. The findings in [22] contribute to the improvement in the relation among the IoE, prosumers, and

VPPs. This study can be extended to investigate the reason for communication delay, uncertain economic dispatch, and disruptive distribution of VPP, etc.

In this section, the Internet of Energy (IoE) is an extended form of the Internet of Things (IoT). The broader idea in the platform of IoT developed the concept of IoE. In addition to sensor technology, IoT takes up a worldwide network to transform data and information via different types of gateways incorporating internet protocols. The energy market also frames its structure by the IoE technology. The electricity market based on renewable energy sources adopts IoE, which brings smart homes, electric vehicles, smart meters, exchange of energy, and sharing information in grids. The study in [25] shows that problems regarding the connection speed and compatibility, etc. can be maintained by using IoE application among households and consumers. IoE plays a decisive role in transitioning the existing electricity system to a high-renewable electricity network suitable to the twenty-first century. The findings in [25] demonstrated that the IoE technology can provide effective control and efficient operation in the decentralized approaches of the energy system. The main objective of this work is to reduce the total cost of the energy system that included the system's operating cost and investment cost and to minimize carbon emissions. Developing a pollution-free technology based on the IoE approach that can offer better energy efficiency, advance strategies for demand-side management, and balanced power flow in both supply and demand side is the actual focus in [25].

Due to the integration of distributed renewable energy sources in the power grids, multi-tapping is seen in the transmission and distribution lines. This increased the complexity in both operation and protection of the power network because a two-way energy flow phenomenon is offered by the multi-tapped lines. The fault current may flow in different directions in the protection relays. Thus, in [33] a novel i-protection scheme has been adopted that works on every single zone instead of multiple separate zones similar to conventional protection schemes. It is shown from the results that the proposed protection scheme is able to detect all types of faults successfully in composite multi-tapped transmission lines with different distributed renewable resources. For sharing the information and real-time based decisions an IoE oriented communication protocol is developed in the infrastructure of grid protection. The proposed work can provide a solution against the complex conditions in transmission and sub-transmission levels due to multi-terminals in the smart grid power network. The result also slows the successful output after integrating the i-protection scheme in integrated grids. But the issues regarding coordination with conventional grid protection schemes do not come across.

In [34] the focus is concentrated on bidirectional energy flow in the energy market. It also investigates the issues of two-way transfer of data and information in the energy system. The concept of IoE integrated with smart grids is beneficial for saving power, optimizing it, and delivering it accurately where it is needed. The future energy networks are possible to be automated through the artificial intelligence (AI) approach.

It is observed that investments into smart grids were increased by about 10% in the year 2018 due to the implementation of IoE in smart grids. But the uncertainty of implementing the 5G network with existing frameworks may slow down the rate. The whole idea of IoE with smart grids truly represented a leading concept in the energy network. Large volumes of information exchanging between the generating companies and the consumers and real-time decision-making platforms are required in an automated feature-based smart grid (i.e. IoE integrated smart grid) to deal with the complex operating conditions in the energy network.

7.3   SOLAR ENERGY GENERATION

Over the last decades, awareness for minimizing greenhouse gases has been highly recommended, which enhanced the use of photovoltaic power generation as it is clean, sustainable, and abundantly available. On the other hand, low-maintenance and minimum operation cost make the solar PV system more attractive to use. However, extended operation of the photovoltaic power generation system would cause high dilapidation rates (such as a median of 0.5%/year). As the solar panels are bonded to deal with the harsh outdoor environment, the power generation operation suffers from various types of faults. Thus, it drastically decreases the power generation and diminishes the durability of solar panels. This also increases the risk of shutdown of the whole system. Hence, to maintain power generation and a reliable power supply, safe, and more efficient proper fault detection and diagnosis are essential. For tracking the operating condition of individual strings, it is important to measure the voltage and current of each PV module in the system [8,52]. The voltage stabilization, power quality, and utilization of efficient energy generated from renewable energy sources are facing different types of challenges when used as distributed energy. In most of the utility grids power, electronic devices are widely used to interface the various energy storing and other types of equipment in the system. The power electronic devices are also integrated with the smart buildings for transmission and distribution of energy from the generating systems. The emerging growth of distributed generation (DG) based on renewable energy sources prolonged and accelerated the function of power electronic converters for proficient electrical utilization. The integration of power electronic devices also enhanced the safety and consistency of the electric utility grid. Also, new applications have appeared for standalone microgrids that increase the attention of using solar photovoltaic (PV) systems, biomass, micro-hydroelectric system, wind energy, etc. with regards to renewable energy utilization. To maintain the availability of power supply in remote villages storage and energy management is also a focusing matter. Power electronic converters are used in both transmission and distribution network of a utility grid based on renewable energy sources (RESs) [9]. Solar photovoltaic (PV) arrays, biomass power plants, micro wind turbines, fuel cells, etc. are the renewable energy-based power generation approaches that use distributed generators and thus utilized in the utility network [10]. The growth of the solar photovoltaic (PV) industry depends on the flexibility, efficiency, application, and reliability of the generated power supply from the PV system. Solar photovoltaic systems have a long life, which is beneficial for large installations [11]. The noticeable qualities associated with solar power utilization are high sustainability, reduced emission of greenhouse gases, and better economic operation[48]. These enhance and encourage the interest of using PV systems in the microgrid with wide penetration. On the other hand, the excessive growth of energy demands and the continuous decline of fossil fuels have aggravated the search for substitute energy sources [49]. Thus, the concept of distributed power generation with renewable energy sources is adopted for providing a reliable power supply that introduced microgrids in the power system. In this regard, as solar energy is easily available, with an easy installation process and easily electricity generated source, this (solar energy) distributed renewable energy gets more attention in the field of a microgrid worldwide than other renewable energy sources based on distributed energy generation [12,46].

7.4   IOE SCENARIO

Recently, the energy sector is becoming a favorite target of application of digital transformation. Collecting data in a huge quantity, analyzing it, and making cross-correlation among those with big data techniques required smart management policies in new businesses. Power grids are continuously dealing with a large number of data to control, optimize, and forecast the real-time information in the energy system [21]. Transactions can be secured by using the blockchain concept. The power companies have a powerful economic background, but they also have to deal with a huge amount of data that include energy generators, providers, and consumers. The concept of "Internet of Energy (IoE)" consists of a smart energy meter for monitoring purposes, smart devices (such as smart power storage, smart electrical tools, etc.) interconnected with smart grids, microgrids, etc. for establishing smart energy networks. The modern energy supply chain may suffer from uncertain cyber-attack and privacy leakage [41] (Figure 7.1).

7.4.1   IOE FOR SOLAR POWER GENERATION

Greenhouse gas emission control is a burning matter of concern now. In this regard, use of renewable energy sources, especially solar energy, plays a vital role. Energy Internet (EI) also faced the challenges regarding power supply for increasing demand for electricity. Due to the lack of green energy management, power generation is not able to fulfill the energy demand at peak load hours. At present, EI has an important position in the third industrial revolution. The Energy Internet is controlling the replacement of fossil fuels with renewable energy sources in the energy market. Thus, it is helping in the sustainable growth of energy systems with a green energy atmosphere that has the least carbon emissions. On the other hand, sustainable growth of energy is hampered due to rising complexity in energy planning, which directly affects the social economy, environmental, and technical media of energy supply. Thus, it is very important to consider every criterion while designing any scheme for power generation. Complex scenarios in power generation may deal with a multiple criteria decision-making (MCDM) network that can give optimal solutions using indicators. The flexibility of this scheme for the decision-making of special objectives and criteria makes it beneficial. The benefits of the modern energy market are not able to reach every corner of the world. Thus, globally most peoples are deprived of enjoying the facilities of a modern energy system. The existing techniques of power generation

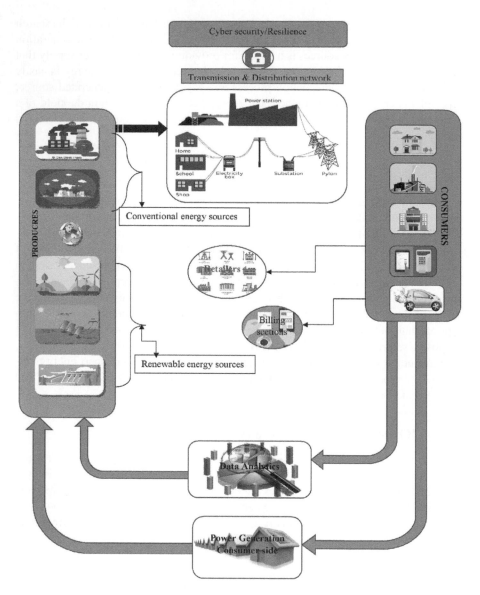

FIGURE7.1   Modern energy supply chain.

from conventional energy sources have a detrimental effect on living things along with the environment by excessive emission of greenhouse gases and global deforestation. Hence, the generation of electricity should have the ability to improve the reliability and sustainable growth of the energy market. Approximately 30% of the energy demand in India is satisfied by renewable energy sources (like solar, wind, hydro, biomass, etc.). MCDM technology is helping with energy planning by dealing with different features that also improve energy generation and supply [22–24].

7.4.2 IoE and Energy Management

Internet of Energy (IoE) is now becoming a highly important concept for designing a realistic electricity market with a high-renewable energy system in the future. The idea of IoE is developed from the broader conception of the Internet of Things (IoT). IoT can integrate household appliances, vehicles, smart meters, and many more things with tiny devices that facilitate real-time bidirectional interflow of information along with keeping a record of the data that optimize their uses. IoE is able to make a real-time cooperative bonding among smart meters, solar panels, electric vehicles, smart homes, wind turbines with a peer-to-peer (P2P) exchange of energy flow between generating units (such as smart grids, microgrids, etc.) and prosumers. Electric vehicles can be charged from the optimized location of charging stations by using the IoE facility [25].

The use of renewable energy sources can be increased by incorporating IoE technology with it. It will improve the level of energy generation to energy consumption allowing freedom in a modified two-way power flow network. All the previous models of power flow follow the top-down approach, i.e. flow of energy from the generator to the consumer (unidirectional flow of energy). But the appearance of IoE will provide bidirectional energy flow in the system and also enhance the battery storage at both the distribution side and transmission side of an energy network. [22,26–28].

Many technologies (such as PLC) are used to detect faults, isolate that faulty part, and restore the system after clearing the fault. For real-time monitoring, controlling, and supervising power stations and sub-stations, SCADA is used. SCADA is a digital system based on computer interfacing devices that collect information, transmit it, and manage data transfer in the different networks coming from various sensors, through a graphical user interface (GUI). It also consists of a human-machine interface (HMI) for controlling the system and supervising the management. But due to sudden changes in environmental conditions energy generation from renewable energy sources are not certain and these changes also lead to complexities in energy production along with the power supply to complex and variable loads. Hence, an advanced communication system is required that can detect any abnormalities in the whole power system and can give an alert signal so that necessary steps can be taken to deal with the situation. The machine-to-machine (M2M) communication system is a similar technology that is able to transfer data and communicate with different embedded devices in the power system network. The combined work of the M2M and SCADA system makes an automatically distributed management in the power system. The use of M2M communication technology enables peer-to-peer energy transfer in a bidirectional way. It is also beneficial for managing power distribution at peak load hours. It makes the power system automated, smarter and energy efficient. In a smart grid, automatic communication technologies are used to interlink various energy devices, variable loads, household appliances, and weather dependent loads. For better energy management, IoE models are able to save the records of power consumption of individual consumers [22,29,30,45,50].

7.5   ROLE OF IOE IN SOLAR INDUSTRY

In the renewable energy market, solar PV energy is playing a crucial role as a source of sustainable energy supply to meet the upcoming energy crisis in the future. The use of rooftop solar PV systems is now integrated with existing grids for bidirectional power supply. Thus, to obtain records of all generation, useable, and transferred data in the PV system real-time assessment is very essential. For better grid stability and efficient performance of the integrated solar energy network, a real-time appraisal system is required [30]. In this regard IoE is providing several advantages to make coordination between solar energy generation sources and existing grids while they are amalgamated. IoE is used for facilitating virtual power plants (VPP) that are introduced by prosumers. Bidirectional energy transactions of prosumers are a crucial feature of the IoE. To incorporate energy devices with one another in the solar PV system, the plug-and-play feature of IoE can be used. This process is similar to transferring information on a computer through a USB. The main advantage of this plug-and-play facility in IoE is that it allows distributed RES and energy storage to connect automatically with the grid. It also assists in contributing to customers' demand-side management without any adjustment to the system. For an immediate transaction of power in a bidirectional way and integration of RES with the grids, an open-standard-based communication protocol is used in IoE platform [30].

7.6   ROLE OF IOE IN PROTECTION OF INTEGRATED GRID

For supplying different types of loads transmission and sub-transmission lines are tapped. Sometimes renewable resources (RRs) i.e. wind or solar farms (medium-size generation farms) are also integrated with the lines through tapping. The use of line tapping can prevent the building of new stations. But it introduces operational and protection challenges. The connection of renewable resources with the feeders acted as transmission lines. Here, flow of energy is bidirectional in protection relays. Thus, fault current flows in diverse directions. Therefore, coordination protection schemes for this configuration have failed. Existing standalone based protection methods are inappropriate in such cases. Hence a new approach for protecting the power network should be devised [31]. For enhancing the performance of energy supply IoE-based technologies are preferable. In the case of transferring information, maintaining communication, and measurements on transmission and sub-transmission systems IoE can provide an accurate platform and optimize the environment in the coordination process. The overcurrent devices incorporated with radial systems can detect faults that flow in one direction. Hence advanced fault detection techniques are required for detecting faults on feeders connected with RRs. [32].

In [33] an i-protection method is presented that uses intelligent electronic devices (IEDs) for accurate fault detection. It also uses IoE with the IEEE 802.16 wireless protocol. To get protection from multi-tapped complex situations this type of technology is first used. I-protection provides the feature of considering a configuration as one zone instead of multiple zones. The i-protection system consists of IEDs, a base station, and a switching center. For protecting the grids a switching center is considered. The decision is made based on the shared information for relays, instead of the data of standalone relays.

7.7 ROLE OF IOE IN AUTOMATION OF POWER SYSTEM NETWORK

To maintain the stability of the grid intelligent energy management systems are playing a crucial role by balancing power generation with power consumption. The supply of power and its demand can be independently synchronized through IoE between consumers and prosumers. In addition, IoE includes a weather forecasting facility, measurement of traffic flows, and much more information related to upcoming needs regarding energy generation and consumption. The automation of the power system can be marked as a self-protection, self-healing, self-configuration, and self-optimizing system. An automatic power system (APS) can give different types of solutions regarding the issues related to volatile energy prices, global warming, the variability of power production and its distribution, increasing population, etc. Moreover, the continuous growth of smart meters, smart vehicles, and smart houses is embedded within one single system via the IoE. IoE-embedded electric vehicles can be interconnected with grids, which may be called grid-to-vehicle and vehicle-to-grid technologies. This technology is based on the concept of a bidirectional flow of energy where the excessive electricity after recharging the electric vehicles gets back to the grid. In this regard, IoE is beneficial as it is useful to sell the extra power to other electrical vehicles or back to the grids remotely. IoE provides various tools and pathways to optimize the exchange of data and power along with other transactions between the grids and users in an effective bidirectional way [34].

Due to the presence of several forms of energy interconnected with the power distributed side through the Energy Internet, it improves capacity, reserve margin, and reduces the unwanted losses in the active distribution network. It gives an indispensable contribution to the improvement of economic operation and maintaining the reliability of the system. The index system incorporated with the Energy Internet in power networks is advantageous to satisfy the demand of power transportation, natural gas, and thermal requirements, need of energy storage, coordination deployment, and information sharing in an automated manner [19].

7.8 ROLE OF IOE ON SECURITY PLANNING IN POWER SYSTEM NETWORK

The IoE has also extended its scope of application in the industrial energy market in the form of the Industrial Internet of Things (IIoT). The integration of numerous IoT devices in the energy network allows a decentralized and diversified power supply in the network. In addition, IoE facilitates a better communication network between consumers and distributed sources of energy generation. Due to the incorporation of Energy Internet technology in the energy market, most of the energy transactions are taking place through the online mode as well as other varied forms of the transaction [42]. This in turn leads to a wide range of problems in the conventional models of energy trading. Some of the major issues encountered are cyber-attacks, scalability issues, insufficient processing effectiveness, etc. Though power supply companies provide a platform for power trade and allied services, a major proportion of the centralized energy trading market is also occupied by them. But they cannot provide guaranteed privacy and security for the trading of energy when it is integrated with a decentralized energy trading platform. Hence, to handle the excessive amount of data in a secured and efficient way, a revolutionary blockchain technology based on the IoE platform needs to be introduced in the field of decentralized energy trading [43–44].

7.9 CHALLENGES

Some socio-technical challenges are:

1. Complex power flow management
2. Intermittency of weather-dependent Renewable Energy Sources (RESs),
3. Maintaining consistency in energy market and resiliency under dynamic situations and
4. Deregulated energy systems.
5. Modern dynamic loads (like electrical vehicles), advanced types of mobile, etc.

These are the common concerning issues that gave an additional layer of challenges in a reliable supply of energy. On the other hand, prosumers are facing problems with communication, transactions, data, and information sharing within the power network due to a poor infrastructure for small-scale power generation. [2,4,35–36]. Moreover, the fluctuations of the price of energy and the uncertainties of power generation due to irregular RESs make small-scale customers susceptible to a burden of economic losses or penalties enforced by the aggregators. Moreover, hacking and cyber-attacks also create issues in IoE technology. A third-party involvement is common in the use of public-key cryptography. The charges per unit of energy consumption are also changing dynamically during the time intervals. Demand management, P2P energy trading, privacy concern, grid operation issues, etc. are the general challenges with centralized IoE technology [37]. Different types of modern methods have recently been adopted in power grids for evaluation of its operation, such as the BP neural network method, fuzzy comprehensive evaluation method, AHP, data envelope method, Gray correlation method, and TOPSIS method, etc. To improve the evaluation of operation in most situations a combined model of the above methods is preferred [15,16]. This makes the calculation process very intricate with a larger amount of data for calculation. It affects the speed of calculation and limits practical applications [19].

7.10 ADVANTAGES AND OPPORTUNITIES

- Bidirectional energy flow between grids and prosumers.
- Real-time cost-effective solution to consumers by controlling flexible loads and shifting the time of operation of the loads from peak to off-peak hours. Thus, minimizes the cost of electricity [38].

- Improving the level of communication by offering reliable transfer of data and information among the power network/ energy market[36,39,40].
- Energy Internet can used to evaluate economic operation in an active distribution energy network [19].
- Energy saving and to make an effective intervention for sharing energy to target oriented locations [22].
- Incorporation of blockchain technology with the IoE domain can give a better platform for handling security issues, privacy problems, and P2P energy trading [37].

7.11 FUTURE DIRECTIONS

IoE plays a vital role in future urban construction as there is a close relation between city and energy consumption. The IoE environment can provide various opportunities for the urban energy market, such as charging stations for electrical vehicles, decentralized energy controlling mechanism, other transportation networks, energy trading platforms, etc. But the challenging parts are system planning, commercial operation, the configuration of equipment, controlling of operation, etc. which should be investigated in the future [47].

7.12 CONCLUSIONS

The energy sector is considered an effective candidate for implementing IoE technology. The aim of this chapter is to provide a holistic view of IoE-based approaches offered in the energy market. It discusses the issues and possibilities with the IoE concept in power grids. The effectiveness of the use of Energy Internet is shown here with different studies in different fields in the energy sector.

The framework of the IoE-based concept enhanced the line of learning and future research work in this domain. The collaboration of artificial intelligence (AI) with IoE can offer an advanced infrastructure in the energy sector. IoE mainly consists of sensors, advanced technologies, high-speed internet connection, and smart configurations that provide better communication among the utilities such as electric vehicles, smart meters, power grid equipment, etc. in the energy network. For maintaining the privacy and security of energy trading blockchain technology is integrated with IoE. But the integration of AI and blockchain with IoE faces different types of issues that can be tried to solve in future research work.

REFERENCES

[1] Derek, D., Wanga, B. and Toshiyuki, S. (2018). Climate change mitigation targets set by global firms: Overview and implications for renewable energy. *Journal of Renewable and Sustainable Energy Reviews*, 94(October), 386–398.
[2] Daisy, I. J., Manimekalai, V. and Hari, S. (2017). *An overview of power generation and scope for renewable energy in India*. In *Proceedings of the 2nd International Conference on Communication and Electronics Systems (ICCES)*, (pp. 19–20). Coimbatore, India.

[3] Foad, H. G., Abdollah, A., Adel, M. S., Pierluigi, S., Josep, P., Branislav, H., and Vassilios, G. A. (2018). Review of FACTS technologies and applications for power quality in smart grids with renewable energy systems. *Journal of Renewable and Sustainable Energy Reviews*, 82(February), 502–514.

[4] Dhanup, S. P. and Rajaseka, N. (2018).A comprehensive review on protection challenges and fault diagnosis in PV systems. *Journal of Renewable and Sustainable Energy Reviews*, 91(August), 18–40.

[5] Simon, J. and Ernst, W. (2019). Regional economic and environmental impacts of renewable energy developments: Solar PV in the Aachen region. *Journal of Energy for Sustainable Development*, 48(February), 11–24

[6] Jyh-Cherng, G., De-Shin, L., Jing-Min, W., Jiang-Jun, H., and Ming-Ta, Y. (2019). Design of a DC series arc fault detector for photovoltaic systems protection. *IEEE Transactions on Industry Applications*, 55(3), 2464–2471.

[7] Zhan, W. and Robert, S. B. (2013). *Arc fault and flash detection in DC photovoltaic arrays using wavelets*. *39th Photovoltaic Specialists Conference (PVSC)* (pp. 16–21). Tampa, FL, USA.

[8] Ahmad, R., Nasrudin Abd, R., Mohamad Fathi, M. E., and Jafferi, J. (2020). Analysis of photovoltaic string failure and health monitoring with module fault identification. *Journal of Energies*, 13(January).

[9] Foad, H. G., Abdollah, A., Adel, M. S., Pierluigi, S., Josep, P., Branislav, H., and Vassilios, G. (2018). Review of FACTS technologies and applications for power quality in smart grids with renewable energy systems. *Journal of Renewable and Sustainable Energy Reviews*, 82(February), 502–514.

[10] Jayamaha, D. K. J. S. and Rajapakse, A. D. (2020). Protection and grounding methods in DC microgrids: Comprehensive review and analysis. *Journal of Renewable and Sustainable Energy Reviews*, 120(March), 109631.

[11] Zhu, Y. and Xiao, W. (2020). A comprehensive review of topologies for photovoltaic I–V curve tracer. *Journal of Solar Energy*, 196(January), 346–357.

[12] Bilal, T. and Cherif, L. (2020). Multivariate statistical monitoring of photovoltaic plant operation. *Journal of Energy Conversion and Management*, 205(February), 112317.

[13] Abhishek, K., Bikas, S., Arvind, R., Singh Yan, D., Xiangning, H., Praveen, K., and Bansal, R. C. (2017). A review of multi criteria decision making (MCDM) towards sustainable renewable energy development. *Journal of Renewable and Sustainable Energy Reviews*,69(March), 596–609.

[14] Jimenez-Delgado, E., Meza, C., Mendez-Porras, A., and Alfaro-Velasco, J. (2019). *Data management infrastructure from initiatives on photovoltaic solar energy*. *International Conference on Information Technology & Systems (ICITS)* (pp. 113–121) Cham.

[15] Famous, O. I. and Jiri, K. (2019). *The prospect of the Internet of Renewable Energy (IoRE) in electricity networks*. In *Proceedings of IEEE International Conference on Symposium on Technology in Society (ISTAS)*, (pp. 33–60), Boston USA.

[16] Cheng, L., Qi, N., Zhang, F., Kong, H., and Huang, X. (2017) *Energy internet: Concept and practice exploration*. *IEEE conference on energy internet and energy system integration (EI2)*. (pp. 1–5), Beijing.

[17] Guan, X., Xu, Z., Jia, Q. S., Liu, K., and Zhou, Y. (2018). Cyber-physical model for efficient and secured operation of CPES or energy Internet. *Sci China*, 61(11), 5–7.

[18] Yang, Y., Fang, Z., Zeng, F., and Liu, P. (2017). *Research and prospect of virtual microgrids based on energy internet*. In *Proceeding of IEEE conference on energy internet and energy system integration (EI2)* (pp. 1–5), Beijing.

[19] Liye, M., Zhiqiang, W., Tao, Z., and Zhigang, L. (2019). Evaluation model for economic operation of active distribution network orienting to Energy Internet. *Journal of Electrical Engineering & Technology*,14(March), 1151–1164.

[20] Arzoo, M., Neeraj, K., Vinay, C., and Sherali, Z. (2020). Blockchain for Internet of Energy management: Review, solutions and challenges. *Journal of Computer Communi cation*,151(February), 395–418.

[21] Dario, A., Clemente, C. and Ottorino, V. (2019). Internet of Energy Training through remote laboratory demonstrator. *Journal of Technologies*, 47(June).

[22] Khizir, M., Behram, K., Jayashri, R., Abdollah, A., and Pierluigi, S. (2020). An internet of energy framework with distributed energy resources, prosumers and small-scale virtual power plants: An overview. *Journal of Renewable and Sustainable Energy Reviews*, 127(March), 109840.

[23] Kasaei, M. J., Gandomkar, M., and Nikoukar, J. (2017). Optimal management of renewable energy sources by virtual power plant. *Renewable Energy*, 114(December), 1180–1188.

[24] Pandzic, H., Morales, J. M., Conejo, A. J. and Kuzle, I. (2013). Offering model for a virtual power plant based on stochastic programming. *Applied Energy*, 105(May), 282–292.

[25] Wadim, S., Dalia, S.. Alena, F., and Elena, S. (2019). Internet of Energy (IoE) and high-renewables electricity system market design. *Journal of Energies*, 12(December), 1-3.

[26] Zafar, R., Mahmood, A., Razzaq, S., Ali, W., Neem, U., and Shehzad, K. (2018). Prosumer based energy management and sharing in smart grid. *Journal of Renewable and Sustainable Energy Reviews*, 82(February), 1675–1684.

[27] Choi, S. and Min, S. W. (2018). Optimal scheduling and operation of the ESS for prosumer market environment in grid-connected industrial complex. *IEEE Transactions on Industry Applications*, 54(3), 1949–1957.

[28] Zepter, J. M., Luth, A., Grespo del Grenado, P., and Egging, R. (2019), Prosumer integration in wholesale electricity markets: synergies of peer-to-peer trade and residential storage. *Energy and Buildings*, 184(February), 163–176.

[29] Zhou, Z., Gong, J., He, Y., and Zhang, Y. (2017), Software defined machine-to-machine communication for smart energy management. *IEEE Communications Magazine*, 55(October), 52–60.

[30] Eissa, M. M., Medhat, H., and Awadalla, A. (2019). Centralized protection scheme for smart grid integration with multiple renewable resources using Internet of Energy. *Journal of Global Transitions*, 1(April), 50–60.

[31] Jijiang, H., Yu, W., and Wenying, C. (2019). *Energy transmission driven by the Energy Internet. Annual Report on China's Response to Climate Change (RSCDCDP)*, (pp. 77–89) Singapore.

[32] Evgeny, N., Seppo, S., and Valeriy, V. (2018), Internet of Energy approach for sustainable use of electric vehicles as energy storage of prosumer buildings. *Journals of Energies*, 11(August).

[33] Cintuglu, M. H., Ma, T., and Mohammed, O. A. (2017). Protection of autonomous microgrids using agent-based distributed communication. *IEEE Transactions on Power Delivery*, 32(1), 351–360.

[34] Ashish, G., Debasrita, C., and Anwesha, L. (2018), Artificial intelligence in Internet of Things. *CAAI Transactions on Intelligence Technology*, 3(4), 208–218.

[35] El-Batawy, S. and Morsi, W. (2018). Optimal design of community battery energy storage systems with prosumers owing electric vehicles. *IEEE Transaction and Industrial Informatics*, 14(5), 1920–1931.

[36] Mahmud, K., Tow, G., Morsalin, S. and Hossain, M. J. (2018). Integration of electric vehicles and management in the internet of energy. *Journal of Renewable and Sustainable Energy Reviews*, 82(February), 4179–4203.

[37] Blom, F. and Farahmand, H. (2018).*On the scalability of block-chain support local energy markets*. In *Proceedings of IEEE international Conference on Smart Energy Systems and technologies (SEST)*, (pp. 1–6), Sevilla, Spain.

[38] Mahmud, K., Hossain, M. J., and Town, G. (2018). Peak-load reduction by coordinated response of Photovoltaics, battery storage and electrical vehicles. *IEEE Access*, 6, 29353–29365.

[39] Zafar, R., Mahmood, A., Razzaq, S., Ali, W., Naeem, U., and Shehzad, K. (2018).Prosumer based energy management and sharing in smart grid. *Journal of Renewable and Sustainable Energy Reviews*, 82(February), 1675–1684.

[40] Nizami, M. S. H., Hossain, M. J., Rafique, S., Mahmud, K., Irshad, U. B., and Town, G. (2019).*A multi-agent system based residential electric vehicle management system for grid support service*. In *Proceedings of IEEE International Conference on Environment and Electrical Engineering and IEEE Industrial and Commercial Power Systems Europe (EEEIC/ I&CPS Europe)*, Genova, Italy.

[41] Doost, Mohammadian H. (2019), *Internet of energy: A solution for energy management challenges*. In*Proceeding, of the IEEE Global Engineering Education Conference (EDUCON)*, (pp. 9–11), Dubai.

[42] Lin, X., Li, J., Wu, J., Liang, H., and Yang, W. (2019), Making knowledge tradable in edge-AI enabled IoT: A consortium blockchain-based efficient and incentive approach, *IEEE Transaction and Industrial Informatics*, 15(12), 6367–6378.

[43] Wu, J., Dong, M., Ota, K., Li, J., Yang, W., and Wang, M. (2019), Fog computing enabled cognitive network function virtualization for information-centric future internet, *IEEE Communications Magazine* 57(7), 48–54.

[44] Guan, Z., Lu, X., Wanga, N., Wub, J., Du, X. and Guizani, M. (2020), Towards secure and efficient energy trading in IIoT-enabled energy internet: A blockchain approach, *Future Generation Computer Systems* 110(October), 686–695.

[45] Bhattacharjee, S. and Nandi, C. (2020), Design of an industrial Internet of Things-enabled energy management system of grid-connected solar-wind hybrid system-based battery swapping charging station for electric vehicle, *Applications of Internet of Things*137(August), 1–14.

[46] Baidya, S. and Nandi, C. (2020), Green energy generation using renewable energy technologies, *Advance in Green Energy Technologies*, 259–276.

[47] Yu, X., Hong, J., and Wang, Q. (2020), *Future development and research prospect of urban Energy Internet*, In *Proceedings of the Asia Energy and Electrical Engineering Symposium (AEEES)*, China.

[48] Kumar, P., Ali, K., and Thomas, M. (2015), *Synchronizing solar cell, battery and grid supply for development of smart power system home*, Annual IEEE India Conference (INDICON), New Delhi.

[49] Kumar, P., Thanki, Vinod D., Singh, S., and Nikolovski, S. (2020). A new framework for intensification of energy efficiency in commercial and residential use by imposing social, technical and environmental constraints, *Journal of Sustainable Cities and Society*, 62(November), 102400.

[50] Kumar, P., Brar Singh, G., and Singh, L. (2019). *Energy efficiency in commercial and residential buildings with demand side management: A review, 8th International Conference on Power Systems (ICPS)*, Jaipur.

[51] DebBarma, M., Deb, S. and Nandi, C. (2010).Maximum photovoltaic power tracking using perturb & observe algorithm in Matlab/Simulink environment, *International Journal of Electrical Engineering &Technology*, 1(June), 71–84.

[52] Nandi, C. and Chakraborty, A. K. (2012), *Wind power plants with VSC based STATCOM in PSCAD/EMTDC environment, 2nd International Conference on Power and Energy Systems (ICPES)* (pp. 7–11), IACSIT Press, Singapore.

KEYWORDS AND DESCRIPTIONS

Solar PV Energy   The solar photovoltaic (PV) energy is one of the fundamental renewable energy sources. For providing a potential solution the solar energy is becoming towards sustainable energy supply in future.

Smart and Micro grid   Smart grids are having smart tools including smart meters, electrical vehicles, smart household devices etc. and micro grid is a self-oriented small-scale power generation unit that can also share power to the other grids.

Decentralized Energy System   Renewable Energy Sources (RES) are insidiously organize across the distribution networks.

Internet of Energy (IoE)   An internet connected approach that can provide better communicating and transforming technology.

Prosumers   The consumers that can generate power, use them for required consumption and transfer the extra power to the nearby interconnected power grid.

8 IoE for Energy Efficient Buildings
Challenges and Solutions

Meet Kumari
Chandigarh University, Mohali, Punjab, India

CONTENTS

8.1 Background 193
8.2 Literature Review 195
8.3 IoE-Based Building Management System 197
    8.3.1 IoE for Energy-Efficient Buildings 197
    8.3.2 Features and Concept of IoE 197
8.4 Applications of IOE in the Commercial and Residential Buildings 199
8.5 Major Challenges for Implementing IOE in Buildings 200
8.6 FoE: A Case Study 203
8.7 Future Directions 204
8.8 Conclusions 204
References 204
Keywords and Descriptions 207

8.1 BACKGROUND

Today, the energy-saving concept has become an important issue for reliable economic development globally. The global electricity challenge is increasing and expected to rise by two-thirds in the year 2035. Further, researchers committed that it further increases the challenges of global warming [1,2]. The electricity demand significantly leads to network congestion and power quality degradation issues. Also, the huge utilization of fossil fuel has a serious environmental impact. Thus, it is essential to replace fossil fuel with renewable energy resources. By 2100, renewable energy sources are estimated to provide about 80% of the total power. Smart grids have been investigated that can provide secure and feasible electricity to users [3]. Further, the effective use of produced electricity is an important factor in the improvement of the world economy. In this scenario, the Internet of Energy (IoE) can be considered as an extension of smart grid for evaluating the full-duplex information and electrical energy flow [4,5]. IoE is the combination of the Internet of Energy (IoT) and smart grid features. IoT means the Internet-based design that provides the transfer of information, services as well as data among trillions of smart things. IoT can be utilized in different areas such as telemetric services, weather forecasting, power distribution, military applications, and home applications. By contrast, the grids provide full-duplex communication between the power management system and grid to control and monitor energy-generating units. Thus, an IoE has been extensively utilized in electric vehicles (EVs), buildings, industrial sectors, and distributed energy sources along with domestic sectors. Here, the Internet can be utilized to control and monitor energy networks. Likewise, the information is transferred through the Internet; energy is transmitted from a transmitter to the receiver side when it needed [6,7].

Currently, the building sector is the emerging energy consuming area. Thus, building energy management has become a focus for modern international technology. It is expected that in the building sector, 40% of total generated energy is consumed and in consequence of that commercial buildings are responsible for the generation of one-third of the total greenhouse gases (GHG) [8]. The major part of energy consumption in buildings takes place in the processes of heating and cooling. Thus, the effects of energy consumption on environmental change are an issue highly disputed in the modern building sector. Various researchers have evaluated building energy by utilizing IoE. IoE with its attractive features of transferring energy between users can importantly drive acceptable power usage by restricted-energy loss, therefore causing the development of sustainable energy globally [9,10].

Further, renewable energy sources are replacing exhaustible sources in the future. Thus, the latest research work has proposed the concept of a smart device, which can provide secure and feasible energy to users. Further, the efficient utilization of energy is a significant consideration in the improvement of the economy. IoT means Internet-based architecture that enables the transfer of information, services, and huge data among trillion smart devices. Subsequently, the full-duplex communication between the smart grid and the energy system can provide controllability of energy-generating systems. Moreover, the Internet has become an inseparable and significant source of information [11]. Thus, the IoE has been extensively utilized in buildings, domestic, industrial, and distributed energy sectors. In IoE, the Internet can be utilized for controlling and monitoring energy networks to transfer the energy from source to destination. For IoE, smart grid devices are used in huge numbers that can send and receive energy information at a short interval of time. The intelligent connection of people, data, process, and devices/components can be treated as a large IoE network. Further, the building sector is the prime energy-consuming sector. Building energy management aims for modern technology. Almost half of the total world energy is consumed by buildings especially commercial and residential. The primary sources of energy consumption in buildings are water heating, heating ventilation, and air conditioning (HVAC), electric vehicles, batteries, and lighting. But reducing the energy usage by buildings leads to lots of benefits such as lower energy bills, a reduction from peak loads, and a reduction in greenhouse gases emission [12]. Therefore, it is imperative to focus on innovative methods that help to optimize and reduce energy consumption by buildings. Improperly controlled and poorly managed devices may greatly increase wasted energy in the energy economy of buildings. Buildings' energy efficiency can be measured for the reference energy model by creating energy setpoints. In buildings, the primary goal of an IoE is energy-saving

[13]. In buildings, IoE helps in promoting energy-saving sources, which connect easily to high-capacity energy storage devices to smoothen and stabilize the energy output. Moreover, it can generate, store, and consume energy at the same time and site for high-efficiency operation. In buildings, IoE consists of two-way energy flow so that users can consume and produce energy [14,15].

In this chapter, Section 8.2 describes the comprehensive literature review of IoE. Sections 8.3 and 8.4 present the IoE for energy-efficient buildings and their potential applications, respectively. Section 8.5 illustrates the issues and challenges existing in IoE-based buildings. A case study is also described in Section 8.6. Finally, the conclusion and future scope are presented in Sections 8.7 and 8.8, respectively.

8.2 LITERATURE REVIEW

In this section various latest literature reviews are discussed as follows:

Nguyen et al. proposed the IoE architecture of net-zero energy buildings (nZEBs) and a smart building energy management (BEMs) framework and find IoE techniques to minimize building power consumption. The significant IoE-based BEMs for improving building performance in terms of efficient energy utilization in the future have been presented. Also, various future applications of IoE in different fields have been described. Also, they found potential applications of IoE in different areas [16].

Dorri et al. presented an architecture of the IoE to identify primary functionalities and the key technical challenges faced in the electricity distribution system. The modern energy and Internet networks as well as services to identify potential functionalities and challenges faced in electricity distribution to the reliable and flexible platform have been compared and contrasted. The results show that for an absolute IoE to be implemented there need to be considerable changes to electricity infrastructure, regulations, and business models [17].

Li et al. reported on the Swarm Decision Table (SDT) learning model and found an appropriate learning model for fog node intelligence. The significance of the IoT-connected building energy demand prediction (BEDP) has been experimentally tested utilizing an energy consumption database. Moreover, they show that SDT presents high accuracy as well as timely performance, investigating it as an appropriate machine learning solution in the fog computing condition. The results show that IoT-connected BEDP and the SDT present the best results in terms of kappa and accuracy [18].

Kaur et al. utilized the nZEB approach to find real-time tracking to monitor instantaneous power generation as well as demand to gain sufficient energy balance in the building. The significance of this study is a real-time controlling and monitoring system to observe the adequate energy achieving demand and instantaneous energy generation in buildings that have been discussed. It is developed as a heterogeneous control system based on a multi-agent system design with user comfort consideration. An intelligent agent namely joint approximate diagonalization of Eigen matrices (JADE) has been optimized for IoE-based applications [19].

Strielkowski et al. presented the flexible and innovative IoE high renewables framework to find and show the issues such as compatibility, speed, and trust in various applications of IoE. The high-renewables electric system that employs IoE has been present. It shows that the decentralized technique for an effective controlled energy system and operation is highly ubiquitous. Also, there may be some other approaches focused to provide development. The results show that a renewables electricity system provides solutions to various issues such as CO_2 reduction and climate change [20].

Hannan, et al. presented various types of IoE-based building energy management system (BEMS) approaches like energy routers, renewable sources, storage systems, and materials to enhance the performance of IoE-based BEMS system. The significance of this study is to review different kinds of BEMS technologies based on IoE like energy routers, materials, plug-and-play interfaces, storage systems and renewable sources. It indicates the already present BEMSs need controllers integrated with hybrid IoE-based technologies for reliable energy building utilization. The main goal is to illustrate various challenges of the traditional controllers as well as BEMSs applications based on IoE. It provides the various key points for the development and research of advanced controlled BEMSs. The results provide an idea for manufacturers and researchers for the future development of advanced IoE-based BEMS [6].

Metallidou reported an IoE and IoT to serve the transformation planning of the European Union into sustainable as well as smart cities to find representative technology approaches for stable short- and long-term energy-efficient buildings constructions by utilizing IoT technology. The significance of this study is building a template using IoT technology to achieve high energy efficiency and to manage the performance of the technical system has been proposed. Also, to enhance the existing building's certification, an automated remote technique with a loud interface has been proposed. It shows that the proposed method reduces the wastage time and stores on the cloud platform for high energy performance. The results show the contribution to Building Certification and compliance checking of buildings [21].

Baccare Lli et al. provided the FoE paradigm to find simulated energy-delay performance of small-scale Fog of Everything (FoE), which is named as the V-FoE prototype. The platforms and technological attributes in the recent review for the IoE and FC paradigms have been presented. Then various opportunities for novel applications with hybrid IoE and FC paradigms along with challenges have been illustrated. The results show that the FoE paradigm and V-FoE prototype to hybrids IoE and FC using the main building blocks services, platforms, and protocols have been proposed. The results are obtained by considering V-D2D as a benchmark technological platform [22].

Moreover, Mohammadian [23] introduced an IoT technology for the novel Internet-driven and its corresponding goals and tools. The results show that present issues to get used and produce energy in energy management most effectively and the sustainable development energy structure show the solutions and opportunities for various types of problems to help the IoE. In [24], the idea behind wireless energy-efficient communication network architecture has been presented. Also, wide taxonomy that tracks the fields of the effect of these methods in the system has been illustrated. Here, prediction-based energy-efficient methods, its challenges, and the latest trends for future networks have been described. Finally, context-specific energy-efficient collaborations to move the energy frontiers in wireless networks have been presented.

8.3   IOE-BASED BUILDING MANAGEMENT SYSTEM

8.3.1   IoE for Energy-Efficient Buildings

Energy-efficient building management is economical and adjustable and therefore can save energy expenses of users. The electricity wastage can be limited by switching off appliances when not used. This can be attained by using a smart building system that impulsively switches off electricity or load when not used. In this way, most of the energy can be saved in commercial and residential buildings [25]. For this IoE provides an effective integrated system that controls and monitors energy consumption. IoE can work on the grid and small scale, providing more efficient energy generation by degrading the usage of fossil fuel [23].

8.3.2   Features and Concept of IoE

IoE for energy-efficient buildings is a method used for predicting, monitoring, and controlling energy consumption in buildings. Electrical devices like electric pumps, chillers, fans, etc. can increase the wasted energy amount in buildings without correct management and control [26]. Thus, an IoE-based building architecture has been proposed in this chapter as shown in Figure 8.1. It consists of storing the building's physical properties, geometric information as well as component information that can be utilized for the energy efficiency of a building [27]. A building's energy efficiency can be investigated by setpoints creation concerning the

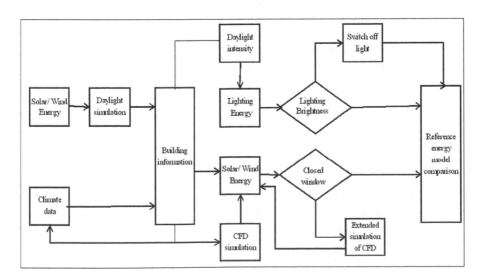

FIGURE 8.1   The framework of IoE-based energy-efficient buildings [16].

reference energy model. With this design, energy-saving and energy efficiency can be observed taking account of cost and energy consumption benefit analysis [16]

Like the Internet, IoE has lots of control-connected nodes and router. These devices are used for different levels of control in buildings. But unlike the Internet, IoE cannot reproduce energy. Thus, there should be a stability between the energy supplier and users' demands [28]

As shown in Figure 8.1, IoE permits energy exchange between various kinds of sources and loads, consists of plug-in electric vehicles, distributed energy storage, renewable energy sources, and domestic etc. The energy system is monitored and managed by the Internet. In this architecture, peer-to-peer transfer of both energy and information occurs. The working principle of the architecture is to direct the energy from sources to loads [17] The key technologies used in this system are as follows:

a. intelligent energy management (IEM) or router
b. plug-and-play interface
c. distributed grid intelligence (DGI)
d. the intelligent fault management unit (IFM)

a. **Router:** It is also known as energy router and it is one of the key devices of IoE. The basic function of the router is to dispatch electricity, convert voltage, and process information. It aims to enhance the efficiency, safety, and reliability to observe the energy usage through balancing demand and supply. It can receive process and transfer the information about current produced electricity and demand. These can be located at various points in IoE network [28]. It also helps in communicating with a huge number of heterogeneous sources as well as loads. When the supply exceeds local consumption, then the router transmits the surplus energy into the smart grid. It can communicate with other routers as well for larger supply and demand balancing on large scale. It consists of three phases: distributed grid intelligent control, solid-state transformer, and communication module [29]. The distributed grid intelligent control is an open operating system standard, which estimates the energy production and distribution within the connected grids. The solid-state transformer is the voltage converter based on power electronics while the communication unit helps in communication between different energy routers [17]

b. **Storage devices:** These lead to an efficient grid by supplying energy quality, stable grid operation, and reliable supply. It is important for the stress grid and also when there is an unbalance between supply and demand. In this case, the grid and battery can provide electricity to restrict blackout. Further, it solves the issue of sag and voltage surge. [30]

c. **Transient energy outages:** As photovoltaic (PV) cannot generate power at night, wind energy can be produced when there is no wind. Thus, power can be stored when they are working. This enhances the robustness, stability, etc. of IoE based buildings. Here, a fuel cell, supercapacitor, compressed air, battery, etc. can be used as storage devices [31].

d. **Distributed renewable energy sources:** To make clean and green energy, IoE-based building systems consist of several connected renewables [32].

e. **Energy resources:** They improve global growth each year. The interconnectivity of these sources needs suitable power converter topologies, fulfill grid code, control and modulation scheme and synchronization issue. The various renewables sources are wind, solar, hydroelectric, biomass, geothermal, etc. with wind and solar being most popular [33].

f. **Plug-and-play interface:** This provides the renewable, storage, and loads connections in IoE. It simplifies the distributed storages and generations. They have distinct interface types, i.e. AC or DC, which are connected through the AC/DC microgrid. It also includes an open-standard-based transmission interface that acknowledges immediately when generating or storage device is connected in the system [34]

8.4 APPLICATIONS OF IOE IN THE COMMERCIAL AND RESIDENTIAL BUILDINGS

An IoE based energy-efficient building management system helps in minimizing the energy consumption in buildings by supplying information based on energy demand. The application of IoE in buildings is shown in Figures 8.2 and 8.3 [16].

As shown in Figures 8.2 and 8.3, IoE includes several renewable energy sources that are interconnected to the smart grids to generate the green and clean energy. However, with new advanced technologies, the cost of these sources is degrading. The various renewable energy resources used in commercial and residential buildings are wind, solar, hydroelectric, etc. In the above-mentioned energy resources, solar and wind power generation have been extensively studied in the smart grid scenario since they are economical and provide clean energy, and, therefore, they are the best substitute for fossil-fuel energy systems [16,35].

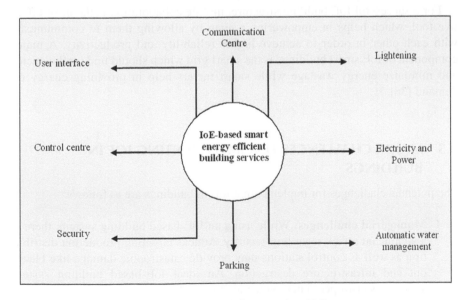

FIGURE 8.2   IoE-based energy-efficient buildings services [36].

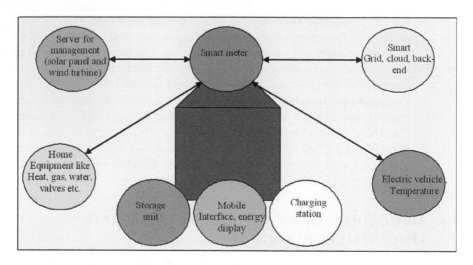

FIGURE 8.3   IoE-based energy-efficient buildings system.

The main function of the IoE-based building system is to adopt the requirements of the residents of the buildings and the way they carry out their work. Its
main goal is improving energy efficiency, enhancing renewable energies permea-
bility, decentralizing, and diversifying energy mixing and industry competitiveness promotion.

The connection between energy and environment, socio-economic development
and social as well as economic security must be recognized to design efficient energy
management strategies [23].

For a successful IoE building structure, mobile collaboration is the most effective tool, which helps in empowering a team by allowing them to communicate
with each other in order to achieve higher reliability and productivity. A major
component of IoE smart buildings is the smart grid which should find inefficiencies
and minimize energy wastage while smart meters help in providing energy on
demand [36].

8.5   MAJOR CHALLENGES FOR IMPLEMENTING IOE IN
BUILDINGS

The potential challenges for implementing IoE in buildings are as follows:

1 **Managerial challenges:** While using an IoE-based building system, there is
a significant attack regarding security. Attacks targeting production distribution as well as control stations may provide catastrophic damage like blackout and infrastructure destruction. An ideal IoE-based building system
supports peer-to-peer interconnection thus if there is a breakdown by a hacker

into the node, user electricity usage, and breach of user confidentiality, etc. can be attached. Thus, security is essential to set up a reliable, sustainable, and secure grid system for proving encryption, integrity protection, and authentication [23].

2 **Technical challenges:** The IoE is a complex network that integrates a decentralized smart grid, sensors, and other devices to monitor and control. The real-time predicting, monitoring, and controlling leads to increase system complexity. Also, the renewable generation intermittent nature and loads variability brings attaining a feasible and intelligent energy management system, which is quite challenging. Moreover, regulating voltage and frequency on the smart grid within the fixed standard brings a technical challenge in IoE [23].

3 **Reliability:** A reliable IoE-based smart building system can lead to the user's attention. Thus, it can ensure the attainment of a sustained building development goal. Incorrect decisions and inaccurate information may lead to maximizing irrecoverable damages and confusion. Also, the energy generation level varies depends on climate conditions and the already present energy network suffers from disparity due to the efficient monitor lacking and fault diagnosis. The energy supply to the users needs to be reliable and stable with optimum power quality. Thus, ESS material selection and smart power infrastructure with control and monitor system for IoE based building design can speed up the smart energy-efficient building structures [6].

4 **Security:** Information collection and analysis is a primary part of the energy-efficient building structure. Here, different kinds of data like replacement or maintenance schedules of the devices, meter data, human resources, billing information, as well as the cost of power consumption of several buildings' devices are stored at a definite interval. This information can be utilized to find the IoE-based building management system like heating, lighting, and cooling [37]. Currently, various advanced information management networks have been presented incorporating sensors, smart meters, and sub-meters to access building structure performance. Thus, the device selection, equipment placement, metering equipment replacing, and circuit identification are responsible for an efficient system. Moreover, privacy, consistency, authentication, integrity, recording, collection, and tracking without data loss are some of the major security needs for IoE-based smart building applications. Also, using a smart grid can increase the chances of a cyber-attack. Thus, it is necessary to store the huge amount of data with advanced security, privacy, and cloud computing. This will enhance users' life quality and their money as well [6].

5 **Scalability:** It presents the system stability while adding new services, applications, and devices to the present system. The system energy quality needs to be enlarged in the future. As users want to achieve new services and applications regularly, the IoE based energy-efficient buildings need to be scalable. [38]

6 **Cost:** For the IoE-based building system the total cost consists of operating costs, energy cost, material cost, smart devices cost, building renovation costs,

construction cost, maintenance cost, and technological cost. Past reviews showed that the cost of integrating solar energy is high, while the integration of wind energy and geothermal energy is very high. Thus, the costs have a great impact on the IoE-based building structure. There should therefore be optimum stability between GHG emission and IoE-based buildings to ensure an effective building [39].

7 **Climate:** In IoE-based building system weather and geographical location are sensitive issues. Cooling, heating, telecommunications, ventilation, thermal comfortability, GHG emission, and Internet supply are highly impacted by weather changes. If the temperature changes, then the corresponding load-based energy consumption varies [40–42]. Thus, the climate is a significant determinant for architecting effective buildings. Moreover, interference of signals depends on the climate conditions of the building thus wireless equipment may not perform well in harsh climate conditions [17]. Figure 8.4 shows the open challenges in implementing IoE in buildings.

8 **Business-related challenges:** The traditional models of grid business are based on large utility companies and centralized generators with a huge market share between generation and users. Thus, due to business reasons, the latest system may not easily put up a large distributed renewable energy generation proportion and not permit billing of the user [43,44]. Therefore, new business models are needed to supply an open market and to allow for energy exchanges. In today's market transformation and deregulation are major challenges for obtaining future energy-oriented market [17].

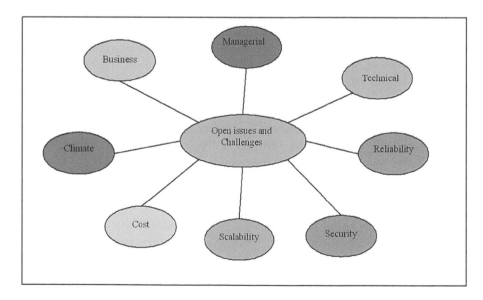

FIGURE 8.4   IoE-based related open challenges.

8.6 FOE: A CASE STUDY

As the IoE paradigm consists of various challenges that cannot be sufficiently addressed by the host and cloud computing models. These challenges are reduced communication delays, resource limitations, self-organizing ecosystems, intermittent network connectivity, etc. These challenges are introduced to the fog cloud (FC) paradigm as described in Table 8.1 [22,40].

Figure 8.5 shows the basic service model under the integrated cloud, fog and IoE layers. On the basis of this figure, the FoE interplay is described as follows in Table 8.2.

TABLE 8.1
The comprehensive FoE parameters [22]

Main attributes	Technological platform	Supported services
Dense virtualization	Input/output buffers	Infrastructure as a Service (IaaS)
Device isolation	Collection of virtual processors (VPs)	Software as a Service (SaaS)
Pervasive spatial deployment	Physical resources	Platform as a Service (PaaS)
Served devices' heterogeneity	Virtual switch	
Served devices' mobility support	Adaptive load dispatcher	

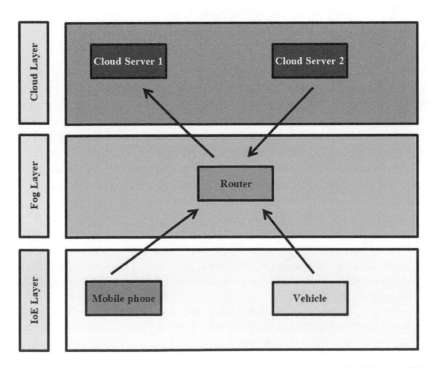

FIGURE 8.5 The basic service model under the integrated clod, fog and IoE layers [22].

TABLE 8.2

FoE interplay: a cooperation opportunity [22]

Fog attributes	FoE support
Proximity of devices	Fog nodes provide support to IoE applications in infrastructure development.
Device mobility support	Spatial clusters fog nodes distribution for single-hop connections.
Context-awareness	Fog nodes contain awareness in real-time applications.
Minimized energy consumption	Stable and energy-efficient communication.
Dense virtualization	Device augmentation is provided on the demand basis.

8.7 FUTURE DIRECTIONS

It is expected that the IoE will extensively be utilized to provide energy efficiency in buildings. This will help to enable novel ways for conducting work, social networks, entertainment etc. and hence it will provide a new lifestyle. As IoE provides various possible applications, the energy-efficient building is an attractive application for future intelligent energy control buildings. In this chapter, an IoE based energy-efficient building system has been presented in which the people, things, and services are connected to facilitate smart building task. IoE-based challenges help to establish a secure, user-friendly, and reliable building system, offering convenience and comfort to users.

8.8 CONCLUSIONS

The future research trends for IoE includes energy resources recognition, replacing renewable sources with their best alternative, understanding the IoE based infrastructure and introducing ways to utilizes the sensors in industrial applications. It is shown that the IoE will change the method of production, transportation, consumption of energy, and impact on human life. IoE can promote energy efficiency and energy transportation, which will enhance the recycling economy and feasible urban development in the future. Also, the use of IoE will protect the environment, as well as promote the significant economic and social benefits for sustainable urban development.

REFERENCES

[1] Strielkowski, W., Veinbender, T., Tvaronavičienė, M. and Lace, N. (2020). Economic efficiency and energy security of smart cities. *Economic Research-Ekonomska Istrazivanja*, 33, 788–803.

[2] Qarnain, S. S., Muthuvel, S., Bathrinath, S. and Saravanasankar, S. (2020). Analyzing factors in emerging computer technologies favoring energy conservation of building sector. *Materials Today: Proceedings* 1–4.

[3] Zor, K., Çelik, Ö., Timur, O. and Teke, A. (2020). Short-term building electrical energy consumption forecasting by employing gene expression programming and GMDH networks. *Energies*, 13, 1–24.

[4] Hyman, B. T., Alisha, Z. and Gordon, S. (2019). Secure controls for smart cities; applications in intelligent transportation systems and smart buildings. *International Journal of Scientific Engineering and Applied*, 8, 167–171.

[5] Hang, M. and Singh, S. (2019). A study of challenges and opportunities of energy efficient housing in Kathmandu: Architects' perspective. *IOE Graduate Conference*, 7, pp 91–98.

[6] Hannan, M. A., Faisal, M., Ker, P. J., Mun, L. H., Parvin, K., Mahlia, T. M. I. and Blaabjerg, F. (2018). A review of Internet of energy based building energy management systems: Issues and recommendations. *IEEE Access*, 6, 38997–39014.

[7] Mahmud, K., Khan, B., Ravishankar, J., Ahmadi, A. and Siano, P. (2020). An Internet of energy framework with distributed energy resources, prosumers and small-scale virtual power plants: An overview. *Renewable and Sustainable Energy Reviews*, 127, 109840.

[8] Khajenasiri, I., Estebsari, A., Verhelst, M. and Gielen, G. (2017). A review on Internet of Things solutions for intelligent energy control in buildings for smart city applications. *Energy Procedia*, 111, 770–779.

[9] Doost, H. (2018). Internet of Energy: A solution for improving the efficiency of reversible energy. *IEEE Global Engineering Education Conference (EDUCON)*, 2018.

[10] Shahzad, Y., Javed, H., Farman, H., Ahmad, J., Jan, B., and Zubair, M. (2020). Internet of Energy: Opportunities, applications, architectures and challenges in smart industries. *Computers and Electrical Engineering*, 86, 106739.

[11] Miglani, A., Kumar, N., Chamola, V. and Zeadally, S. (2020). Blockchain for Internet of Energy management: Review, solutions, and challenges. *Computer Communications*. 151, 395–418.

[12] Rathor, S. K. and Saxena, D. (2020). Energy management system for smart grid: An overview and key issues. *International Journal of Energy Research*,. 44, 4067–4109.

[13] Khatua, P. K., Ramachandaramurthy, V. K., Kasinathan, P., Yong, J. Y., Pasupuleti, J. and Rajagopalan, A. (2020). Application and assessment of Internet of things toward the sustainability of energy systems: Challenges and issues. *Sustainable Cities and Society*, 53, 101957.

[14] Singh, P., Nayyar, A., Kaur, A. and Ghosh, U. (2020). Blockchain and fog based architecture for Internet of everything in smart cities. *Future Internet*, 12, 1–12.

[15] Jindal, A., Kumar, N. and Singh, M. (2020). Internet of energy-based demand response management scheme for smart homes and PHEVs using SVM. *Future Generation Computer Systems*, 108, 1058–1068.

[16] Nguyen, V. T., Luan Vu, T., Le, N. T. and Min Jang, Y. (2018). An overview of Internet of Energy (IoE) based building energy management system. In *9th International Conference on Information and Communication Technology Convergence: ICT Convergence Powered by Smart Intelligence, ICTC 2018*, pp 852–855.

[17] Dorri, A., Kanhere, S. S., and Jurdak, R. (2017). Towards an optimized blockchain for IoT. *Proc. - 2017 IEEE/ACM 2nd Int. Conf. Internet-of-Things Des. Implementation, IoTDI 2017 (part CPS Week)*, 173–178.

[18] Li, T., Fong, S., Li, X., Lu, Z. and Gandomi, A. H. (2020). Swarm decision table and ensemble search methods in fog computing environment: Case of day-ahead prediction of building energy demands using IoT sensors. *IEEE Internet of Things Journal*, 7, 2321–2342.

[19] Kaur, E., Sharma, S., Verma, A. and Singh, M. (2019). An energy management and recommender system for lighting control in Internet-of-energy enabled buildings. *IFAC-PapersOnLine*, 52, 288–293.

[20] Strielkowski, W., Streimikiene, D., Fomina, A. and Semenova, E. (2019). Internet of energy (IoE) and high-renewables electricity system market design. *Energies*, 12, 1–17.

[21] Metallidou, C. K., Psannis, K. E., and Egyptiadou, E. A. (2020). Energy efficiency in smart buildings: IoT approaches. *IEEE Access*, 8, 63679–63699.

[22] Baccarelli, E., Naranjo, P. G. V., Scarpiniti, M., Shojafar, M. and Abawajy, J. H. (2017). Fog of Everything: Energy-efficient networked computing architectures, research challenges, and a case study. *IEEE Access*, 5, 9882–9910.

[23] Mohammadian, H. D. (2019). IoE – A solution for energy management challenges. *IEEE Global Engineering Education Conference (EDUCON)*, 2019, 1455–1461.

[24] Ogbebor, J. O., Imoize, A. L. and Atayero, A. A. A. (2020). Energy Efficient design techniques in next-generation wireless communication networks: Emerging trends and future directions. *Wireless Communications and Mobile Computing* 2020.

[25] Lorincz, Josip and Antonio Capone, J. W. (2019). Greener, energy-efficient and sustainable networks: State-of-the-art. *Sensors*, 19, 4864.

[26] Desai, S., Alhadad, R., Chilamkurti, N., and Mahmood, A. (2019). A survey of privacy preserving schemes in IoE enabled Smart Grid Advanced Metering Infrastructure. *Cluster Computing*, 22, 43–69.

[27] Brindha, T. and Vincent, P. M. D. R. (2017). BESM based approach to build energy efficient smart homes. In *2017 Innovations in Power and Advanced Computing Technologies, i-PACT 2017*, pp 1–6.

[28] Aazam, M. and Huh, E. N. (2016). Fog computing: The cloud-IoT/IoE middleware paradigm. *IEEE Potentials*, 35, 40–44.

[29] Vermesan, O. and Blystad, L. (2011). Internet of Energy – connecting energy anywhere anytime. *Advanced Microsystems for Automotive Applications* 2011, 33–48.

[30] Janani, P., Verma, S., Natarajan, S. and Sinha, A. K. (2020). Communication using IoT. In *Information and Communication Technology for Sustainable Development, Advances in Intelligent Systems and Computing*, pp. 659–668.

[31] Fan, X., Liu, X., Hu, W., Zhong, C. and Lu, J. (2019). Advances in the development of power supplies for the Internet of Everything. *InfoMat* 130–139.

[32] Zhong, W., Xie, K., Liu, Y., Yang, C., Xie, S. and Zhang, Y. (2019). ADMM empowered distributed computational intelligence for Internet of Energy. *IEEE Computational Intelligence Magazine*, 14, 42–51.

[33] Queralta, J. P., Nguyen Gia, T., Tenhunen, H. and Westerlund, T. (2019). Collaborative mapping with IoE-based heterogeneous vehicles for enhanced situational awareness. In *SAS 2019 – 2019 IEEE Sensors Applications Symposium, Conference Proceedings*.

[34] Yue, X., Kauer, M., Bellanger, M., Beard, O., Brownlow, M., Gibson, D., Clark, C., MacGregor, C. and Song, S. (2017). Development of an indoor photovoltaic energy harvesting module for autonomous sensors in building air quality applications. *IEEE Internet of Things Journal*, 4, 2092–2103.

[35] Roasto, I., Husev, O., Najafzadeh, M., Jalakas, T. and Rodriguez, J. (2019). Voltage source operation of the energy-router based on model predictive control. *Energies*, 12, 1–15.

[36] Vermesan, O. and Friess, P. (2014). *Internet of things applications: From research and innovation to market deployment*.

[37] Kim, Y. M., Jung, D., Chang, Y. and Choi, D. H. (2019). Intelligent micro energy grid in 5G era: Platforms, business cases, testbeds, and next generation applications. *Electronics*, 8, 468.

[38] Serrano, A. Á. R. and Álvarez, S. P. (2016). Life cycle assessment in building: A case study on the energy and emissions impact related to the choice of housing typologies and construction process in Spain. *Sustain*, 8, 287.

[39] Amaxilatis, D., Akrivopoulos, O., Mylonas, G. and Chatzigiannakis, I. (2017). An IoT-based solution for monitoring a fleet of educational buildings focusing on energy efficiency. *Sensors (Switzerland)*, 17, 1–15.

[40] Awan, K. M., Sherazi, H. H. R., Ali, A., Iqbal, R., Khan, Z. A. and Mukherjee, M. (2019). Energy-aware cluster-based routing optimization for WSNs in the livestock industry. *Transactions on Emerging Telecommunications Technologies*, 1–18. https://doi.org/10.1002/ett.3816

[41] Kumar, P., Brar, G. S., Singh, S., Nikolovski, S., Baghaee, H. R. and Balkic, Z. (2019). Perspectives and intensification of energy efficiency in commercial and residential buildings using strategic auditing and demand-side management. *Energies*, 12, 4539.

[42] Kumar, P., Thanki, D. V., Singh, S. and Nikolovski, S. (2020), A new framework for intensification of energy efficiency in commercial and residential use by imposing social, technical and environmental constraints. *Sustainable Cities and Society*, 62, 102400.

[43] Kumar, P., Brar, G. S. and Singh, L. (2019), Energy efficiency evaluation in commercial and residential buildings with demand side management: A review. *8th International Conference on Power Systems (ICPS)*. 1–6.

[44] Kumar, P., Ali, I. and Thanki, D.V. (2018). Demand-side management: Energy efficiency and demand response. *Handbook of Research on Power and Energy System Optimization*, 453–479.

KEYWORDS AND DESCRIPTIONS

Internet of Energy (IoE)   It refers to the automating and upgrading of electricity structures for energy manufacturers and producers.

Internet of Things (IoT)   It is system of interconnected computing devices, digital and mechanical machines supplied with specific identifiers and the capability to transmit information over a network lacking human-to-human as well as human-to machine communication.

Sustainable energy   It connects the requirements of the present without lacking the ability of future networks to reach their own requirements.

Renewable Energy Sources   These are the energy sources that are naturally and continuously replenished such as wind, sunlight, water etc.

Building energy management system (BEMS)   An architecture where optimization balances envelope retrofits along with high efficiency and renewable.

9 Battery Management of Automated Guided Vehicles Via System Dynamics

Arzu Eren Şenaras and Onur Mesut Şenaras
Bursa Uludag University, Bursa, Turkey

CONTENTS

9.1 Background 209
9.2 Literature Review 210
9.3 System Dynamics 211
    9.3.1 SD Model for AGV Batteries 211
    9.3.2 Manual Charge 212
    9.3.3 Automatic Fast Charge 213
    9.3.4 Charging Continuously from the Ground 214
9.4 Future Directions 214
9.5 Conclusions 214
References 215
Keywords and Descriptions 216

9.1 BACKGROUND

Owing to advances in laser scanner-based navigation and safety technology, Automated Guided Vehicles (AGVs) are becoming increasingly common in warehouses and factories [11].

Material handling is an important part of the manufacturing systems. This is due to the fact that there are aims today to automate this process, which is seen as an non-value-added process, and the performance of enterprises is measured with this aspect. For automating material handling the AGV system is first among these methods. This material handling system, which has been successfully implemented in many sectors, is increasingly used in our lives, and by adding many other features, it will increase the usage area of AGV.

AGVs' management has to address two main problems. These problems are [11]:

- the job allocation
- the energy management.

As defined in [9] the two basic distinctions on how to ensure the energy supply of vehicles are changing batteries (manual or automatic) and charging batteries at stations or while driving.

Energy management for AGVs is a crucial issue for managers. Efficient use of AGVs is also related to AGVs' energy management. As shown in the next section, there are lots of studies in the literature for AGVs' battery management. In this chapter a system dynamics model was developed for testing different scenarios of AGVs' battery management.

9.2 LITERATURE REVIEW

Parry et al. [12] simulated the pre-defined path of AGVs, and examined the effects of operating conditions on perception of hazards in virtual and real operating conditions.

Pagani et al. [11] proposed a neural network-based algorithm to simultaneously allocate orders to vehicles and decide which vehicles should visit a charging station.

Zhan et al. [13] proposed two dual-stage battery charging strategies of AGVs, equipped with lithium-ion batteries for improving utilization. A real case was adopted to illustrate the applicability and effectiveness of the proposed approach.

Hamdy [6] developed a simulation model to determine the optimized number of AGVs that is capable of increasing throughput while meeting the material handling requirements of the system. This model incorporates the battery management aspect and issues, which are usually omitted in AGV research. This includes the charging options and strategies, the number and location of charging stations, maintenance, and extended charging. The analysis entails studying various scenarios by applying different charging options and strategies, and changing different parameters to achieve improved throughput and an optimized AGV fleet size.

Dehnavi-Arani et al. [1] developed an integrated model of scheduling of parts, routing of Automated Guided Vehicles (AGVs), and location of Battery Charging Storage (BCS) in a job shop environment. Since the proposed model was nonlinear, it could not achieve an optimal, global solution. As a result, the nonlinear model was transformed into a linear form to be efficiently solved in GAMS software.

Kabir and Suzuki [8], made a comparative analysis of different routing heuristics for the battery management of AGVs at a manufacturing facility. Those heuristics were modified to make them applicable and distinct for a manufacturing system.

Greve et al. [5] studied how reducing greenhouse gas emission plays a virtual role in the logistics sector. They provided a systemized overview of the cost drivers arising in the transformation process of a smart electrified container terminal.

Menyhárt and Szabolcsi [10] suggested the use of AI to optimize battery use and performance in military equipment.

Frivaldsky et al. [4] designed a precise measuring circuit that is responsible for the determination of SOC levels based on selected methodologies.

İnanç and Şenaras [7] developed a program for AGV routing via ACO. The program was developed using C# programming language. The shortest path was calculated via ACO.

9.3   SYSTEM DYNAMICS

As defined in Forrester [3], system dynamics deals with how things change over time [3]. System dynamics is basically a process modeling technique. System dynamics strives to reproduce existing decision-making processes within the system, rather than finding equations that predict the value of specific variables at the most satisfying level. In other words, the efforts of the system dynamics approach focus on a description and policy design rather than a prediction [2].

9.3.1   SD MODEL FOR AGV BATTERIES

An important issue in AGV systems is the energy management of AGV systems. Since AGVs are mobile machines and they use electrical energy, AGV is generally the most battery-powered machines of the factories. Today, there are dozens, perhaps hundreds, of AGVs in factories, and there should be at least one battery for each AGV.

Finding a battery creates a problem: How will the battery be charged? The strategies that exist today are listed as follows. From top to bottom, from simple to complex. Likewise, it can be considered as cheap to expensive.

1. Manual charging strategy
2. Automatic fast charging
3. Charging continuously from the ground

The system dynamics model illustrated in Figure 9.1 shows the general situation of the battery level. The charge level of the battery (SOC: state of charge) is the sum of charge and discharge currents. In this respect, SOC is a level and charge and discharge is a flow. Charging is determined by charging current, charging period, and charging frequency. The charging method used changes these parameters.

If we start with a simple case study; let AGV run 24 h in a system with 1 AGV 2 batteries. It should be calculated how much battery consumption is realized in the AGV cycle. This is specific to the relevant cycle.

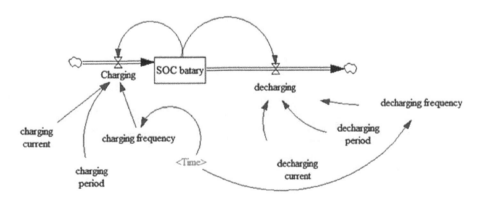

FIGURE 9.1   System dynamics model of general battery.

- Consumption current at 0 speeds A
- Low-speed consumption current A
- Medium-speed consumption current A
- High-speed consumption current A
- Consumption time at 0 speed
- Low-speed time
- Medium-speed time
- High-speed time
- The cycle time
- How many cycles does it perform in 24 hours?

But for a medium-size cycle, which is generally encountered, let us assume that 1.3 Ah/tour is used in one cycle, and that it performs one tour in 20 minutes and 72 turns in 24 hours. Therefore, it will be subject to discharge current of 3.9 Ah / hour per hour.

9.3.2 MANUAL CHARGE

The manual charging operating mode works as follows: The AGV comes to the charging station; the operator receives the finished battery over AGV, connects the newly charged battery to the AGV and the AGV goes. The empty battery is connected to the charger.

The battery is mostly 24 V in AGVs. Manual charging usually charges with 20 A. If the battery capacity is 80 Ah, charging will take 4 hours. Although the system dynamics seems to be quite simple for 1 AGV 2 batteries in the system shown below, the question becomes confusing while calculating how many additional battery and manual charge station are needed for multi-AGV. The model illustrated in Figure 9.2 shows the basis for questions such as which hours should we change the battery.

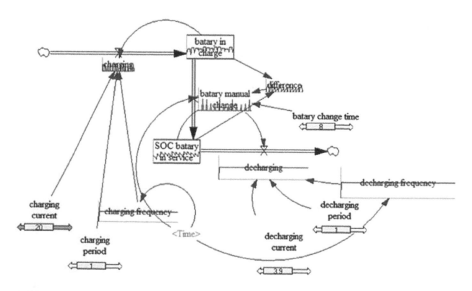

FIGURE 9.2   System dynamics model of manual charging battery.

As with the difference between the first system dynamics model with manually charging a battery, here there are two batteries – one battery for discharging on an AGV and the other battery is on a manual charging station.

For multiple AGVs, SOC service levels should be increased and the system's response should be evaluated accordingly.

The good thing about manual charging is that the cost of the manual charging station is low but the system requires labor time for battery replacement; and also, the cost of the additional battery should be taken into account.

9.3.3 AUTOMATIC FAST CHARGE

Fast charging units allow the battery to be charged automatically by transferring high voltage in a short period of time, allowing the battery to be charged without leaving the AGV. The charging current is usually determined as three to four times that of manual charging.

Since fast charging is used in every cycle, it should be considered when determining the number of AGVs.

The parameters related to automatic charging are as follows:

- How many automatic charging units are required in the cycle?
- How long should the charging time be?
- Charging current, some units adjust the unit current automatically according to time, where it also takes into account the cell temperatures of the charged battery.

Figure 9.3 illustrates the system dynamics model of an automatic charging battery

The condition of an AGV system with a charging time of 2 min. and a cycle time of 20 min. is observed above. The charge amount varies between 40% and 70% instead of being completely depleted in a fast charge. While the need for a spare

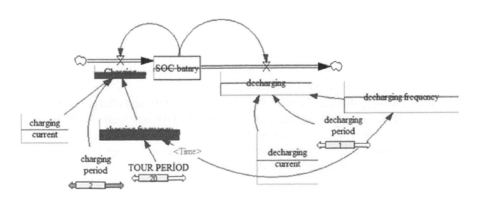

FIGURE 9.3   System dynamics model of automatic charging battery.

battery is not required for normal situations in the automatic charging system, the fast charging unit has an installation cost and in some cases it may increase the number of required AGVs.

9.3.4 CHARGING CONTINUOUSLY FROM THE GROUND

This method uses contactless energy transfer: Energy is transferred from metal cables embedded in the ground the ground to the AGV receptor over a short distance. This method is very expensive when compared with other methods.

Cables are embedded in the ground and are covered with coatings such as epoxy. There is no battery requirement in the system. With this method, if there are unpowered partitions in the system, super capacitor prediction is made for these places. No matter how long the system operates, it takes the same amount of energy from the system. It is very costly today. The flexibility of the system is greatly reduced.

9.4   FUTURE DIRECTIONS

Current charging strategies can increase the efficiency of the system with a system that collects information such as the states of the batteries, SOC, and station states. For example, fast charging can also be dynamic, or an automatic charging station can be added to the system and can send information to the AGV with a low level of SOC battery so that the battery can be charged for a long time. This will be developed as an IOT project and the requirements of the method will be examined in later studies.

9.5   CONCLUSIONS

In this study, different strategies of battery charging were analyzed with the system dynamics approach in to analyze systems requirements. In this investment decision the economic aspect is important so economic evaluation of the system also analyzed. Determining system requirements with SD and evaluating economically, helps decision makers to perform their project effectively.

Nowadays, economic efficiency becomes much more important. Increasing economic pressure leads projects manager to select accurate solutions. So, evaluating changing strategies also determines charging capacity and battery type that influence investment costs and project performance. A higher battery capacity with an expensive charging strategy increase cost; on the other hand, insufficient capacity and charging strategy leads projects to failure.

Another method that can be used for choosing a battery and charging strategy is multi-criteria decision-making methods. A TOPSIS AHP application will be carry out in a later study. Unlike the system dynamics method, TOPSIS analysis investigates the optimum solution by comparing choices with many factors such as cost, labor requirement, charging strategy, durability, and so on.

REFERENCES

[1] Dehnavi-Arani, S., Sabaghian, A., and Fazli, M. (2019). A Job shop scheduling and location of battery charging storage for the automated guided vehicles (AGVs). *Journal of Optimization in Industrial Engineering*, 12(2), 121–129.

[2] Erkut Haluk (1983), *Sistem Dinamiğinin Temelleri, İTÜ Fen Edebiyat Fakültesi Ofset* Atölyesi, İstanbul.

[3] Forrester, Jay Wright (1995), The beginning of system dynamics, *The McKinsey Quarterly*, 4, 4.

[4] Frivaldsky, M., Sedo, J., and Pipiska, M. et al. Design of measuring and evaluation unit for multi-cell traction battery system of industrial AGV. *Electr Eng* (2020). 10.1007/s00202-020-00982-z

[5] Greve, M., Harnischmacher, C., Lichtenberg, S., and Kolbe, L. (2019). *Smart Grid in Container Terminals–Systematization of Cost Drivers for Using Battery Capacities of Electric Transport Vehicles for Grid Stability. Twenty-fifth Americas Conference on Information Systems*, Cancun, 2019, pp. 1–10.

[6] Hamdy, A. (2019). Optimization of automated guided vehicles (AGV) fleet size with incorporation of battery management. PhD dissertation, Engineering Technology, Old Dominion University, DOI: 10.25777/n2vs-4122. ODU Digital commons.

[7] İnanç, Ş., Eren Şenaras, A. (2020). AGV routing via ant colony optimization using C#. *Optimization Using Evolutionary Algorithms and Metaheuristics: Applications in Engineering*, Kumar, K., and Davim, P. (eds.), CRC Press Taylor & Francis Group, 2–23.

[8] Kabir Qazi, Shaheen, Suzuki, Yoshinori (2019). Comparative analysis of different routing heuristics for the battery management of automated guided vehicles, *International Journal of Production Research*, 57:2, 624–641, DOI: 10.1080/00207543.2018.1475761

[9] McHaney, Roger. (1995) Modelling battery constraints in discrete event automated guided vehicle simulations. *International Journal of Production Research*, 33, 11: 3023–3040.

[10] Menyhárt, J., and Szabolcsi, R. (2019). Artificial intelligence applied for technical status diagnostics of the batteries of automated guided vehicles. In *2019 International Conference on Military Technologies (ICMT)* (pp. 1–8). IEEE.

[11] Pagani, Paolo, Dominik Colling, and Kai Furmans. (2018). A neural network-based algorithm with genetic training for a combined job and energy management for AGVs. *Logistics Journal: Proceedings*, 2018, 10

[12] Parry, P .W., Yücel, G., and Duffy, V .G., (2009). "Modelling The Effect of AGV Operating Conditions on Operator Perception of Acceptability and Hazard", Volume 22(12).

[13] Zhan, X., Xu, L., Zhang, J., and Li, A. (2019). Study on AGVs battery charging strategy for improving utilization. *Procedia CIRP*, 81, 558–563.

KEYWORDS AND DESCRIPTIONS

Automated Guided Vehicle   An automated guided vehicle or automatic guided vehicle (AGV) is a portable "https://en.wikipedia.org/wiki/Robot" robot that follows along marked long lines or wires on the floor, or uses radio waves, vision cameras, magnets, or lasers for navigation.

SOC   State of charge (SoC) is the level of charge of an electric battery relative to its capacity.

Stocks   The present values of the variables that are formed by the accumulated difference between the inflow and outflow.

System Dynamics   The basis of system dynamics is to understand how system structures cause system behavior and system events.

Decision Functions   States of the policy that determines how to convert available information in stock into a decision.

Delays   A characteristic of dynamic systems and affect both material and information flow.

Flow   It is defined as the increase or decrease in the unit time interval in stocks and denoted by $f(t)$.

System Dynamic Language   This language consists of four components: stocks, flows, decision functions and information flow.

Index

Page numbers in *italic* indicate figures. Page numbers in **bold** indicate tables.

A

Abdelwahed, Ahmed S., **5**
abstract communication service interface (ACSI),
64, *64*
active energy boosters (AEBs), 3, **4–6**, 12, 31, 33,
35, 39
actuation layer (IoT), 164, *165*
adaptive power management, 90
aerodynamics, 113, 123, *123*, 132–134
Aftab, Mohd Asim, **44**
aggregators, 99, 186
definition, **83**
Ahuja, Hemant, **5**
air cooling, 109
air pollution, 73, **75**, 108, 110
Ali, Ikbal, **4**, **44**
alternating current, 72, 82, 163, 199
AC charging levels, 82
AC distribution system, 7, 8, *8–9*
Anand, M. P., 110
Andervazh, Mohammad-Reza, **44**
ant colony optimization (ACO), 42, 43, **44**, 57,
58, **62**, 210
flowchart, *58*
Anvari-Moghaddam, Amjad, **5**, 90
Apache, 121, *122*, 135
application layer (IoT), 165, *165*
arc faults, 177
arc flash, 177
architectures and fusion, 163–167
blockchain and IoT architectures, 163–164
blockchain energy framework, 167
computing, 165
energy systems architecture, 163
functional perspectives, 164–165, *165*
IoT-based energy framework, 167
physical perspectives, 165–167
Arora, Seema, **5**
artificial intelligence (AI), 42, **44**, 70, 142, 179,
187, 210
artificial neural networks (ANNs), 42, 53–55, **62**,
66, 142
concept, *54*
framework, 54–55
automated guided vehicles (AGVs)
battery management via system dynamics,
209–214
literature review, 210
results and conclusions, 214

automatic fast charging, 211, 213–214, *213*
automatic power system (APS), 185
automation: role of IoE, 185
auxiliary subsystem, 125, *126*
Azizian, Davood, **44**

B

Baccare Lli, E., 196
Baidya, Sanghita, 175–191
Banerjee, Binayak, **4**
Baran, Mesut E., **4**
Baredar, Prashant, 107–137
base entropy, 127–131
batteries, 72, **74**, 76, *77–79*, *83*, 90, 100, *110–111*
operational life, 84
problems, 75
rechargeable, 73, 90
thermal management (literature review),
108–109
battery capacity, 99, **119**
Kaplan-Meier survival curve, 118, *121*
battery capacity and range
box-cox transformation, *120*
cross-correlation, *120*
data, **119**
density plot, 118, *121*
3D plot, *122*
battery charging, 75, 76, 77, **127–131**, *132*
entropy calculation, 127–128, **127–129**
information system, **127–128**; *see also*
charging
battery charging data, 123, **125**
battery charging storage (BCS), 210
battery charging time, 118
battery discharging, 118, 123
battery management (AGVs), 209–216
battery management system (BMS), 81, 82,
91, 98
battery performance (PHEVs), 80–81
state-of-charge (SoC), 81
state-of-health (SoH), 81
battery-only electric vehicles (BEVs), 75, 76, *76*
big data, 135, 181
definitions, 111, 137
HEVs, *112*
HEV depository (dataset), 113
Bitcoin, 163
blackouts, 72, 198, 200

blockchain, 163, 181
　　clear legal rules wanting, 170
　　execution layer, 170
　　future considerations, 171
　　governmental policies, 170
　　P2P architecture, 166
　　policy and regulations, 170
　　public and private protocols, 169
　　security, 168–170
　　smart contracts, 170
　　use-cases, 168, *169*
blockchain categories
　　types according to access and transaction
　　　　processing, *169*
blockchain energy framework, 167
blockchain technology, 160, *160*, 186, 186, 187
　　recent advances in energy sector, 161–162
Borges, Carmen L. T., **4**
Bose, Bimal K., **44**
Bouchekara, H. R. E. H., **44**
BP neural network method, 186
branch numbers, 25, *26*, **26**
building energy demand prediction (BEDP), 195
building energy management system (BEMS), **44**,
　　65–66, *66*, 91, 92, 98, 99, 196
　　definitions, 70, 207
building energy monitoring system, 90
building sector
　　energy demand, 194
buildings, **34**
　　commercial and residential (USA), 82
　　energy consumption, 31
　　energy efficient, 193–207
　　energy management (flow chart for IoE
　　　　framework), *32*; *see also* energy-efficient
　　　　buildings
business understanding, 114
Byzantine Generals' Problem, 166, *167*

C

C# programming language, 210
CAN bus, 85, 86
centralization, 97, 161, 164, 167, 186, 186, 202
centralized principle architecture, 165, *166*, 170
CHAdeMO, 99
charging, *33*, **34**, 80, 90, 95, *96*, 99, 100, 113; *see
　　also* battery charging
charging schemes (PHEVs), 81–82
charging stations, 73, *83*, 90, 99, 168, 187, 210,
　　212, 213
Chiu, Wei-Yu, **5**
cities, 170, 196
client-server architecture, 166, 171
climate, *197*, 202, *202*
climate change, 170, 175, 177, 196
clock line, 87, *87*, 88

cloud computing, 201, 203
coefficient of road adhesion
　　auto-correlation for wet roads, *118*
　　data, **116**, 117
　　data variation for wet roads, *118*
　　logarithmic data, **117**
commercial buildings, **5**, **45**, 197
　　IoE applications, 199–200
commercial loads, 3, **20**, 20, 91
commercial smart grid (CSG), *92*, 97, *98*, 98
communication, 42, 64, 90
communication concept, *64*
communication module (CM), *83*, 198
community energy management systems
　　　　(community EMSs), 65, *67*
complex HEV, 78, *79*
consensus, 166, *167*, 168
constant current, 7, 20, **20**, 81
constant impedance, 20, **20**
constant power, 15, 19, 20, **20**
constant voltage, 8, 16, 23, *30*, 81
construction costs (CAPEX), 115, 124
consumers, 9, 10, 11, 30, *66*, 72, *124*, 167, 169,
　　182, 183, 185
control centers, 66, 140, *144*, 144, 157
control system, 42
　　EVs (literature survey), 109
conventional HEVs, 76, *76*
conventional residential microgrid (CRM), 91,
　　92, *98*, 98
converters, *110–111*, **125**
Copenhagen, 99
Costanzo, Giuseppe Tommaso, **5**
coulomb counting, 81
cryptocurrencies, 163, *169*
current integration method, 81
current phasors, 149
currents, 7, *150–151*
customer choice approach, 90
Customer Relationship Management (CRM), 113,
　　113
cyber physical system (CPS), 139, 141, 157
cyber security, 181, *182*, 186, 187, 201
cyclic redundancy check (CRC), 87

D

data clustering, 132–135
data envelope method, 186
data layer (DLT), 164, *164*
data length code (DLC), 87
data line (SDL), 88
data logging, 85, 86–89
　　frame format of I²C, *88*
　　interconnected master–slave configuration, *88*
　　master to slave connection, *87*
　　UART data connection, *88*

data map, 125
data objects (DOs), 63
    definition, 64
data preparation, 115
data understanding, 115
data volume, 113
Davenport, Thomas, 73
De Salis, R. T., 90
decentralization, 160–165, *166*, 168, 171, 176,
    179, 186, 196, 200
decentralized principle architecture, 165, *166*, 171
decentralized renewable energy sources (DRESs),
    163
decision tree, 126, 131, 132, 137, 142
Deepa, S. N., **44**
Dehnavi-Arani, S., 210
demand-side management (DSM), **5**, **6**, 23,
    30–31, **34**, **45**, 63
    definition, 40
    direct versus indirect techniques, 72
    IoE framework, 31, *30*
Deshmukh, Rohit R., **44**
Dietrich, Dietmar, **5**
direct current, *80*, 99, 163, 199
    DC distribution system, 7, 8, *8*
    DC fast charging (DCFC), 82
    DC high-voltage lines, 72
    DC-link voltage, *29*
    DC loads, 160
    DC voltage, 177
distributed applications (DApps), 161
distributed automation system (DAS)
    definition, 70
distributed energy, 40
distributed energy resources (DERs), 26–28, *27*,
    31, 39, 43, 63, 65, *67*, 178
distributed generation (DG), 3, **4**, 33, **35**, **44**, 180
distributed grid intelligence (DGI), 198
distributed information processing and power
    control (DIPPC), 92, *93*
    house and vehicle count, **94**
distributed ledger technology (DLT), 163
    access and permissions, 168
    functional architecture principle, *165*
    rooted in evolution of ledgers, 168
    taken into realm of energy systems, 168
    three core layers, 164, *164*
distributed principle architecture, 165, *166*
distribution automation system (DAS), 43, 65,
    66–67
distribution grid, 23, *30*, *33*, 35
distribution lines, *12*, *24–25*, 179
distribution systems, 91
    fault scenarios, 140
distribution upgrade deferral, **80**
distributors, 6, *6*, *8–10*
    definition, 7

Doorsamy, Wesley, 159–174
Dorri, A., 195
double line (LL) fault, 141, 149, 151–154
double line to ground (LLG) fault, 141, 149–154
dual axle transmission, 78, *79*
dynamic voltage restorer (DVR), 3, **6**, 28–30, *29*
    components, 28
    dynamic model, *28*
    equivalent circuit, *29*
    topology, *29*

E

Electric and Hybrid Vehicle Act (USA, 1976), 73
electric power system, 72–73
electric vehicles (EVs), 31, **34**, 72–101, 160, 168,
    179, 183, 185, 187, 194
    battery modules, 108
    classification based on type of propulsion
        system, *76*
    control system (literature survey), 109
    definition, 137
    fundamentals, 73–74
    grid integration, 90
    historical background, 73–74, **73**
    versus ICEVs, 73, *75*
    leading manufacturers and models (1900–
        1920), 73, **73**
    literature survey, 90
    onboard data logging facility, 85
    optimum design (literature review), 108
    popular (1960s–), **73**
    power storage equation, 94
    reasons for decline in popularity (1920–1960),
        73–74
    service as storage system, 90, 90–91
    types, 75–76
electrical current, **127–131**
    information system, **129–130**
electrical link (EV system), 124, 126, *126*
electrical propulsion unit, 125, *126*
electricity, **4**, 7, 8, 26, **34**, 63, **62**, 70, **75**, **80**, 84,
    110, *123*, 178, 181, 185, 186, 197, 198,
    201, 207
electricity demand, 11, 140, 175, 176, 181, 193
electricity market, 140, 179
electricity system, 163, 196
Electronic Controller Unit (ECU), 86
end users, *30*, *33*
end-of-frame (EoF), 87
Enel, 99–100
energy conservation, 72
energy currency, 92
energy demand, 2, 84
energy efficiency, 2, **4–6**, 23, 27, 31, **44–45**,
    84, 91
    definition, 40

energy efficiency parameters (mathematical
　　formulation), 11–17
　　calculation of power losses, 17
　　equivalent representation of distribution line
　　　between two nodes, 12
　　node voltage calculation, 13–15
　　phasor diagram of distribution line between
　　　two nodes, 13
　　power flow equation, 15–17
energy efficiency performance (EEP), 3, **4–6**, 24,
　　27, 31, 33, **35**, 43
　　definition, 40
energy flow, *30*
　　bidirectional, 97–98, *98*, 183–185
Energy Internet (EI), 90, 176, 177–178, 181, 185,
　　187
energy management, 28, 35, 63–66
　　buildings (BEMS), 65–66, *66*
　　communication protocols, 64, *64*
　　definitions, 63, 70
　　distribution automation system, 65, *66–67*
　　IEC 61850 standard, 63–64, *63*
　　IoE, 181–183
　　IoE framework, **34**
energy management system (EMS), 43, **44**, 63, 163
energy resources, 199
energy router, 198
energy source subsystem, 125, *126*
energy storage, *29–30*, 90
energy systems architecture, 163–164
energy wastage, 70, 84, 196, 200
energy-efficient buildings, 193–207
　　business-related challenges, 202, *202*
　　costs, 201–202
　　future research trends, 204
　　IoE applications, 199
　　IoE for, 197
　　IoE framework, *197*
　　IoE-based building management system,
　　　197–199
　　IoE-based services, *199*
　　IoE-based system, *200*
　　literature review, 195–197
　　managerial challenges, 200–201, *202*
　　technical challenges, 201, *202*
Enterprise Resource Planning (ERP) NoSQL
　　database environment, 113, *113*
entropy, 127–131
entropy calculation for
　　battery charging, 128–129, **128–129**
　　coefficient of performance of IC, electrical
　　　current, 130, **131**
　　engine, 129–130, **131**
　　motor speed, 128–129, **129**
Ethernet, 63, 64, 70
Evolved Packet Core (EPC), 86
EVSE (Electrical Vehicle Supply Equipment), 82, 99

F

Facchini, Alessandro, **5**
factories, 170, 209, 211
Falcao, Djalma M., **4**
Fast Fournier Transform (FFT), 141, 145, 149,
　　152
　　error in fault location estimation, **151**,
　　　152–153, 153
fault diagnosis, 201
fault location estimation
　　asymmetrical fault solution, 146–148,
　　　151–152
　　background, 140–141
　　four-step method, 143–144, 154
　　future directions, 154
　　literature review, 141–143
　　modelling transmission line network,
　　　144–145, *145*
　　phasor extraction for faulty network, 145
　　positive and negative sequence circuit of
　　　faulty line, *147*
　　sequence network components (calculation),
　　　144
　　simulation and result, 149
　　symmetrical fault, *148*, *151*
　　symmetrical fault solution, 148, 153
　　using CPS in WAMCP, 140–157
　　using equations for different types of fault,
　　　146–148
　　using IoE under different fault types, 143–153
feeders, 6, *8–10*, 16, 18, 19
　　definition, 6
Fernando, Kurukulasuriya, **44**
flexibility, 83, 84, 142, 159, 160, 161, 163, 165,
　　166, 169, 171, 180, 181, 186, 195, 214
flow battery, 72, 97–98, *98*
Flume, 123–124
　　assessment of HEV system, *123*
fog cloud (FC) paradigm, 196, 203, **203**
fog node intelligence, 195
Fog of Everything (FoE), 196
　　basic service model, 203, *203*
　　case study, 203
　　interplay, 203, **204**
forecasting, **44**, **62**, 66, 101, 110, 112, 135, 181,
　　185, 193, 201
Forrester, Jay Wright, 211
fossil fuels, 108, 110, 175, 181, 175, 177, 193,
　　197, 199
fraud risk, 168
Frederiksberg Forsyning, 99
Frivaldsky, M., 210
fuel cell system, 108–109
fuel tanks, *77–79*, *83*, *110–111*, **125**
fuel-cell electric vehicles (FCEVs), 75, *76*
full HEVs, 75, **75**, 76, *76*

full-duplex communication, 194
fuzzy logic (FL), 42, 45, **44**, 142
fuzzy logic systems, 55–57, **56**, **62**
    benefits, 57
    components, 57
    framework, *56*
    input signal, 55, **56**
    steps, 57

G

Game Theory, **5**, 166
Gautam, Durga, **4**
generators, *110–111*
genetic algorithm (GA), 42, 45–46, **62**, 108, 142
    flowchart, *46*
geothermal energy, 72, 202
Global Positioning System (GPS), 143, 144, 157
Goswami, S. K., **4**
graphical user interface (GUI), 183
Gray correlation method, 186
great electric car race (1968), 73
greenhouse gases (GHGs), 65, 108, 176, 180, 194,
        202, 210
Greve, M., 210
grey wolf optimization (GWO), 42, **44**, 50–53, **62**
    flowchart, *61*
grid to vehicle (G2V) technology, 30, *30*, 31, *33*,
        34, 185
    definition, **83**
grid-connectable HEVs, 76, *76*
GSM, 142, 165
Guan, Jen-Chiun, 90
Guarnieri, M., 90
Guo, Yuanxiong, **5**
Gupta, Nikhil, **4**

H

Hadoop, 112, 120, *122*
    definition, 137
Hadoop distributed file system (HDFS), *122*, 135
Hadoop distributed HEV system, 120–124
Hamdy, A., 210
Hannan, M. A., 196
Hao, He, **5**
Haque, M. H., **4**
hardware, 55, 137
harmony
    definition, 47
harmony memory (HM), 47–48, *48*
harmony search algorithm (HSA), 42, 45, 47–48, **62**
    flowchart, *48*
Hbase, 121, 123, *122–123*
heat pipe with copper sheet (HPCS), 109
heating, ventilation, air-conditioning (HVAC),
        70, 194

Hemdan, Nasser G. A., **4**
heuristics and meta-heuristics, **4**, 43, **44**, 47, 50
hierarchical data clustering, 132–134
    agglomerative approach, 132–133, *133*
    divisive approach, 132, 133, *133*
high-renewables framework, 195
human brain, 42, 53–55
human-machine interface (HMI), 183
Hung, Duong Quoc, **4**
hybrid electric vehicles (HEVs), 90, *113*
    assisted by IC engine, 77–78, *76–79*
    configurations, 76
    final layout, *126*
    load demand, 126, **127–131**, *132*
    modus operandi, 113
    power output of motors, **76**
    types, 75–76, **75**, *76*
hydraulic link (EV system), 124, 125, *126*
hydrogen fuel cells, 72, 108
hydropower, *23*, 26, 63, 72, *83*, 84, *92*, *98*
Hyundai, 84

I

i-protection method, 179, 184
identifier extension (IDE), 86
IEC, **44**
    international standard used for communication
        between substations, 63
IEC 61850: 43, **44**, 63–65, 68
    communication protocols, 64, *64*
    definition, 70
    distribution automation system, 65–66
    overview, 63–64
Iman-Eini, Hossein, **6**
impedance, 15, 19, **20**, 143, 146, 153
İnanç, Ş., 210
India, 176, 182
Industrial Internet of Things (IIoT), 185
industrial loads, 3, 18, **20**
information and communications technology
        (ICT), *83*, 140, 141, 142, 143, 144
information flow, *23*, *30*, 84–89
integration of distributed energy resources, 26–27,
        27
integration of dynamic voltage restorer (IDVR),
        24, 28–30, **34**
integration of renewable energy sources (IRES),
        24, **34**
intelligent electronic devices (IEDs), *63*, 70,
        184
intelligent energy management (IEM), 185, 198
intelligent fault management (IFM), 198
inter-frame space (IPS), 87
Inter-Integrated Circuit (I^{2}C), 86, 88
    frame format, *88*
    modes, 89

internal combustion (IC) engine, 73, 75–76,
        76–79, *83*, 90, *110–111*, 122, 125, 126,
        128–131, *132*
    coefficient of performance, **127**
    data, **125**
    information system, **131**
internal combustion engine vehicles (ICEVs), 73
    versus EVs, 75, **75**
International Energy Agency (IEA), 3
International Mobile Subscriber Identity (IMSI),
        86
Internet of Energy (IoE), 140, 142, 144, 146, 148,
        157, 160, *160*, 162
    access technology, *23*
    advantages and opportunities, 186–187
    big data analysis, 108
    challenges, 186
    coordinated operation in power delivery, 2–40
    core characteristic, 161
    definitions, 40, 70, 84, 157, 207
    energy-efficient buildings, 193–207
    extension of smart grid concept, 84
    flowchart for fault location estimation, *144*
    formula, 23
    future directions, 187
    implementation in buildings (challenges),
        200–202, *202*
    infrastructure, 100
    plug-and-play feature, 184
Internet of Energy (building management system),
        197–199
    energy-efficient buildings, 197
    features and concept, 197–199
Internet of Energy (overview), 84–89
    information flow, 84–89
    NAN, 89
    wireless communication, 89
Internet of Energy framework, 23–31
    demand-side management, 31, *32*
    integration of distributed energy resources,
        26–28, *27*
    load and energy management, *23*, 24, **34**
    primary distribution system, 24–30
Internet of Energy framework
    development, 42–70
    literature, 42–43, **44–45**, 66
    soft computing, 42
Internet of Energy for plug-in hybrid
    electric vehicles, 72–106
    case study, 99–100, *100*
    future directions, 100
    proposed approach, 90–100
    sample system, 91–99
    test scenario, 95–99
Internet of Energy role in: automation of
    power system network, 185
    protection of integrated grid, 184–185

    security planning, 185–186
    solar industry, 184
Internet of Energy scenario, 181–183
    energy management, 183
    modern energy supply chain, *182*
    solar power generation, 181–182
Internet of Renewable Energy (IoRE), 178
Internet of Things (IoT), 23, 40, 84, 91, 141,
        143, 154, *160*, 163, 176, 179, 183,
        196, 214
    definitions, 157, 207
    energy framework, 167
    future considerations, 171
    generalized functional architecture, 164–165,
        165
    infrastructure, 140
    future directions, 170
    literature review, 161–162
    security, 168–170
Islam, M. S., 90
Islam, Syed M., **4**

J

Japan, 73, 176
Jarial, R. K., 72–106
Jaya algorithm, 42, **44**, 45, 60–61, **62**
    flowchart, *61*
Jayaprakash, Pychadathil, **6**
Jedlik, Ányos, 73
Jiang, Tianhua, **44**
joint approximate diagonalization of Eigen
        matrices (JADE), 195
Jowder, F. A. L., **6**

K

Kabir Qazi, Shaheen, 210
Kamruzzaman, M. D., 109
Kaplan-Meier survival curve, 118, *121*
Kaur, E., 195
Khare, Cheshta J., 107–137
Khare, Vikas, 107–137
Kong, Weicong, **44**
Kumar, Pawan, 1–70
Kumari, Meet, 193–207
Kurrat, Michael, **4**

L

lead-acid batteries, 73
Li, T., 195
liberalization (of energy markets), 162, 163, 167,
        168, 170
Lin, Chin-Teng, **44**
Lin, Zhilong, 90
line tapping, 184

line to ground (LG) fault, 141, 149, *150*, 151–153, **151**
linear regressions, *120*
Linux, 86
lithium-ion batteries, 92, 108, 210
load balancing, 91
load demand, 28
load following, 98
load management, 35
 IoE framework (key features), **34**
load models, 19–20, **20**, **35**
load profile, 25
load shifting, 72
loads, 2, *9–10*, 15, 72
Logenthiran, Thillainathan, **5**
logging (transfer of data), 85
logical nodes (LNs), 63, *63*
 definition, 64
LTE (long-term evolution), 86, *89*
Lyu, Y., 109

M

machine-to-machine (M2M) communication,
 84–85, 183
 architecture, 85, *85*
 data logging system, 86–89
Mansiri, Kongrit, **44**
manual charging, 211–213, *212*
manufacturing message specification (MMS),
 64
Mao, Meiqin, **44**
MapReduce, 112, 120, 125, 135
 data requirements, **125**
 definition, 137
 HEV framework, *126*
Marini, Federico, **44**
market basket model, 112, 135
Markov chain process, 110
master in, slave out (MISO), 87, *87*
master out, slave in (MOSI), 87, *87*
master stations, 65, *66–67*
MATLAB code, 149
mechanical link (EV system), 124, 125, *126*
megabyte (MB), 113, 113, *113*, 123
membership functions (fuzzy logic systems), 57
Mendoza, J. E., **4**
Menyhárt, J., 210
Metallidou, C. K., 196
micro HEVs, 76, **76**, *76*
microcontrollers, 55, 87, 88
microgrids, 3, **5**, **44**, 63, 72, 90–92, 154, 161, 163,
 176–178, 180, 181, 183, 199
middleware layer (IoT), 164, *165*
mild HEVs, 76, **76**, *76*
Mishra, Mahesh K., **6**
Mitsubishi Outlander PHEV, 99, *100*

Mobile Station International Subscriber Directory
 Number (MSISDN), 86
Mohagheghi, Salman, **44**
Mohammadian, H. D., 196
monitoring, 86, 143, 160, 183, 194, 195, 197, 201
Monte-Carlo simulation process, 110
motor speed, 123, **125**, **127–131**, *132*
 entropy calculation, 128–130
 information system, **129**
motors, *110–111*, 122
MTC (machine-type communication), 85, *85*
multi-point-to-point (MP2P) traffic, 89
multi-tapping, 179, 184
multiple criteria decision-making (MCDM)
 network, 181, 182
musical techniques, 47, **47**
MVA load, 21, 21, **22**, *22*

N

Nakamoto, Satoshi, 163
Nandi, Champa, 175–191
Nara, Koichi, **4**
Nefedov, E., 90
neighbourhood area network (NAN), 89
Nema, Savita, 107–137
net-zero energy buildings (nZEBs), 195
network configuration
 definition, 40
network configuration management (NCM),
 24–25, *24–25*, **26**, **34**
network layer (DLT), 164, *164–166*
network reconfiguration, 3, 24
network topology, 2, 3, 25
neural fuzzy systems, **44**
neural network braking control system, 109
neuron components, 53–55
Newton's second law of motion, 110
Nguyen, V. T., 195
Nissan, 73, **74**, 84, 99–100, *100*
Nissan Evalia, 99, *100*
Nissan Leaf, 99, *100*
node transfer, 24
node voltage, *22*
node voltage calculation, 13–15, **22**
nodes, *24–27*
NoSQL database environment, 113
nuclear energy, 72, *83*, *92*, *98*
Nuvve, 99

O

office microgrids, 91
off-peak load period, *33*
on-site generation
 identical to 'network configuration', 40
online load management, 35

Oozie, 120, *122*
operating costs (OPEX), 115, 124
optimal power flow algorithm, 43
optimal reactive power dispatch, 43
optimization, 48, 65, 178
optimization process, 47, **47**
outages, **80**, 140, 198

P

Packet Data Network Gateway (PDN-GW), 86
Pagani, Paolo, 210
Palensky, Peter, **5**
parallel HEV, 77, *111*, *124*, 124
parameter estimation techniques, 20
Parker project, 99
Parry, P. W., 210
particle swarm optimization (PSO), 42, 42, **44**,
    48–50, **62**
    flowchart, *50*
particle velocity, 48, *50*
Parveen, Nisha, 139–157
passive energy boosters (PEBs), 3, **4–6**, 12, 31,
    35, 39
Paul, Babu Sena, 159–174
peak load factor (PLF), 33
    calculation, 18–19, 21–23, *22*
peak load generators, 91
peak load hours, 10, *33*, 183
peak load reduction, 186, 194
peak loading, 2, **3**, 24, 25
peak power surcharge, 96, *97*
peak shaving, 72, 90–92, 94, 96, 98
peer-to-peer (P2P) architecture, 166
peer-to-peer energy transfer, 183, 186, 198, 200
permissioned and permissionless systems, 169,
    169
petabyte (PB), 113, *113*, 123
Peugeot, 73
    Peugeot iON, 99, *100*
phasor data, 143
    different types of fault, 149
phasor data concentrators (PDCs), 140
    definition, 157
phasor diagram, 13, *13*
phasor extraction (faulty network), 145
phasor measurement units (PMUs), 140–143
    applications, 142
    definition, 157
    protection scheme, 142
phasor values calculation of sequence network
    components, 145–146
pheromone model, 43, 57, *58*
PHEVs [plug-in hybrid electric vehicles], 76, *76*,
    79–82
    AC charging levels, 82
    battery performance, 81

charging schemes, 81–82
DC fast charging, 82
future directions, 100
grid applications, 80, **80**
optimum battery utilization, 100
V2G technology, 82–84
PHEVs (big data analysis), 107–137
    background, 108
    decision tree, 126, 131, *132*
    Hadoop distributed HEV system, 120–124
    hierarchical data clustering, 132–134
    literature review, 108–110
    MapReduce algorithm, 120, 125, *126*, 135, 137
    modeling HEV system, 125
    prefeasibility assessment, 112–118, **119**,
        121–122
    proposed approach, 110–112
PHEVs (big data analysis: literature review),
    108–110
    control system of EVs, 109
    optimum design of EVs, 108
    reliability assessment of EVs, 109–110
    thermal management of battery, 108–109
PHEVs (test scenario), 95–99
    bidirectional power flow with provision of
        flow batteries for storage, 97–98, *98*
    EV charging curve, 95, *96*
    load curve for domestic household, *95*
    load curve from domestic household, *97*
    power demand from grid, 96, *96–97*
    solar power generation, *95*
pig and mahout, 121, *122*
Pipattanasomporn, Manisa, **5**
plug-and-play interface, 196, 199
point-to-multiple-point (P2MP) traffic, 89
population, 43, 48, 58, *61*, 84
power converters (PCs), 28, *76–79*, *83*, 176
power delivery, 1–40
power demand, 11, 19–21
power distribution
    connection schemes, 8–10
    interconnected system, 10, *10*
    radial system, 8–9, *8*
    ring main system, 9–10, *9*
power distribution systems, 6–7
    classification, 7–8
    definition, 6
    energy efficiency parameters (mathematical
        formulation), 11–17
    low-tension type, 6, *6*
    objectives, 7
    primary, 24–29, *30*
    requirements, 11
    secondary, 23, 30–31
power flow equation, 15–17, 22
    backward, 16–17
    forward, 16

power generation, *30*, *32*
power losses, **4**, 24, 33, 43
    calculation, 17
power quality, 98, 176
power system network
    automation (role of IoE), 185
    security planning (role of IoE), 185–186
prefeasibility analysis, 112–118, **119**, *121–122*,
        124, 130, 135
    key points, *114*
prefeasibility report, 114
Prisoner's Dilemma, 167
privacy, 89, 111, 160, 161, 162, 164, 171, 177,
        181, 186, 187, 201
propulsion systems, 75, 76, *76*, 110, 137
propulsion unit, 110, 113, 125, *126*
prosumers, 91, 162, 163, 178, 183, 184–186
protocol layer (DLT), 164, *164*
PSCAD model of transmission line, 149, *149*
Pure Electric Vehicles (PEVs), 82
    types, 75, *77*

R

R-connectors, 121, *122*
radial distribution systems, **4**, **5**, 18, 31–33, **35**
radial networks, *15*, 21–23, 24, *26*
Rahman, Md Aminur, **5**
Rana, Ankur Singh, 139–157
range-extended HEVs (REVs), 76, *77*
Rao, R. Jaya, **44**
Rao, R. Venkata, **44**
receiving-end nodes, 25, **26**
receiving-end voltage, *21*, 21, 23
regression analysis, 116, 121
    definition, 137
reliability, 2, **4–5**, 10–12, 31, **34**, 40, 43, **62**, 77,
        80, 84, 109, 135, 140, 159, 160, 165, 166,
        171, 177, 178, 193–204 *passim*
    electric vehicles, 110
    energy market, 181
    hybrid electric vehicle system, 132
    ICT, 140, 142–143, 144
    power supply, 24, 178, 180, 186
remote terminal units (RTUs), 66, *66–67*
remote transmission request (RTR), 86
renewable electricity network, 179
Renewable Energy Sources (RESs), 143, 175,
        176, 180, 184, 186, 193, 194
    definition, 207
residential buildings, **5**, **45**, 197
    IoE applications, 199–200
residential loads, 3, **20**, 20, 91
residential smart grid (RSG), *92–93*, 94–98, *98*
    power generation equation, 94
    total power demand equation, 94
resilience, 84, 160, 163, 167, 171, *182*, 186

resource allocation, 121
road condition, 113, 115–117, **116–117**, *118*, 123
Rockefeller and Udren algorithm, 141, 145, 149
    error in fault location, 151–154, **151**
router, 198

S

Safdarian, Amir, **4**
safety concerns, 177
Salomons, David, 73
Sasitharan, S., **6**
scalability, 162, 163, 165, 166, 169, 186, 201,
        202
security, 89, 159–161, 168–170, 171, 200, 201,
        202
    authentication, permission, tokenization,
        168–169
    public and private protocols, 169
    smart contracts, 160
    trustless platforms, 168
security vulnerabilities, 166, 171
Şenaras, Arzu Eren, 209–216
Şenaras, Onur Mesut, 209–216
sending-end voltage, *21*, 21
sending-end nodes, 25, **26**
Senke, Noriyuki, **44**
sensing layer (IoT), 165, *165*
sensors, 70, 86–88, 140, 178, 179, 183, 187, 201,
        204
series HEV, 77, *77*, *110*, *124*, 124
series-parallel HEV, 77, *78*, *111*, *124*, 124
server layer (IoT), 165, *165*
service mains, 6, *6*
    definition, 6
Shao, Shengnan, 90
Sharma, Saurabh Ranjan, 72–106
Shen, C., 90
shunt capacitance, **4**, 13
shunt devices, 43
Singh, Arush, 72–106
Singh, Chanan, **44**
Singh, Rajesh Kumar, **4**
Singh, Surjit, **4–5**, **44**
sinusoidal waveform, 153
Sivanagaraju, S., **4**
Sivanandam, S. N., **44**
slave select (SS), 87, *87*
smart buildings, **5**, 176, 180, 195, 197, 200
smart computing (concept), 42
smart contracts, 170
smart grids, **5**, **44**, 63, 65, 68, 84, 85, 89–92, 140,
        143, *144*, 154, 160, 163, 176–183 *passim*,
        193, 198–201
smart homes, **5**, 177, 179, 181, 185
smart meters, *83*, 92, 165, 169, 179, 183, 181,
        185, 200, 201

soft computing methods, 45–61, *61*, 67
   ant colony optimization, 57, **62**
   application in power and energy systems,
     62, **62**
   artificial neural networks, 53–55, **62**, 66
   definition, 70
   fuzzy logic systems, 55–57, **56**, **62**
   genetic algorithms, 45–46, *46*, **62**
   grey wolf optimization, 50–53, **62**
   harmony search algorithm, 47–48, **47**, *48*, **62**
   identical to 'artificial intelligence', 42
   Jaya algorithm, 60–61, *61*, **62**
   particle swarm optimization, 48–50, **62**, *50*
   teaching learning-based optimization,
     58–60, **62**
software, 2, 55, 111, 115, 140
Solanki, Deepanshu Singh, 72–106
solar energy, **5**, *23*, 26, **34**, 72, *83*, *92*, 94, *95*, 97,
   97, *197*, 199, 199, 202
solar energy generation, 175–191
   fault detection and diagnosis, 180–181
   IoE, 181–182, 184
   literature review, 178–180
solar panels, 180–182
   price, 176
solar photovoltaic (PV) system, 63, *67*, 91, 92,
   169, 176–177, 180–181, 184
solid to moisture ratio, **128–129**
SPI, 86–88
Sqoop, 123
start-of-frame (SoF), 86
state-of-charge (SoC), 81, 85, 86, 91, 93, 95,
   97–99, 210, 211, *211*, 214
state-of-health (SoH), 81, 86
static load model, 19–20, **20**
storage devices, 28, 66, 97–98, *98*, 198
Strielkowski, W., 195–196
substation automation system (SAS), 64
   definition, 70
substation bus-bar, 9
substation communication, 43
substations, 6, *8–10*, 16, 23, **44**, *144*
super data concentrator, *141*
supervisory control and data acquisition
   (SCADA), 66, *66–67*, 159, 163, 183
supply and demand, 31, 179, 184, 198
supply-side management, 24–29, *30*
sustainable energy, 2, 184, 194
   definition, 207
Suzuki, Yoshinori, 210
Swarm Decision Table (SDT), 195
swarm intelligence, 42
synapses, 53–55
synchrophasor technology, 140, *141*, 141
system dynamics (SD)
   AGV battery management, 209–216

automatic fast charging, 211, 213–214, *213*
charging continuously from ground,
   211, 214
definition, 211
general battery model, *211*
manual charging, 211–213, *212*
model for AGV batteries, 211–212
future directions, 214
system voltage profile, 11
Szabolcsi, R., 210

T

teaching learning-based optimization (TLBO), 42,
   43, **44**, 58–60, **62**
   flowchart, *60*
   steps, 59
   student phase, 59–60
   teacher phase, 58–59, *60*
terabytes, 113, 123
TES systems, 65, *67*
Tesla, **74**, 82
Thanki, Dip V., **5**
thermal energy, 72, *83*, *92*, *98*
thermal management system, 108–109
thermoelectric surge control, 109
thermoelectric cooling, 109
Thevenin's equivalent and line parameters, 142
Third Generation Partnership Project (3GPP),
   85, *85*
Thomas, Mini S., 139–157
three-phase faults, *145*, 146, 153, 154
tie lines, *24–27*
time, 12, 25, 35, 42, 57, 80, **80**, 81, 82, 86, 115,
   140, 142, 157, 211, 213
time-of-use pricing, 72
TOPSIS, 186, 214
Toyota Prius, **74**, 79
transient energy outages, 198
transmission lines, *83*, 140–142, 144
   faulty (three-phase representation), *145*
   multi-tapped, 179
   PSCAD model, 149, *149*
   use of IoE to estimate faults, *144*
transmission systems, 6, *77–79*, 91, *110–111*, 114,
   142, *182*, 184
   fault scenarios, 140
transparency, 162, 168, 170
Tripathi, Vivek Kumar, 72–106
trustlessness, 155, 167, 168, 171
Tsagarakis, George, **5**

U

ultra-capacitor electric vehicles (UCEVs), 75,
   76, *78*

ultra-flywheel electric vehicles (UFEVs), 75,
        76, *78*
United States, **73**, 73, 99, 176
Universal Asynchronous Serial Receiver and
        Transmitter (UART), 86, 88, *88*, 88
University of Delaware, 99
Uppal, Anjali, 1–70
user interface app, 91, 98

V

V2B (vehicle-to-building), 98
V2G (vehicle-to-grid), 30, *30*, 31, *33*, **34**, 80, 81,
        82–84, 91, 92, 98, 185
    challenges, 84
    components, *83*
    definition, **83**
    grid-requested power and power delivery by
        each car, *100*
    terminology, **83**
V2G Hub, 99–100, *100*
Venkatesh, B., **4**
virtual power plants (VPPs), 178, 184
virtual processors (VPs), **203**
voltage collapse, 18, *22*
voltage difference, 11
voltage exponents, **20**
voltage phasors, 142, 145
voltage profile, 24, 28, 30, 33, **34**
voltage support, **80**, 98
voltage transducers, 165
voltage waveform, 149
voltages, 2, 16, 43, *150–151*

W

Walczak, Beata, **44**
Wang, Lingfeng, **42**
Wani, Shufali Ashraf, 139–157
wave velocity, **134**
wheels: front, *77–79*, *83*
    rear, *78–79*, *83*
Wi-Fi, 89, *89*, 165
Wide-Area Monitoring Control and Protection
        (WAMCP), 140–143, 154
    architecture, *141*
wind power, *23*, 26, **34**, 63, 72, 182, *197*, 198,
        199, 202
wireless communication, 89, *89*, 140, 141, 143,
        196
Wiriyasart, S., 108
World Bank Group, 163
World Wide Web, 113, *113*
Wu, Felix F., **4**

Y

Yarn, 121, 123, *122–123*

Z

Zahedi, A., 90
Zhan, X., 210
Zhang, Jiancheng, **44**
Zhao, Zhuang, **5**
ZigBee, 89, *89*
Zookeeper, 120, *122*
Zou, Kai, **4**

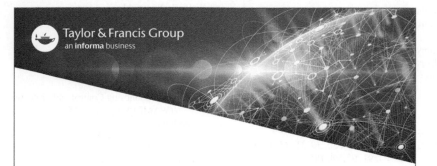